Consumer Behavior Dynamics

A Casebook

M. Wayne DeLozier

University of South Carolina

CHARLES E. MERRILL PUBLISHING COMPANY
A Bell & Howell Company
Columbus   Toronto   London   Sydney

Published by
CHARLES E. MERRILL PUBLISHING COMPANY
A Bell & Howell Company
Columbus, Ohio 43216

This book was set in Helvetica.
The production editor was Jo Ellen Diehl.
The cover was prepared by Will Chenoweth.

International Standard Book Number: 0–675–08504–7

Library of Congress Catalog Card Number: 76–52679

2 3 4 5 6 — 81 80 79 78 77

Printed in the United States of America

To Janice

Preface

This casebook is the product of the contributions of a number of outstanding scholars in the marketing field. Its strengths lie in the diverse background of the contributors' experiences and writing styles. The cases follow no set format, and the editor has been careful to retain the idioms, jargon, and writing styles of the authors. By not imposing a standard format or his own writing style on these cases, the editor hopes he has provided student case analysts with a more realistic set of business situations.

It is evident in this book that business people use different approaches to describe a situation, emphasize certain points and philosophies while excluding others, and express themselves with different word choices and phrases. Obvious examples are the cross-cultural buying behavior cases written by two people of British background. The editor was tempted at first to "Americanize" their writing, but instead recognized the value of exposing students to cultural variations in writing styles. The same holds true of the other cases to a lesser degree.

Although cases are categorized as "attitude" cases, "learning" cases, or "diffusion-adoption" cases, students should realize that other behavioral concepts and principles should not be excluded from their analyses. The interrelationships of human behavioral concepts are undeniable and quite complex. Although a particular case emphasizes a specific behavioral notion, the student should not exclude from consideration other behavioral dimensions pertinent to the problem. In fact, the student is encouraged to examine the case problem in every aspect.

This casebook is designed to supplement any introductory consumer behavior book. You will note that a correlation chart keying the cases to other consumer behavior books has been prepared by the editor.

The editor is indebted to all the contributors who made this casebook possible. Thanks go to Mr. Jack McHugh of Charles E. Merrill Publishing Company who encouraged the editor to undertake this project. Special appreciation is given to Dr. John B. Stewart, University of Miami, who first provided the editor with insights into consumer and human behavior.

A matrix of cases and relevant chapters of several major consumer behavior textbooks

Case Chapters

Textbook*	1	2	3	4	5	6	7	8
Runyon, Consumer Behavior, 1977	Ch. 13	Ch. 9	Ch. 8	Ch. 12	Ch. 10	Ch. 11	—	Ch. 4
Walters, Consumer Behavior: Theory and Practice, 1974	Ch. 8	Ch. 10	Chs. 6, 7	Ch. 9	Ch. 11	Ch. 5	—	Chs. 17, 18
Markin, Consumer Behavior: A Cognitive Orientation, 1974	Ch. 8	Ch. 9	Ch. 7	Chs. 10, 11	Ch. 12	Chs. 5, 7, 8	Ch. 15	Ch. 16
Engel, Kollat, Blackwell, Consumer Behavior, 2nd ed., 1973	Ch. 8	Ch. 9	Chs. 1, 2, 8, 10, 15, 17	Ch. 14	Ch. 12	Chs. 5, 6, 11	Ch. 6	Chs. 4, 6
Block, Roering, Essentials of Consumer Behavior, 1976	—	Ch. 8	—	Ch. 10	Ch. 7	—	—	Ch. 4
Louden, Della Bitta, Consumer Behavior (forthcoming), 1979	Ch. 15	Ch. 16	Ch. 14	Chs. 17, 18	Ch. 19	Ch. 19	—	Chs. 7, 8, 9
Schiffman, Kanuk, Ray, Consumer Behavior (forthcoming), 1978	Ch. 3	Ch. 4	Ch. 2	Ch. 6	Ch. 5	—	—	Chs. 12, 13
Reynolds, Wells, Consumer Behavior, 1977	Ch. 9	—	Chs. 10, 12	Chs. 9, 10	—	—	—	Ch. 8

*Chapter correlations are subject to changes in revisions of books indicated.

Case Chapters

Textbook	9	10	11	12	13	14	15	16	17	18	19
Runyon	Ch. 5	Ch. 6	Ch. 7	Ch. 6	Ch. 15	Ch. 14	Ch. 16	Ch. 16	Ch. 4	Ch. 4	All Chs.
Walters	Ch. 16	Ch. 18	Ch. 13	Ch. 12	Chs. 22, 24	Chs. 24, 29	Ch. 23	Ch. 23	Ch. 17	Ch. 17	All Chs.
Markin	Ch. 15	Ch. 14	Ch. 15	—	Ch. 17	Ch. 17	Ch. 11	Ch. 11	Ch. 16	Ch. 16	All Chs.
Engel, Kollat, Blackwell	Ch. 5	Ch. 6	Ch. 7	Ch. 24	Ch. 19	Chs. 3, 12	Ch. 13	Ch. 21	Ch. 4	Ch. 4	All Chs.
Block, Roering	Ch. 5	Ch. 5	Ch. 6	Ch. 15	Ch. 13	Chs. 9, 11, 12	Chs. 10, 12	—	Ch. 11	Ch. 4	All Chs.
Louden, Della Bitta	Ch. 10	Ch. 12	Ch. 13	Ch. 11	Chs. 20, 21, 22	Chs. 20, 21, 22	—	—	Ch. 7	Ch. 7	All Chs.
Schiffman, Kanuk, Ray	Ch. 11	Ch. 8	Ch. 9	Chs. 10	Ch. 15	Ch. 15	Ch. 7	Ch. 7	Ch. 12, 13	Ch. 12, 13	All Chs.
Reynolds, Wells	Ch. 8	Chs. 9, 12	Ch. 11	Ch. 12	Chs. 13, 14	Chs. 13, 15	Ch. 10	—	—	—	All Chs.

About the
Contributors

M. Wayne DeLozier. Dr. DeLozier earned his Ph.D. at the University of North Carolina at Chapel Hill and is presently a faculty member at the University of South Carolina. He is the author of a textbook, *The Marketing Communications Process,* and has published articles in the areas of self image—brand image relationship, M.B.A. education, and advertising in such journals as *The Journal of Advertising, Business Horizons,* and the *Journal of the Academy of Marketing Science.*

Denis F. Healy. Dr. Healy holds both a Ph.D. in marketing from The Ohio State University and an S.B. in engineering from M.I.T. He has had over ten years of industrial engineering, sales, marketing management, and consulting experience. His publications report results of studies of the impact of changing environments on marketing practice and the cost of foster child care in the U.S. Presently teaching at the University of Delaware, Dr. Healy is also involved in the design and implementation of marketing strategy and planning programs in industrial firms and the banking industry.

James M. Clapper. Having earned his Ph.D. at the University of Massachusetts, Dr. Clapper is a faculty member at Wake Forest University. He has been actively engaged in consulting advertising agencies, trade associations, and state government.

Paul S. Hugstad. Dr. Hugstad presently is a faculty member of the School of Business Administration and Economics at California State University (Fullerton). He earned his Ph.D. degree in marketing at the University of Wisconsin. Dr. Hugstad has written numerous articles and papers in the area of business education. His major research interests include social stratification, the family, cross-cultural buyer behavior, and new product development.

Dale M. Lewison. After receiving his Ph.D. from the University of Oklahoma, Dr. Lewison joined the faculty at the University of South Carolina. Dr.

Lewison's research interests include channel decision making, retail site evaluation, transportation, and the use of experiential learning in marketing education.

Andrew C. Ruppel. Dr. Ruppel is a faculty member at the McIntire School of Commerce, University of Virginia. Before earning his Ph.D. in business administration at the University of North Carolina at Chapel Hill, Dr. Ruppel was Market Analyst, Supervisor of Forecasting, and Assistant Director of Market Research for the New York Central System. His publications include a textbook, management cases, numerous articles, and conference papers. Dr. Ruppel has recently returned to his academic position at the University of Virginia after having served for one year as a resident consultant to the National Aeronautics and Space Administration.

Billy J. Silver. Mr. Silver is Vice-President of Marketing Communications at the Citizens and Southern National Bank, Columbia, South Carolina. Mr. Silver has previous experience with a national advertising agency and is a past president of the Columbia Advertising Club.

Brian Toyne. Dr. Toyne received his Ph.D. from Georgia State University, after which he joined the University of South Carolina faculty in international marketing. His research interests include U.S. multinationals, the impact of foreign competition, and cross-cultural comparisons of developing countries. Dr. Toyne currently is the director of the Center for International Business Studies at the University of South Carolina.

John F. Willenborg. Professor Willenborg earned his D.B.A. at Washington University, after which he joined the faculty at the University of South Carolina where he currently is an associate professor. Dr. Willenborg is director of the Center for Marketing Studies and director of the University's Consumer Panel. He is a co-author of *Marketing Management Strategy* and has published articles in a wide range of business journals including *Journal of Marketing, Journal of Business Research, Southern Journal of Economics,* and the *Journal of Risk and Insurance.* Dr. Willenborg is very active in executive development programs and as a marketing consultant.

Arch G. Woodside. After receiving his Ph.D. from the Pennsylvania State University, Dr. Woodside joined the faculty at the University of South Carolina where he currently is Professor of Business Administration and Academic Program Director for Marketing. He has served as a Fulbright Professor in Consumer Behavior and has numerous articles appearing in many publications including the *Journal of Advertising Research, Journal of Marketing Research, Journal of Applied Psychology, Journal of Retailing,* and the *Journal of Small Business Management.*

Roger E. Cannaday. Mr. Cannaday presently is completing his Ph.D. in Business Administration at the University of South Carolina. Mr. Cannaday has several years of business experience with Wilbur Smith and Associates, where he became Director of Marketing. His interests include retail site evaluation, real estate, and urban geography.

Peter Doyle. Dr. Doyle, a faculty member at the University of Bradford in England, earned his Ph.D. at Carnegie-Mellon University. Dr. Doyle is co-author of *Advertising Management, Product Management, Marketing Management,* and *Inflation.* He has written numerous articles for *Journal of Retailing, Advertising Quarterly, Journal of the Market Research Society, European Journal of Marketing, Economic Journal,* and the *Oxford Economic Papers,* among others. His interests include household decision making, brand positioning, advertising, and salesmanship.

Creighton Frampton. Professor Frampton received his Ph.D. from the University of South Carolina and currently is on the faculty at the University of Richmond. Dr. Frampton's research interests include communications theory and direct selling approaches. He also has an interest in curriculum evaluation about which he has published several articles and papers.

Donald H. Granbois. Professor Granbois is a professor of marketing at Indiana University where he has also earned his D.B.A. in marketing. He has published articles on brand evaluation and brand choice, the black consumer, and family decision making in such journals as the *Journal of Marketing,* the *Journal of Marketing Research,* and the *Journal of Consumer Research.*

Carter L. Grocott. Professor Grocott currently is a faculty member in the College of Business and Economics, West Virginia University. He has done graduate work at W.V.U. and at the University of North Carolina (Chapel Hill). His areas of research interests include small business promotional problems, sex in advertising, and the application of communications theory to marketing. He has served on the staff of the *Journal of Small Business Management* and *The Business Law Review.*

James E. Littlefield. Professor Littlefield is a member of the graduate faculty of business administration at the University of North Carolina (Chapel Hill). After working several years in industry, he completed his Ph.D. at the University of Wisconsin. Dr. Littlefield is co-author of *Advertising: Mass Communications in Marketing,* co-author of *Marketing: An Environmental Approach,* and the editor of *Readings in Advertising.* Dr. Littlefield also is very active in national and international consulting.

Robert E. Pitts. Mr. Pitts currently is completing his Ph.D. in business administration at the University of South Carolina. He has published several articles and papers in journals such as the *Journal of Marketing, Journal of Travel Research,* and the proceedings of national and regional associations. Mr. Pitts has served as assistant director of the University of South Carolina Consumer Panel.

Benson P. Shapiro. Professor Shapiro received his D.B.A. from Harvard University where he is currently on the faculty of the Harvard Graduate School of Business. He has published articles on the psychology of pricing.

Daniel L. Sherrell. Professor Sherrell is a faculty member at Georgia Southern University. His research interests include consumer choice behavior, marketing communications, and advertising strategy.

Gordon L. Wise. Professor Wise is a faculty member at Wright State University in Dayton, Ohio. His research interests include advertising, sales promotion, and retailing, and he has published articles in numerous journals including *The Journal of Business, Journal of Retailing, Journal of Advertising Research,* and the *Journal of Advertising.* Professor Wise also has consulted with a wide range of firms engaged at both wholesale and retail levels, as well as in the areas of advertising and sales promotion. He received his formal education at Miami University and Indiana University.

Contents

part 8
Complete Analysis of Consumer Behavior

part 1

Student Guidelines to Using the Case Method

Prepared by **Denis F. Healy,** College of Business and Economics, University of Delaware.

The case method is a teaching approach in which the learner is presented with a description of some situation confronting an organization. In addition, a set of facts and opinions about the organization, its markets, and its environment in general are supplied. The student is asked to analyze the situation, to answer a set of questions regarding the type of action to be taken, to evaluate the merits of a set of alternatives, and to defend the approach chosen.

The case method places intellectual demands on the student that are substantially different and more taxing than one experiences under other educational methods. The principal objective of the approach is to reduce the amount of time it takes to become skillful in decision making.

Case analysis, if approached properly, places the student in a simulated business environment. There is usually little structure to a business problem, and one must draw on a wide range of experiences and formal educational tools to attack a case. The analyst usually has limited time and incomplete information in dealing with the case. And, finally, the student is obliged to present his analysis and findings as a complete unit in written and oral forms for evaluation.

Each individual has had a different set of experiences and has been exposed to a different pattern of courses and formal educational experiences. As a result, the alternatives that one evaluates and recommends for implementation may vary from those selected by others. There is no one "best" answer to a case. Each analysis and set of recommendations is based on a unique set of perceptions, analytical skills, and effort expended. Each

1

analysis must therefore be appraised with this in mind. That is to say, while there may be no one best answer, there are vast gradations in the quality, completeness, substantiation of claims, and creative content of the analysis and presentation. This is an important observation which should be remembered as you attack cases and reflect on how your performance has been evaluated.

As you progress and become sophisticated in case analysis, you will find that short cases of a page or two in length can be just as difficult as those of fifteen or twenty pages. Moreover, you will find that the time spent developing a solution will increase as your skill grows. The same can be said for the depth and quality of your work.

Frequently, students complain that they have to spend too much time on casework, or that they cannot find how to attack a particular case problem in the textbook. Others comment that there must be an easier, more structured way to learn how to deal with such problems. Unfortunately, little comfort can be offered on these points. Case analysis takes considerable time and a special kind of time at that! One cannot possibly do a respectable job on a case when tired or only partially committed to the problem.

Textbooks are useful in case analysis when used as a tool to supply information about the merits of one analytical approach or decision alternative over another. In a sense, a text is a bag of tools. The selection of which set of tools to use to fix a problem, however, is *up to you,* the analyst, *not the book.* Thus, it is often useful to scan the text after reading a case to glean ideas and to refresh your memory about possible alternatives. However, never depend on the text to do the intellectual work for you. You, not the book, have a brain. So use it!

Finally, in dealing with student objections, it is difficult to suggest an easier route to the acquisition of knowledge at the analytical and integrative level. The case method, by simulating real business situations, offers the student a very efficient method for gaining decision-making skills in a low risk setting.

With today's high speed pace of business decision making, one can ill afford to be a novice in this area. Although luck is a decided factor in the successes and failures one experiences in organizational life, there is no question that the most successful people are those who are sophisticated analysts and decision makers. The case approach is designed to help you gain these skills early in your career, and at a low total personal cost.

Guidelines on Case Analysis

Although they may vary in length, scope, and degree of difficulty, cases have many things in common and can be approached using a general analytical framework. This section is devoted to a discussion of ways to approach a case analysis.

There are five main elements to a well-developed case analysis as follows:

1. Identification and specification of the problem.

2. Appraisal of the facts and opinions expressed in the case.

3. Development of alternative approaches to the case problem.

4. Selection and justification of best approach.

5. Discussion of implementation schedule and organizational responsibilities.

A brief discussion of the contents of each stage of the analysis follows.

Step 1: Identification and Specification of the Problem

Often a beautifully prepared case analysis will be worthless because the analyst failed to identify the basic problem(s) contained in the case. Instead, attention was directed at a symptom, and analysis dealt with how to make the symptom go away. Just as an elevated body temperature is symptomatic of a more fundamental problem, so too in a business case, a decline in sales or profits is merely symptomatic of more basic problems. For instance, the fundamental problem may be a breakdown in the organization, a new competitor may have entered the market, or perhaps tastes or needs of the target market have changed.

Problem definition activity should constitute the single most important aspect of case preparation. To accomplish this task, one must read and think about the case several times. Next, a list of potential problems should be prepared. Then, the list should be purged of all items which are symptomatic of more fundamental problems. Finally, the remaining items which truly constitute the problem areas should be organized in terms of degree of importance, or by topical area. A precise, tightly written statement of the case problem(s) should be presented for every case.

Step 2: Appraisal of Facts or Opinions

Every case deals with the behavior and relationships between people and organizations. Moreover, virtually every case contains bits and pieces of fact, information, opinion, and conjecture. It should be apparent, then, that some of the material presented is extraneous, incorrect, or improperly organized. The analyst must be sensitive to the hazards of accepting such information as "gospel."

A useful way to net out the substantive from the spurious is to (a) sift out the interrelationships that exist among the participants, (b) develop a profile of the likely postures, attitudes, and reactions of the key figures in the case, (c) separate the facts from the opinions, (d) arrange the facts in sequence of importance to the case, (e) arrange the opinions in terms of their plausibility or centrality to the case, and (f) present the above in outline form as part of the case write-up.

The list of facts, opinions, and relationships become the essential informational ingredients drawn on in alternative evaluation and choice. Well-developed cases are built on a careful appraisal of the *relevant* facts and upon a cautious and selective interpretation of the opinions and organizational interrelationships uncovered in this step. Never forget that human beings, with all of their biases, prejudices, and perceptual hang-ups, are involved. A business is not a machine.

Moreover, energetic and ambitious students will want to locate additional sources of information concerning the structure and practices of the industry, government legislation and regulatory agencies which affect the industry, current consumer behavior data related to the product or service discussed in the case, and other pertinent information that might be useful in developing the analysis.

Step 3: Development of Alternative Approaches

The typical case asks the analyst to propose a course of action to rectify the problem or achieve some objective. The potential action areas may cover a wide range of specific possibilities but all can be placed under the general headings of organization and the marketing mix.

Organizational changes may include such items as change in the personnel who staff a particular marketing function or change in the structure of a particular function such as a shift from a product management to a market management arrangement. Marketing mix changes involve alterations or changes in emphasis of the product, promotion, pricing, and channel of distribution areas.

For any problem, there may be several organizational and marketing mix combinations that have a reasonable potential for overcoming the problem and for achieving objectives. A well-developed case presentation will display *not less than three nor more than six* alternative action plans. Each alternative should contain a description of the organization scheme and marketing mix combination to be used and comments on the "how" and "why" aspects of the choice.

Step 4: Selection and Justification of Most Promising Alternative

Ultimately, a decision must be made about the direction to take. In "real world" situations, the decision maker operates with incomplete information and often under excrutiatingly painful time pressures. Often, there is lingering doubt about the chosen action and, frequently, information about the impact of a strategy is incomplete, late, confused, or nonexistent.

Case analysts find many of these characteristics in dealing with a case situation and are tempted to avoid making a decision by resorting to excuses about incomplete information and lack of time or experience. These excuses, although understandable, are unacceptable in the real world and so, too, in case analysis. The only justifications for no action is that "no action" is the preferred strategy or that there is a *cost justified* basis for seeking additional information before committing to a strategy. In either of these cases, a well-documented rationale must be presented.

Should additional information be needed to complete a strategy or action plan, the following support information must be contained in the case write-up:

1. Precise statement of the kind of information needed including dummy displays to show formats.

2. Source(s) and expected time and dollar costs to obtain information.

3. Discussion of how the information is to be used in shaping a decision.

4. Course of action to be taken if information is favorable.

5. Course of action to be taken if information is unfavorable.

For each action alternative (strategy) the analyst should list its strengths and weaknesses using a ledger (T-account) format. Using this approach and a summary statement, the chosen alternative should be highlighted and justified over the others.

Step 5: Implementation of Strategy

An important ingredient to all managerial activity is the finesse with which decisions are put into action. Timing, sensitivity to human relations issues, and the ability to concentrate resources to impact on a situation have a great bearing on success or failure of strategies. Thus, implementation considerations are an essential part of the decision-making process.

In this section of the case development, the analyst must plan and make explicit the implementation steps. Consideration should be given to timing, organizational reaction, competitive reaction, resource requirements and availability, methods of measuring and tracking performance, and the like. Useful questions to ask oneself in developing this area are: Who should be involved? When should action be taken? How can performance be measured? What market responses are expected?

Case Presentation

Cases may be presented in both written and oral forms and may be prepared by individuals or by groups of peers. Throughout your use of the method you will be asked to prepare and present a case analysis using each mode. This section is devoted to a discussion of the more important aspects of each mode. Hopefully, some time-saving tips can be gleaned from a careful reading on this topic. At the onset, it should be stressed that the prime criteria for evaluating the merits of a presentation are the quality of the analysis *and* the communication power of the presenter. Weakness in either detracts from the other.

Written Presentations

In some cases, you are asked to respond to a set of questions while in others you may be left to unravel the problems and alternatives without any clues. In either case, the format for presentation is essentially the same. A good topical outline for written or oral case analysis is that used in the previously presented discussion of case analysis. For most write-ups, the steps listed could be subheadings. For cases where questions are specified, specific addressing of the question should be organized using a similar format but tailored somewhat to the situation. Should it be necessary to develop the case, assumptions may be made and must be stated explicitly. The student must be prepared to defend his assumptions; otherwise, many problems could be assumed away. Finally, diagrams, tables, charts, and the like should always be considered as a means of improving the communicating power of the presentation.

The analyst should assume one of several postures in developing and presenting the case. For most cases, the appropriate role is that of a line manager responsible for planning and implementing strategy. In other situations, a plausible role might be that of a staff analyst or outside consultant. Regardless of the role assumed, the analyst should *not* assume the student or the innocent bystander role.

The case write-up should be concise, organized with liberal use of subheadings, employing outline or list formats, tables, and so forth. A general format for written case development follows:

1. Analysis and presentation of pertinent facts, opinions, etc., of present situation.

2. Statement of objectives (desired situation).

3. Statement of problems.

4. Statement of alternative approaches to the problem.
   (a.) Advantages of each.
   (b.) Disadvantages of each.

5. Statement of criteria in selecting approach.

6. Statement of implementation of selected approach.

7. Statement of how to monitor progress and measure results.

8. Statement of additional research needed.

9. Conclusions.

Evaluation of the presentation will consider the following dimensions:

1. Appearance, grammar, organization, and form. Such items as clarity of expression, sentence and paragraph structure, and readability will be judged.

2. Problem definition and fact identification. Such items as ability to distinguish between problems and symptoms and between fact and opinion will be assessed.

3. Alternative selection and evaluation. Such elements as completeness, substantiation of decision, and creativity of alternative identification and selection will be reviewed. The skill used in critiquing each alternative will be judged.

4. Selection and implementation. Such items as the precision of strategy statement and the completeness of implementation considerations will be made. Weakness in this area is as harmful as weakness in the problem definition area.

Oral Presentation

Although written analysis is important in many situations, the ability to verbalize one's ideas frequently is critical to gain acceptance of ideas. Oral presentations are often difficult for students but are an important aspect of the learning process. Portraying ideas *persuasively* but *tactfully* is a delicate process, the mastery of which can only be achieved through practice. As a result, much of your work in case analysis will involve the use and development of verbal skills. Therefore, you will be called on frequently to present either a partial or full case analysis. This exercise normally will be associated with the written development of a case.

The oral presentation requires a slightly different format and set of considerations than does a written one. The principal differences are in the character and environment of the audience. Written presentations typically are analyzed under less distracting conditions than oral ones. In addition, the audience for the oral presentation is likely to be considerably more passive, uninformed, and disinterested than the audience of the written report. Thus, attention to the communication task normally is greater in oral work. Care should be taken to organize your presentation so that the audience is constantly aware of the sequence or direction of your comments and where you are in the sequence. Furthermore, the use of visual aids is *essential* for an effective oral presentation. Every major presentation should include a judiciously chosen set of aids. Even a more informal individual presentation should contain some visual treatment to capture attention and to clarify a point.

The following aspects of oral presentation are subject to evaluation:

1. Organization of presentation.
2. Content (quality and thoroughness).
3. Quality of visual aids.
4. Speaking voice (delivery).
5. Courtesy to audience.
6. Ability to answer questions.
7. Posture, poise.
8. Ability to defend position.
9. Persuasive impact.
10. Mannerisms.
11. Practicality of recommendations.

Group versus Individual Presentations

Group and individual work will be treated along the dimensions listed above with the further proviso that within any group presentation, each member is expected to make a visible impact on the group output. Group case development is for the more involved cases and may require numerous meetings, division of labor, rewrites, presentation rehearsals, and visual treatments.

Group work is part of the learning process in the case method because it puts the students into a role relationship which more closely parallels the "real world" than does individual work. Without question, the group assignments are more demanding than others if for no other reason than it is difficult to schedule meeting times, extract commitments from peers, divide the work, and perform other activities. Every instructor who has assigned group work is confronted with the objections listed above; however, the problems involved with group work are not exclusive to students. They extend far into the "real" business work where one must contend with them on a daily basis. Most instructors are tolerant of the problems associated with the process but few are willing to eliminate group work from their courses because of the high learning value of the approach.

Every member of a group should define his role with group concensus and with the understanding that his peers as well as the instructor will evaluate both the quantity and quality of his inputs. In other words, it is very important that the group task be subdivided and the responsibilities be communicated in writing to each member within the group and to the instructor. Failure to do this task early in the group case development process will detract from the smooth functioning of the group and the evaluation of group performance. Finally, it should be remembered that roles should be traded from case to case to the extent possible. Each individual should have a turn at presenting a portion of the group's findings.

part 2

Fundamental Processes in Consumer Behavior

This section deals with the basic human behavioral processes of attention, perception, learning, need and motivation, and attitude formation and change. Attention to and perception of both physical and mental stimuli are the focal points of the first three cases. The next two cases concern the roles of *prior* learning in consumer decision making and consumer information sources in making a purchase decision.

The motivation and need arousal case forces students to look beyond consumer "wants" in developing a bank marketing strategy. And, finally, the last two cases in this section focus on development and change in consumer attitudes for a new product and a well-known retail chain.

Students should remember that although these cases emphasize a specific aspect of consumer behavior, the case analyses should include discussion on other pertinent behavioral dimensions used in answering the questions at the end of each case and developing a marketing program to cope with the case problems.

chapter 1

Attention to and Perception of Market Stimuli

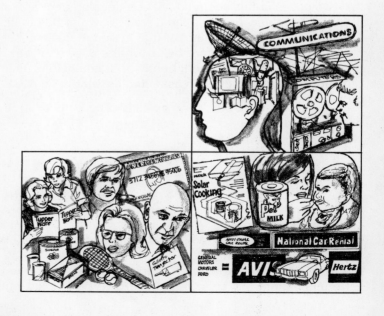

Quench
Fruit Punch Mix

*This case was prepared by **James M. Clapper**, Babcock Graduate School of Management, Wake Forest University. The case was made possible through the cooperation of Henderson Advertising Agency and one of the agency's clients; the scenario and the product have been changed to provide anonymity for the client. This case is intended to serve as the basis for classroom discussion rather than to illustrate either effective or ineffective handling of an administrative situation.*

Early in September 1975, Product Manager Dennis Johnston sat at his desk reviewing the results of the recently completed packaging research study undertaken for his product, Quench Fruit Punch Mix. The test had been conducted to determine whether a change should be made to make packaging more consistent with the overall marketing strategy for the product.

The strategy outlined in the 1976 annual plan called for a more direct positioning of Quench Fruit Punch Mix as a drink for mealtime consumption by the whole family. If any packaging changes were to be made in the upcoming year, final decisions would have to be made in a week or so. Lead times required by Production, Advertising, Merchandising and Sales dictated a decision within this time if all marketing efforts were to be coordinated and all outlets fully stocked with the new package in time for the beginning of the strong spring-summer selling season for soft drinks. Accordingly, the division president had asked the marketing group to have their recommendations to him within the week. This left Johnston with only two more days in which to develop his assessment of the costs and benefits of such a package change and to make his report to Jeanne Ray, the group product manager to whom he reported.

Background

Quench Fruit Punch Mix is a product of the Snack Foods Division of Kestor Corporation. Quench is Kestor's entry in the $450 million powdered soft drink market, a market dominated by General Food's Kool-Aid and Borden's Wyler's.

The powdered soft drink market before 1974 was unspectacular with little innovation and only ordinary growth. However, spurred by consumer resistance to rapidly increasing prices for canned and bottled noncarbonated soft drinks, sales of powdered mixes rose at a rate of 50 percent in both 1974 and 1975. This growth has not gone unnoticed, and several firms are thought to be studying ways to cut themselves in for a share of this market.

At the national level, Kool-Aid and Wyler's each now claim about 40 percent of the business with another 10 percent going to Pillsbury's Funny Face, the only other brand of a major company in the field. Within the trade, however, it is known that RJR Foods, a subsidiary of R. J. Reynolds Industries, is planning the introduction of a mix version of its popular Hawaiian Punch. RJR Foods apparently plans to introduce this new product early in 1976 with heavy promotional spending (approximately $6 million) which promises to bolster promotion industry wide, draw more consumer attention to the product class in general, and, hopefully, expand industry sales even further.

Kestor Corporation has been a beneficiary of this increased activity in the powdered drink market. Kestor's Snack Foods Division manufactures and markets several prepared foods, distributed only in the southeastern states. Although only a regional marketer, Kestor has managed to achieve prominence within its region, and several of its brands have significant market shares within their geographic territory. Kestor introduced Quench in 1972 with little marketing and promotional support, relying instead on a slight price advantage to appeal to consumers. In mid-1974, when the growth trend for this product class became evident, the decision was made to become more aggressive with Quench. Dennis Johnston was assigned exclusively to the product. Promotional support was stepped up, and the price differential between Quench and the major brands was eliminated gradually. Late in 1975 it was estimated that Quench had captured an approximate 10 percent share of the market in its eight-state marketing area. Exhibit 1 con-

EXHIBIT 1   *Comparative income statement 1974–1975 (in thousands)*

	1974	1975[1]
Sales	$4,190	$6,280
Less: Cost of goods sold[2]	1,470	2,200
Gross margin	$2,720	$4,080
Less: Marketing administration and sales[3]	900	1,400
Less: Media advertising	485	725
Less: Sales promotion	260	400
Less: Research and development[4]	65	125
Before tax contribution to general overhead and profit	$1,010	$1,430

[1] Year-end figures estimated on basis of first nine months of year.
[2] Transferred from production at full production cost.
[3] Includes direct costs of product management, allocated cost of sales department and allocated marketing department overhead.
[4] Includes both product and process improvement research as well as market research.

tains an income statement for Quench with 1974 figures compared with estimated 1975 year-end totals.

The Package Change Study

Rationale

In developing the 1976 marketing plan for Quench, the company decided to seek greater sales for the product by encouraging greater mealtime consumption of Quench by all members of the family. During discussion of how this strategy might be implemented, questions arose as to whether the existing package should be redesigned, perhaps around a mealtime theme, so that it would communicate a message to consumers more consonant with the intended marketing strategy. As a result of these discussions, $40,000 was budgeted for the development and testing of alternative package designs, the goal being to find a suitable replacement for the current package that could help communicate the desired product position without damaging the existing brand franchise.

A New York package design firm was retained at a cost of $33,000 to develop two alternative designs. Two designs were developed, both of which were felt to be superior to the existing package in communicating the mealtime message. These new designs are identified here as the "Red" and the "Gold" designs.

Instituting a package change is a costly undertaking. It was estimated by the production department that changeover costs in that department would amount to $2,000. In addition, there would be added costs of producing new media ads, new point-of-purchase materials, and new sales aids for the sales force. Johnston estimated the total cost of a change would be approximately $35,000. With this much money at stake, it was decided to test consumer reactions to both new designs before making any decision.

Consumer Test Design

Henderson Advertising Agency, Kestor's Agency for Quench and several other products of the Snack Foods Division, was given the assignment of testing the new package designs. The test program developed by Henderson was designed to answer four basic questions:

1. Which design is better able to achieve brand identification?

2. Which design is better able to communicate brand characteristics?

3. Which design will stimulate interest in purchase more effectively?

4. Which design will have greatest acceptance among current Quench users?

A two-part test was used to answer these questions. The first part used a tachistoscope to measure brand identification. The second part determined consumers' perceptions of Quench as influenced by the different packages and also determined their interest in purchasing the product.

Personal interviews were conducted with female household heads who purchase powdered soft drink mixes. These women were recruited via shopping center intercepts in three cities: New Orleans, Atlanta, and Greenville, South Carolina. In each city the women were divided into three groups as they were recruited. A tachistoscope was used to show each woman a color slide of a simulated supermarket aisle display of soft drink mixes; the three products displayed were Kool-Aid, Wyler's, and Quench. Positions of the different products were rotated in different slides so that although each woman saw one slide, all six possible product position combinations were shown. Women were exposed to the Red, Gold, or current package designs depending upon the group to which they were assigned.

The slides were shown to the women at eight different exposure lengths from 1/125 of a second to one full second, or until the products were correctly identified. The exposure length at which the respondent correctly identified each product was recorded. Prior to seeing the test slide, each subject was shown a control slide containing a popular floor wax product, and the exposure length at which the respondent was able to identify this product was recorded. The data from the control slide showing were used in the analysis to weight the samples to remove the effects of different distributions of perception thresholds in the three groups.

In the second part of the test each respondent was exposed to the two packages she did *not* see in the first part of the test. If she had seen the Red design in the tachistoscope slide, then she now saw the Gold package and the current package. One of the two packages was placed on a table in front of the respondent together with packages of Kool-Aid, Wyler's, and Funny Face. Each woman was asked to rate Quench (on the basis of what she thought it would be like, if untried) on a list of attributes associated with the basic marketing strategy. Table 2 contains this list of attributes. When the rating task was completed, the Quench package was removed from view and replaced by the second package. The respondent was asked to rate the product contained in the second package using the same set of attributes. Next, the woman was shown both packages together and was asked to rate them on a list of comparative statements about the same attributes.

Each woman was then asked a battery of demographic and powdered soft drink usage questions. Finally, each respondent was shown the two Quench packages together with the competitive products and offered 50¢ toward her next purchase of soft drink mix. She was asked to indicate which of the products in front of her (or any other soft drink mix) she would like the allowance for.

A total of 379 interviews were completed in the test, approximately one third of which came from each city. Of these, 155 women were former triers of Quench while 224 were nontriers. Tables depicting the major results of this test follow.

TABLE 1 *Brand identification test results*

Exposure Time (Seconds)	Red Package			Gold Package			Current Package			Kool-Aid	Wyler's
	All Respondents	Quench Triers	Non-triers	All Respondents	Quench Triers	Non-triers	All Respondents	Quench Triers	Non-triers	All Respondents	All Respondents
1/125	22%	20%	22%	12%	13%	11%	19%	22%	17%	54%	28%
1/60	12	11	12	12	18	7	12	16	9	20	17
1/30	13	17	11	15	13	17	22	30	17	9	10
1/15	12	13	11	15	18	13	13	8	17	7	12
1/8	11	6	15	10	9	11	12	12	12	4	8
1/4	10	6	14	9	7	10	10	8	11	3	11
1/2	7	4	9	13	15	12	6	2	8	1	5
1	3	2	4	7	7	7	2	—	4	1	5
Did not recognize	10	21	2	7	—	12	4	2	5	1	4
Sample sizes	128	54	74	125	52	73	126	50	76	97	81

15

TABLE 2　　*Monadic opinion ratings (Percent rating each design "excellent" on a six-point scale)*

	All Respondents	Quench Triers	Non-triers
Overall opinion			
Red	16%	14%	17%
Gold	15	17	13
Current	7	14	3
Good w/meals			
Red	20	23	17
Gold	17	20	15
Current	9	12	4
Thirst quenching			
Red	18	24	15
Gold	19	20	19
Current	12	20	7
Real fruit flavor			
Red	16	20	13
Gold	15	23	15
Current	13	25	5
High quality drink			
Red	19	22	17
Gold	17	20	14
Current	13	22	7
Refreshing drink			
Red	16	20	14
Gold	17	20	15
Current	11	21	4
Good between meals			
Red	10	18	8
Gold	15	18	10
Current	11	23	9
Nutritious			
Red	13	20	8
Gold	13	16	11
Current	12	20	6
Good value			
Red	16	15	13
Gold	16	20	16
Current	13	21	7
Something children will like			
Red	21	23	19
Gold	20	21	19
Current	10	17	5
(Bases) Triers:	Red (100)	Gold (103)	Current (106)
Nontriers:	Red (149)	Gold (151)	Current (149)

TABLE 3   *Paired comparison (Product preferences)*

Prefer:	Total Respondents	Quench Trier	Non-trier
Overall opinion			
Red	64%	56%	69%
Gold	46	39	51
Current	36	49	28
Good w/meals			
Red	73	71	75
Gold	54	49	58
Current	17	24	13
Thirst quenching			
Red	74	70	77
Gold	54	46	59
Current	18	26	11
Real fruit flavor			
Red	62	59	64
Gold	41	35	25
Current	37	48	29
High quality drink			
Red	62	55	66
Gold	42	35	47
Current	34	47	25
Refreshing drink			
Red	71	69	72
Gold	54	46	59
Current	21	29	14
Good between meals			
Red	41	40	42
Gold	31	26	35
Current	67	72	64
Nutritious			
Red	65	64	66
Gold	49	43	53
Current	23	28	19
Good value			
Red	47	44	50
Gold	34	30	37
Current	51	59	45
Something children will like			
Red	73	69	75
Gold	53	49	55
Current	18	26	12

TABLE 4   *50¢ offer brand preference (Total sample)*

Prefer:	All Respondents	Quench Triers	Non-triers
Quench			
Red	27%	31%	24%
Gold	14	14	14
Current	7	8	6
Kool-Aid	40	35	43
Funny Face	3	4	3
Wyler's	7	5	8
Other	2	3	2
Sample sizes	379	155	224

TABLE 5   *50¢ offer brand preference*

Chose:	Red vs. Current			Gold vs. Current			Red vs. Gold		
	Total Respondents	Quench Trier	Non-trier	Total Respondents	Quench Trier	Non-trier	Total Respondents	Quench Trier	Non-trier
Quench									
Red	35%	38%	32%	—	—	—	42%	47%	39%
Gold	—	—	—	29%	30%	27%	15	14	15
Current	7	8	7	14	18	12	—	—	—
Kool-Aid	48	40	52	40	38	41	34	29	37
Funny Face	3	4	3	3	5	1	4	4	4
Wyler's	6	6	5	11	7	14	3	2	4
Other	1	2	1	2	2	3	2	4	1
No answer	—	2	—	1	—	2	—	—	—
Sample size	125	50	75	131	55	76	124	49	75

TABLE 6   *Demographics*

	Total Respondents	Quench Trier	Non-trier
Respondents	379	155	224
Age: Female head of household			
Under 25	27%	24%	29%
25—34	33	36	30
Under 35	60	60	59
35—49	25	23	26
50 and over	15	17	15
Over 35	40	40	41
	100%	100%	100%
Household income			
Under $5,000	10%	8%	12%
$5,000—$8,000	19	24	15
$8,000—$10,000	12	10	13
Under $10,000	41	42	40
$10,000—$15,000	28	31	26
$15,000 and over	31	27	34
Over $10,000	59	58	60
	100%	100%	100%
Race			
White	75%	74%	75%
Black	25	26	25
	100%	100%	100%
Employment female head of household			
Not employed	54%	54%	54%
Employed part-time	6	5	6
Employed full-time	40	41	40
Total employed	46	46	46
	100%	100%	100%
Marital status			
Married	79%	76%	80%
Never married	10	11	10
Widowed	6	8	5
Divorced	5	5	5
	100%	100%	100%
Number in household			
1—2	35%	34%	35%
3—4	43	41	45
5 or more	22	25	20
	100%	100%	100%

TABLE 7   *Soft drink mix awareness/usage*

	Total Respondents	Quench Trier	Non-trier
Respondents	379	155	224
Brand awareness			
Quench	90%	100%	84%
Kool-Aid	100	100	100
Funny Face	88	87	89
Wyler's	82	80	83
Brand(s) ever used			
Quench	42%	97%	4%
Kool-Aid	98	100	97
Funny Face	39	48	33
Wyler's	52	56	49
Brand used most often			
Quench	11%	26%	—
Kool-Aid	67	56	74
Funny Face	5	5	6
Wyler's	14	10	17
Others	3	3	3
	100%	100%	100%
Drinking family members			
Female HHH	40%	42%	39%
Husband	27	30	24
Teens	96	96	96
Children	74	74	75
Others	14	13	15
	100%	100%	100%
Member who drinks most			
Female HHH	8%	7%	8%
Husband	3	2	4
Teens	58	64	52
Children	27	23	31
Others	4	4	5
	100%	100%	100%
Times drunk			
At meals	46%	53%	42%
Between meals	17	12	20
Both same	37	35	38
	100%	100%	100%

Questions

1. How do you interpret the results of the tachistoscope test? What are the implications of these results for the package design decision?

2. How do you interpret the results of the opinion questions? What are the decision implications of these results?

3. What other powdered drink mix attributes do you feel might be important to consumers?

4. If the tachistoscope test results and the opinion measurement test results are in conflict, how should this conflict be resolved?

5. What changes, if any, would you have made in the design of this study?

6. What additional information would you find useful in making this package decision?

7. If you were Johnston, what would be your recommendations to Ray? Why?

Stanton
Chemical Company

*This case was prepared by **Daniel L. Sherrell,** School of Business Administration, Georgia Southern University.*

Stanton Chemical Company produces and distributes a liquid laundry bleach under its own brand, Clo-White, on a regional basis. The company was founded in 1950 by its current president, Robert M. Stanton. From a modest beginning, the company has grown in size until it now has annual sales of over $6 million out of an estimated total industry sales in 1975 of $130 million. Clorox, Purex, and Fleecy White, brands of three major consumer goods manufacturers sold nationwide, control about 55 percent of total industry sales. The remaining 45 percent is spread among some twenty-six companies, including Stanton Chemical, who primarily sell their products on a regional basis.

Stanton Chemical has its headquarters in a large southern city and operates several mixing and bottling plants in the southeast region. Stanton's major competitor is Allison Products, Inc., whose bleach is produced and distributed from its plant in Tennessee. The respective market shares for Stanton, Allison, and another regional competitor are shown in Table 1.

TABLE 1   *Average market share*

	1972	1973	1974	1975
Stanton Chemical	3.9%	4.2%	4.8%	5.0%
Allison Products	2.0	3.4	4.9	6.5
Coastal Chemical	1.9	2.5	3.6	4.5

Laundry
Bleach

Liquid laundry bleach is used primarily by homemakers to remove stains and whiten clothes. Bleach and detergents are also used to help take out stains and yellowing due to age.

Trade association estimates place the percentage of bleach sold through grocery stores and related food outlets at around 94 percent. The regional brands generally are similar in price to the national brands, and in 1975 both sold for the following average retail prices:

Gallon container	$.84—$.88
Half-gallon container	$.43—$.47
Quart container	$.22—$.26

Prior to 1960, laundry bleach was sold mainly in heavy glass bottles with a handle at the top to assist in lifting and pouring. In late 1960, Clorox came out with a plastic bottle that cost slightly more than a glass bottle but was less costly overall because its use reduced the breakage problem of glass containers to practically nothing. By 1963 plastic containers were the standard package used for bleach.

The manufacture of bleach is simple since it is merely sodium hypo-chlorite and water mixed together in a solution. All of the bleaches on the market contain 5.25 percent sodium hypochlorite and 94.75 percent inert ingredients (water), but bleach produced in this manner is subject to an "aging" problem. When first produced, laundry bleach has no odor and is at its highest potency level. However, once it has been on the shelf for a length of time (five to eight days), the solution begins to break down chemically. The chlorine in the mixture is given off as a gas; hence, the strong smell that certain bleaches exhibit. When a bleach breaks down in this manner, it loses some of its potential for whitening and stain removal, but smells "stronger" to the consumer.

Stanton's
Distribution Strategy

Because mixing and bottling plants are relatively simple to build and inex-pensive to operate in cases where large volumes of a product are concerned, Stanton has built plants close to several of its major market areas. Another factor in this distribution strategy decision is the relatively low unit value and heavy weight per unit of product which cause transportation costs to be characteristically high. Stanton's regional competitors have been reluctant to follow this strategy so far, choosing instead to place more emphasis in their marketing strategy on the promotion of their brands.

The management of Stanton Chemical has always emphasized a somewhat higher than average customer service level on the theory that "The consumer can't buy our products if they aren't on the shelves when they look for them!" In other words, management feels that an efficient distribu-tion system is just as important in the marketing of their bleach as price, promotion, or the product itself.

As a result of this emphasis by top management, Stanton has developed the capability to deliver its bleach quicker and more consistently than any of its competitors by locating mixing and bottling plants close to its markets. This capability has provided Stanton with a good reputation among retailers and helps make the job of Stanton's sales force easier.

Industry Conditions

The industry which Stanton is in may be described as extremely competitive. No one producer is able to command a price premium without risking the loss of substantial market share. Promotional activities engaged in by the companies generally consist of a heavy emphasis on advertising through broadcast and print media and the use of personal selling to gain distribution and retailer participation in company promotional campaigns. As stated before, the only real competitive advantage that Stanton currently enjoys in the market place is its ability to deliver its product quicker to the retail outlets.

Stanton's Distinctive Competence

Stanton's distribution system has provided another advantage that management has been unwilling or unable to focus on until now. In tests, using samples of Clo-White, Snowy-White, and a third regional brand, Clo-White outperformed the other two bleaches a significantly higher proportion of the time. The samples were selected at random from local grocers' shelves and tested for their stain removal power and whitening ability. Clo-White performed better than both of the other brands.

As noted before, laundry bleach is identical in composition, regardless of the brand. The variation in performance was attributed to the lower average shelf age of Clo-White as compared to its competitors. A survey disclosed that Clo-White was two to three days fresher when it arrived on the shelf due to Stanton's distribution system. Because it is fresher, it has more cleaning power for a short period of time before it, too, begins to break down.

The previous vice-president of marketing, who had helped found the company with Stanton and had retired five years earlier, had been unwilling to make use of this knowledge. His belief was that "Consumers can't tell the difference in strength between bleaches. They are mainly interested in price." As a result, he had developed the current distribution system as a means to deliver the product quicker and cheaper to the retailer and thus gain a price advantage over competitors. This initially was the case, but the competition for market share quickly forced down prices to Stanton's level.

Consumers

Despite the availability of detergents with bleach additives, homemakers, according to industry estimates, still look to the chlorine-based laundry bleach as the means to remove stains and whiten clothes. The female who is married, has children, and has her own washer and dryer generally represents the heaviest-user segment of the laundry bleach market. Independent research studies have been done that suggest the woman's attitude toward domestic activities and the degree of family orientation are primary determinants in brand selection. Women who possess a strong domestic orientation are more likely to perceive real or imagined differences in the quality of various bleaches, while women who possess weaker orientations will tend to rate all brands equal in quality and prefer to shop for the lowest priced brands.

Corporate Management's Concern

Top management has expressed concern over the apparent ability of Snowy-White to outsell Clo-White in the market place, particularly since the price and promotional expenditures for both products are approximately equal. In an effort to find a remedy for the situation, the vice-president of marketing recommended that a marketing research study be conducted to determine what consumers actually thought of Clo-White compared with other brands and, if possible, some reasons for the particular brand image.

Marketing Research

A sample of 1,000 homemakers was selected at random from several large southern cities where Clo-White enjoyed a large market share. They were asked to rank pairs of leading regional brands in terms of their perceived similarity, then to rank the brands according to their own individual preferences. Finally, the respondents were asked to give reasons why they ranked the bleaches in that particular order. While the answers to the final part did not represent "hard" enumerative data, nevertheless, it was felt that a consistent interpretation of the information might yield some useful results. The compared brands and the results of the data analysis are shown in Figure 1.

A computerized, nonmetric, multidimensional scaling program was utilized to show the positions of the brands relative to each other and to the consumer's ideal image of what a bleach should be. The labeled axes represent the two main dimensions on which the brands of bleach appear to have been evaluated.

As shown, the top three brands come closest to the ideal point, representing the position of the ideal bleach. Of particular interest to the researchers at Stanton was the fact that Snowy-White was perceived by the respondents as being the strongest bleach on the market. In light of the results from the earlier laboratory tests, the respondents' reasons were examined to see if any possible explanations for the situation could be found. Some of the typical comments received from the respondents were:

"All the bleaches are the same. I just buy the cheapest one."

"There's not much difference in price, so I usually buy the stronger bleach. It gets my clothes cleaner and that's what I want."

"Well, you can take the cap off this one (Snowy-White), and smell the bleach. The other brands just don't have that kind of smell. I always buy the stronger bleach to get my clothes cleaner."

FIGURE 1   *Marketing Research Results*

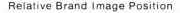

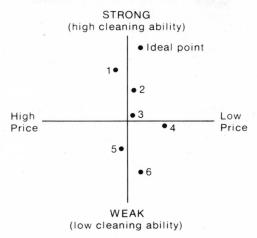

Composite Brand Ranking:

1. Snowy-White
2. Blue Sky
3. Clo-White
4. Dixie Day
5. Miracle-White
6. Quality

Current Situation

Allison Products has launched its fall promotion campaign one month early this year, and preliminary indications are that a bigger-than-usual campaign is planned. The current campaign features television and magazine advertisements stressing the cleaning and whitening power of Snowy-White bleach. In addition, a 10¢-off deal on the gallon container of bleach is being run simultaneously with the advertising campaign.

Mr. Pearl, current vice-president of marketing at Stanton, feels certain that Allison is starting an intensified promotional effort to increase Snowy-White's market share. Furthermore, he believes that it will succeed in further eroding Clo-White's position in the market unless Stanton reacts quickly. Pearl feels that what most consumers want is the strongest bleach on the market and that they are willing to pay at least the competitive price for it. He points out that the research proves Clo-White is the strongest bleach on the market due to Stanton's quick delivery time. Thus, he feels that Stanton should mount an advertising campaign which "educates" the consumer about the superiority of Clo-White over its competitors. "Tell them the research results and that smell doesn't make any difference. We must maintain our quality."

Mr. Lawrence, brand manager for Clo-White, feels that the research results indicate the importance the consumer attaches to smell as an indicator of strength. "Telling them that Clo-White is the strongest bleach won't convince them once they take the cap off and smell it. They just won't believe that kind of advertising."

Mr. Lawrence feels that Stanton Chemical must allow its bleach to "age" and to develop a stronger smell. "Most consumers go by the smell. Let's give them what they want." Lawrence's plan is to introduce "Clo-White Plus" and advertise it as a new and stronger bleach. "Shoot, we won't be lying to them; it will have a stronger smell and that's what they want. Gentlemen, we're dealing with consumer perceptions. How do you think Snowy-White got ahead of us?"

Mr. Stanton has heard both ideas. He doesn't want to reduce the product's quality; but, on the other hand, he does see the merits of Mr. Lawrence's arguments. He has asked Mr. Pearl and Mr. Lawrence to develop additional alternatives before making a decision.

Questions

1. What other alternatives might Stanton Chemical consider?

2. What would be the short versus long run effects of each strategy?

3. How important is olefactory perception in the consumer's evaluation of bleach and other similar products? How easy (difficult) would it be for a company to "educate" consumers about product characteristics which are contradictory to their own perceptions of the product?

4. Is Mr. Lawrence's suggestion ethical? Or is he right in giving consumers what they "want?"

Lefty's, Ltd.

This case was prepared by **Carter L. Grocott,** *College of Business and Economics, West Virginia University.*

Lefty's, Ltd. is a men's clothing store located in a midwestern college town. In twenty years Lefty's has grown from little more than a storefront operation to a 3,200 square foot men's specialty shop and college student boutique. Almost since entering town, Lefty's assumed the leadership position in retailing for men in the under-40 age group and the college student.

While Lefty's has been profitable over the years, the last two years have shown a decline in sales and profits. (See Table 1.) Norman Mathews, the owner, feels the problem is that Lefty's does not project the same image to the market that was so carefully cultivated over the years. In an effort to ascertain what the community thinks of Lefty's, Mathews hired Kingman and Associates, a small advertising agency, to find out how consumers perceive his store.

TABLE 1   *Sales and profits of Lefty's (1972–1975)*

	1972	1973	1974	1975
Net sales	$251,255	$302,717	$299,247	$282,134
Net profit	75,950	81,128	79,147	74,927

Background

Lefty's, Ltd. was opened in 1956 by Norman Mathews after he had spent five years learning the business in his brother's men's wear shop. Lefty's began with a store layout of little more than 1,000 square feet and used display fixtures. In the next ten years Mathews modestly expanded his store area and upgraded its facilities by always buying used items. Such frugality provided Lefty's with a pleasing if unexciting decor, at a fraction of normal cost.

In 1965 Lefty's was able to acquire second floor storage space above the store, which allowed for an expansion of the sales area to almost 1,500 square feet. While new carpeting was added throughout the store, again only used cabinets and fixtures were purchased.

Although Mathews desired more space, Lefty's expansion was blocked at the current location by existing leaseholders on both sides of the store. Because the location was ideal for his customers, Mathews looked to other alternatives to satisfy his space requirements, so in 1969 he opened the fore-runner of his student boutique in the basement of a nearby building. The new 288 square foot store had very simple appointments and operated under the name of "The Downstairs Shop." The store carried jeans, shirts, belts, sandals, and other items of interest to the male and female college student. The Downstairs Shop operated successfully until early 1973 when Lefty's was able to obtain additional floor space next door.

The acquisition of the new space allowed for a doubling of sales space and a vast increase in much needed storage areas. With the expansion of the store, Mathews completely redecorated the facilities. With new carpets, display and lighting fixtures, cabinets, and wall and ceiling treatments, the store was a changed operation from top to bottom. The exterior also was refurbished with brick veneer and new signing. About 800 square feet of the new area was allocated to the student boutique, designed in a rustic fashion. The boutique carries many of the same items offered in the former The Downstairs Shop. Although often a hardship, Lefty's operated throughout the redecoration process. The store had its "Grand Opening" in October 1973.

Merchandising Practices

Until recently Lefty's carried a wide range of nationally advertised brands. This broad selection of merchandise seemed to enable Lefty's to meet the needs of all its customers. Over the last several years, Mathews, who does all the buying, has been able to obtain some excellent buys on unbranded merchandise. As a result, the Lefty's brand name now appears more frequently on suits, sport coats, shirts, and other items. During this process, the number of national brands carried was sharply reduced. Mathews suggested that the unbranded was the same quality level as the national brands, but privately some of his salespeople did not agree with his assessment.

Along with the increased use of the Lefty's brand there was a shift in the type of national brands offered; the store now is stocked with unfamiliar national brands. Mathews again claims no change in quality, but rather just good buying on his part. Within the past year Mathews has begun to purchase some irregulars and extras to offer as specials in the college boutique. While this policy has not been extended to the rest of the store, Mathews indicated it might be possible in the future.

When compared with stores in other communities, Lefty's has always tended to be rather conservative in its offering of styles. But this policy matches the character of both the student market as well as the community as a whole and Mathews feels it has made Lefty's successful.

The Mathews pricing philosophy has changed in the last several years from one with moderate prices with few price lines to that of high prices with few price lines. In a practical sense, the prices are fictional, for Lefty's runs what amounts to a continuous sale on at least some of the store's merchandise. It has become almost a standing joke in the community that no one would buy an item from Lefty's unless it were on sale, and that seems to be all the time. Mathews feels that the sales add excitement to the store and that people like them.

The only advertising Lefty's does is through the local newspapers, morning and evening, and the student paper. All of Lefty's advertisements stress the same thing—a sale. Mathews accepts no cooperative advertising. He feels that sales items are what bring the customer into the store, not any fancy copy with its pseudo-sophisticated pictures.

Competition

The competitors have come and gone over the twenty years Lefty's has been in operation, but only one full-line men's store, Gordon's, is providing serious competition. Gordon's caters to the same market as Lefty's but its student-oriented clothing is included within the rest of the store's merchandise. Gordon's is located only one block away, and Gordon's management suggests that the only reason Mathews remodeled Lefty's is because Gordon's redecorated the year before. Competition between the two stores has become quite intense in the last several years. In an effort to counter Lefty's pricing policies, Gordon's has run advertisements in the local papers stressing their normally low prices. Copy in other ads has suggested that customers need not wait for a sale to obtain a good buy. Both advertisements have been directed toward Lefty's customers.

Additional local competition comes from two "jeans shops" and two men's wear shops in a nearby mall. While the "jeans shops" do offer strong competition in their specialty, their merchandise lines are very limited. The two men's shops appear to be having a good deal of difficulty generating any type of business. The two mall shops offer merchandise at the same price and quality level as Lefty's and Gordon's, but have generated little interest in the community. Most people seem to feel that the two men's stores provide a much higher quality and style level than the rest of the mall stores and as a result are of little interest to the typical "value conscious" mall customer. Rumors have spread that the owners of these two men's shops have realized their mistake and plan to relocate next year within the downtown area. Mathews has some concern over this possibility.

Consumers

The consumers in this community have been and continue to be very mobile. Even with the recent recession, the community had a much higher population turnover than the national average. The city has a population of 40,000 with an additional 30,000 suburban residents. There also are 16,000 student consumers who play an important role in the clothing market. (Although Mathews is unsure how important the student is to Lefty's business, it would be safe to assume that 50 percent of sales emanate from the student population.) Both the community and student populations have increased about 33 percent over the last twenty years.

As one would expect of a college town, the population is well educated with a college degree being the rule rather than the exception. It should be noted that the high educational level is the result not only of the university, but also of several federal agencies which operate facilities in the area. These operations require highly educated personnel.

For some unexplained reason, members of the community tend to be very localized in their shopping behavior. Little shopping is done outside of town, even though there are many shopping areas in a twenty-five to seventy-five mile range of town reachable by an excellent new highway system. The majority of television viewing in the community comes from this twenty-five to seventy-five mile range via cable television. Although the community is exposed to advertising from large retailers in neighboring areas, it seems to make little difference in the shopping patterns.

Regarding the tendency to shop locally, the student population operates in much the same fashion as the townspeople. However, the majority of students make only 50 percent of their clothing purchases in town. The remainder of their clothing is usually obtained in their hometowns. While the student population is not very affluent, its size alone makes it an attractive market.

Image
Study

Because Mathews felt uncomfortable about the image his store might be projecting to the community, he decided to hire Kingman and Associates to conduct an image survey for him. Jim Kingman suggested the following:

1. Compare Lefty's advertised image with the customers' image of the store.

2. Compare Lefty's store image with Gordon's store image.

3. Compare the image of Lefty's customers who used a charge account with those who did not use one.

To conduct the survey, Kingman decided to test three kinds of consumers: those who preferred to shop at Lefty's, those who preferred to shop at Gordon's, and a group of consumers from another community who were unfamiliar with Lefty's.

Over a two-week period, subjects for the first two groups were selected randomly from individuals shopping in the downtown area. Shoppers were assigned to one of two groups on the basis of their answers to the following question: "When considering a clothing purchase, at what store in town do you prefer to shop?" The subjects were then asked to complete a seventeen-item, six-point semantic differential questionnaire. Those who preferred to shop at Lefty's were asked if they generally used a Lefty's charge account in making purchases there. Demographic data was obtained at the end of the interview.

Lefty's advertised image was generated by interviewing subjects drawn from a nearby city. The subjects had no knowledge of the store. They were

EXHIBIT 1 *Lefty's image versus Gordon's image (Mean values)*

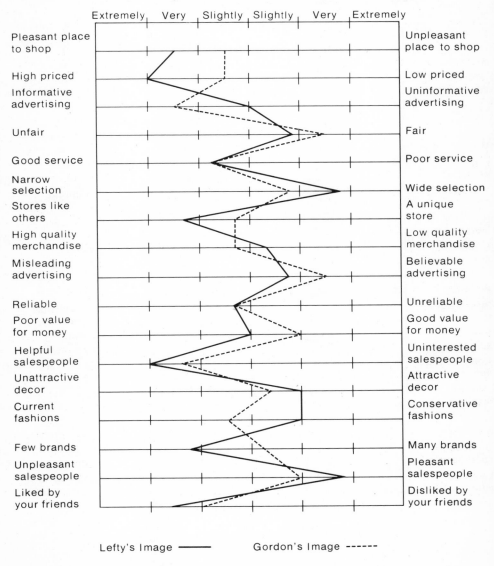

Lefty's Image ——————   Gordon's Image ------

shown a series of Lefty's advertisements and were asked to form a mental picture of the store which did the advertising. With this picture in mind, the subjects were asked to complete the same seventeen-item semantic differential scale.

EXHIBIT 2   *Lefty's advertised image versus actual customer image (Mean values)*

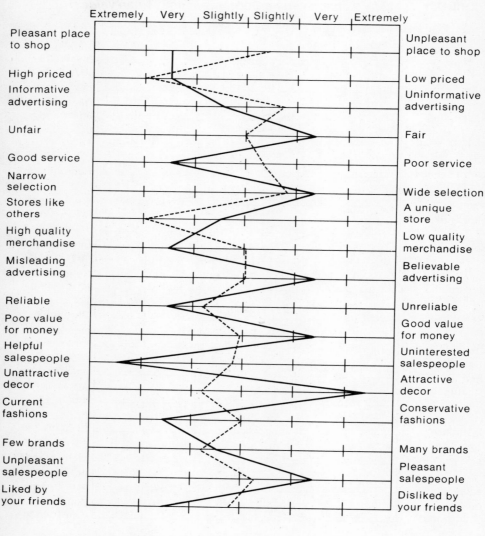

Survey Results

The data generated from the three subject groups were analyzed, and arithmetic means for scale values were calculated. A summary of the results is

EXHIBIT 3   *Lefty's customers' image: Charge account versus no charge account (Mean values)*

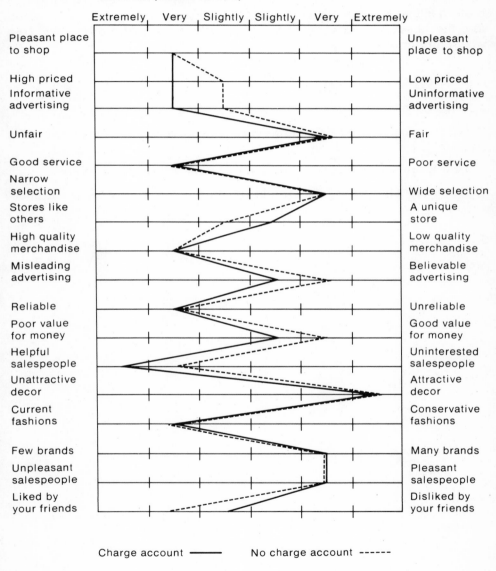

provided in Exhibits 1 through 3. These exhibits provide image profiles for Lefty's, Gordon's, and Lefty's advertising.

Kingman's report to Mathews was basically a descriptive report on his research procedures and the data. Very little interpretation of results were included. Mathews had the report, but was uncertain of just what it meant or what to do. He felt something was wrong and that he must decide what changes to make in his marketing effort if he were to reverse the sales and profit decline. A quick decision was especially important since he believed that the possible relocation of the two mall stores to the downtown area would further erode his business.

Questions

1. What do you see as the problems, if any, with Lefty's image?

2. What action should Mr. Mathews take to make a turnabout in Lefty's sales and profits?

3. How would you evaluate the research that Mr. Kingman performed?

4. What additional image data would you have collected? For what purpose?

chapter 2

Consumer
Learning

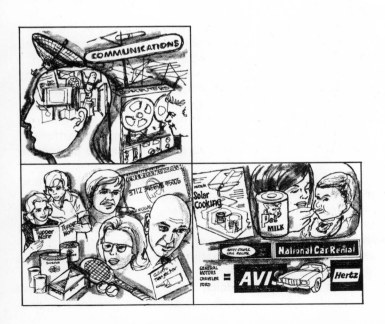

Lumpkin's
Cosmetics, Inc.

*This case was prepared by **M. Wayne DeLozier,** College of Business Administration, University of South Carolina. Copyright © 1976 by M. Wayne DeLozier. Permission granted by author.*

Lumpkin's Cosmetics, Inc. is a large "personal care" firm established in 1922 by John Lumpkin. The company initially developed lipsticks, powders, lotions, and bath oils for women of all ages. The Boston-based company rapidly grew into a national leader in the personal care market, having distribution in all forty-eight states by 1942. During World War II, Lumpkin's supplied the U.S. government with lotions and "lipsticks" that protected soldiers against sunburn, frostbite, wind chapping, and general skin deterioration. After the war, sales dropped dramatically to this purchaser as might be expected. However, the government continued to purchase these product lines for its peace-time army.

In 1968, John Lumpkin retired as president and chairman of the board of the family-owned company, and his son Robert took over as president. Robert Lumpkin worked his way up the corporate ladder after receiving his MBA degree from Harvard. Although Robert was the son of the company founder, he was most capable and deserving of his newly acquired position.

Robert Lumpkin acquired the helm of the company at a most difficult time. Intense competition from Revlon and other domestic and foreign firms was cutting severely into Lumpkin's market share. Profits were not suffering, but they definitely had leveled and Lumpkin feared that a period of decline was imminent.

In 1972, Lumpkin hired Janice Morris, an account executive of Colb and McIntire Advertising Agency which had been handling Lumpkin's advertising. Lumpkin was impressed with Morris' credentials. She had handled the accounts of major cosmetics companies and was experienced in developing communications strategies for a variety of personal care products. Since Lumpkin felt she was an imaginative and creative individual, he created for her the position of consultant to the president.

Since Lumpkin's lines included lipsticks, hand lotions, mascara, eye shadows, eye liners, rouges, base makeup, moisturizers, cleansers, and other related products, Lumpkin felt that an imaginative female was needed to advise him and his staff on these product lines.

The Current
Situation

By the end of fiscal year 1974, Lumpkin's was still in stalemate. Some product lines had improved slightly, while others had declined. Lumpkin realized that an advance in traditional markets or product lines would be costly. He felt reasonably satisfied to hold present market shares for his company's products if new markets could be developed to improve corporate sales and profits.

In early 1975, Lumpkin called his executive board together to discuss expansion, diversification, and potential markets for present products. All agreed that an increase in market shares of present products in present markets would not be worth the cost and effort. Thus, new proposals were suggested for consideration. Ms. Morris suggested that present lines of makeup, mascara, lipsticks, facial creams and moisturizers, rouges, etc. be reformulated and packages redesigned for the male market.

Harry McQuillen objected most strenuously to her proposal as did other male members of the board. "Men do not use makeup, lipstick, mascara, and other lines that we produce."

Morris believed her idea was sound and would create a totally new market for their present lines of products without the costs of adding new product lines or acquiring new production facilities for diversification. In her proposal she stated the following:

"Traditional male-female product barriers have broken down—not to the extent they could, but nevertheless have broken down. Who in the 1950s would have dreamed that men would, a few years later, use hair spray? Who in the 1960s would believe that men would carry purses, make appointments for hair styles, or buy hair dryers? Along with feminine hygiene deodorants came male hygiene deodorants (Braggi, for example).

"Men are just as concerned as women are about their personal appearance—perhaps more so. They are just as vain as women are about how they look. Sex barriers have been broken down. All we would be doing is extending a trend in the unisex revolution.

"Male actors use makeup. They use cleansing creams, moisturizers, rouge, lipstick, powders, eye makeup, etc. They are opinion leaders. We could use them and athletes in ads to show it is not effeminate to use our personal care products to improve personal appearance.

"We can show them that a little dab here and a little dab there covers up blemishes, wrinkles, and highlights their best facial features.

"Remember, gentlemen, that our forefathers wore wigs and used powders. What we have to do is break down the prior learning experiences of men that these products are for "females only"—that they are effeminate! We must educate the mass male market that these are personal care products, not feminine products. They deserve, and indeed owe it to themselves, to look their best. We must emphasize that women will find them more appealing and that other men will not consider them effeminate.

"Through the socialization process, men have learned what is masculine and what is feminine. This is a lot of hogwash. We must educate the male market that there is nothing wrong and that it is all right for them to use personal grooming products to enhance their appearance. Lumpkin's will go down in history as the personal-care company that broke down the sex barriers and developed a new market for personal care products.

"If we are to expand and innovate, we must be willing to take risks."

Tom Robertson: "As vice president of marketing, I am most interested in innovation and expansion. But I am afraid that by implementing this proposal, we'll go down in history as the 'queer' company in the personal care market!"

Robert Lumpkin: "Tom, I understand your concern, but I believe that Janice has come up with an idea that we should explore. As she has pointed out, other traditionally female products have come into popular use by the male market.

"My initial inclination is to go along with her proposal. After all, we have expanded as far as we can in our present markets. Her idea has merit. I feel we should study it."

Questions

1. This case suggests several behavioral notions. Attitude change is one. However, Janice Morris believes that a change in prior learning is the basis for changing attitudes. Discuss the relationship between learning and attitude change and attitude formation.

2. How easy or difficult is it for a company to change consumers' prior learning, both in general and specific product situations?

3. Assuming that Lumpkin's decides to introduce male makeup products, how would you "educate" the market to the use and acceptance of male makeups?

4. What principles of learning would you suggest to Morris and Lumpkin's marketing management as useful in educating the male market for cosmetics?

Crampton Auto Sales, Inc.

This case was prepared by **M. Wayne DeLozier** *and* **Arch G. Woodside,** *College of Business Administration, University of South Carolina. Copyright* © *1976 by M. Wayne DeLozier and Arch G. Woodside. Permission was granted by the authors.*

Crampton Auto Sales was established by Bill Crampton in 1954 after his return from Korea. Bill learned automotive mechanics in the service and decided to open an automotive service center and dealership after the Korean Conflict.

Bill opened Crampton Auto Sales for business in his hometown of Atlanta with a used car lot and auto repair service. With the population growth in Atlanta and the surrounding area, Crampton Auto Sales became a booming business.

Recalling the words of his former Army commander, "Seize the opportunity," Crampton opened a dealership which sold new and used cars while continuing to service all makes of automobiles. With the rising prosperity of Atlanta and the South, Crampton decided to expand operations. During the 1960s he opened dealerships in Birmingham, Augusta, Columbia, Jacksonville, Charleston, and New Orleans.

In 1974, Crampton's experienced a decline in new car sales as did other dealers in the automotive industry. Moreover, Crampton noticed a shift in sales from his dealerships to other dealerships selling other new cars. Although many consumers were buying smaller, fuel-economy cars, Crampton believed that his sales were shrinking more rapidly in the intermediate to luxury size cars than those of his competition. This fact became more evident as consumers began to resume their purchases of larger cars in 1976. Furthermore, dealerships in other parts of the country which sold the same make of car were not experiencing the same decline as Crampton.

At a meeting of the Sales and Marketing Executives International (S.M.E.I.) Club in Atlanta, Crampton discussed his situation with Bill Maggard, a marketing professor at Emory University. Maggard told Crampton about a recent article he had read concerning automotive purchasing in the local retail market. The article described a study which stated that although advertising by auto producers created certain images and informational characteristics in the minds of consumers, purchasers at the local level were more influenced by the marketing activities of local dealers in arriving at a purchase decision for the kind of car they were interested in.

Maggard explained to Crampton that within specific classes of automobiles, image projections of quality, styling, and handling were perceived by consumers as "about the same" among models offered by General Motors, Ford, Chrysler, and A.M.C. The difference in local sales primarily was a function of local dealership promotion.

In clarifying his statement, Maggard offered the following examples: "In consumers' minds the Pontiac Grand Prix, the Chrysler Cordoba, the Chevrolet Monte Carlo, and the Ford LTD are perceived as very similar by consumers. The Mercury Monarch, the Ford Granada, and the Oldsmobile Omega also are perceived as similar by consumers. Once a consumer decides the *class* of car he wants, local dealerships play a major role in influencing the final purchase decision. The study revealed that the amount and kind of information which dealers conveyed to potential customers directly influenced the customer learning process and, thus, local dealer sales."

Crampton was intrigued by this idea and asked Maggard to conduct a study in his market areas to determine the major informational sources for cars which affect his customers' learning behavior.

The
Maggard Report

Maggard conceptualized his task as one of determining the prepurchase information-seeking behavior of automobile consumers. He decided to assess the relative importance which automobile consumers attach to the variety of personal and impersonal information sources.

In November of 1976 Maggard conducted interviews in all seven of Crampton's markets. Three-hundred-fifty personal interviews were conducted with recent new car purchasers (i.e. those who had purchased a 1976 model within the past ninety days). Table 1 shows the results of the study in terms of the relative weight of importance which new car purchasers attach to each of the stated information sources.[1]

Maggard also collected data on what kinds of information that new car purchasers sought and the relative importance that each kind of information had in the purchase decision. Table 2 summarizes the results.

Maggard felt that in writing his report for Crampton he needed to provide an interpretation of the data and recommendations for a course of action for Crampton Auto Sales. Moreover, he believed that he should include several behavioral principles related to learning and explain to Crampton how he could adopt these principles to facilitate consumer learning about Crampton's dealerships and their new cars.

TABLE 1   *Sources of information used by new car purchasers*

Information sources	Weight
Dealer visit [a]	20
Expert opinions [b]	16
Consumer Reports	14
Friends' opinions	12
Spouse	11
Dealer advertising	10
Brochures	8
Manufacturers' advertising	6
News articles	3
TOTAL	100

[a] Information from salespeople, service personnel, personal inspection of cars and facilities, etc.

[b] Auto repair and service people and others perceived by purchasers as knowledgeable about cars.

TABLE 2   *Information sought and its relative importance in purchasing new car*

Information	Weight
Price [a]	11
Dealer service and reputation	28
Warranty	5
Convenience of dealership location	20
Physical product features [b]	22
Options available	14
TOTAL	100

[a] Importance of price information after consumer had determined affordable price range.

[b] Refers to styling, comfort, handling, horsepower, gas economy, etc.

Questions

1. What marketing strategy decisions are most critical for Crampton Auto Sales?

2. What marketing problems have been identified by the Maggard Report?

3. How would you advise a new car buyer in evaluating automobile brands?

4. What learning principles would you suggest that Crampton use in facilitating his customers' learning? How would you implement them?

Notes

[1] The weights shown in Table 1 are average scores for the 350 respondents who allocated 100 points to each of the nine information sources according to their perceived importance.

Videogames:
You Ain't Seen Nothin' Yet

*This case was prepared by **Denis F. Healy**, College of Business and Economics, University of Delaware.*

The Revolution in Consumer Electronics

Who ever heard of Intel Digital Equipment, Fairchild Camera and Instruments, National Semiconductors, or Texas Instruments over a few years ago? Who ever expected to be able to purchase a hand-held calculator for less than $10 or an accurate wrist watch for under $20? How absurd it would have been for anyone to even think that it would be possible to play ping-pong on the TV screen, or to be able to purchase a gadget for the TV set that would allow one to play several sophisticated games for about the cost of a good ping-pong table!

Well, in the past five years, the consumer electronics industry has accomplished this and then some, but not without numerous shakeouts of competitors and a major change in the buying behavior of customers. The diversity of developments and the rate of change of this industry is startling as is the rate of acceptance of such items by consumers.

Whether it is recognized or not, the U.S. market is currently in the midst of a significant revolution in its acceptance and usage of electronic gadgets, and this is just the beginning! The pace has become so hectic that several generations of products have come and gone on the market before there has been significant acceptance of the first generation of ideas. In addition, many of the original innovations and firms responsible for developing markets either have died or have been acquired by more market-sensitive firms.

Clearly, the activities in these consumer electronics markets will be of great importance to the total market of the next decade and will provide many employment and investment opportunities. Thus, appraisal of the current and future marketing activities of leading firms is warranted.

The Development of Videogames

In 1972, Magnavox introduced its videogame Odyssey to the home market. Pong and other coin-operated games began to be seen in hotel lobbies, bars, and amusement parks.[1] Today, the videogame is one of the hottest consumer electronic items to hit the market. The games all employ some form of semiconductor device. Most of the games on the market are variations of ping-pong in which a moving image is hit by electronic paddles from one edge of the screen to the other. With the use of more sophisticated silicon chips or microprocessors, game capabilities may be expanded to the point that the games become smart. Thus, games involving logic and memory such as chess are feasible and will appear on the market by 1977, and at affordable prices.

The Competitive Environment

Characteristic of the hand-held calculator and digital watch businesses, the first video games were high-priced and of limited capability. Product innovation and initial development has been the domain of companies who are comparatively unknown or are newcomers to the business. Pinball manufacturers, for example, have had little if anything to do with videogames. Magnavox in the home market and Ataria in the coin-operated area have been the dominant suppliers. In 1976, the major semiconductor firms such as Fairchild Camera and Instruments, National Semiconductors, and Texas Instruments had products either under development or about to be marketed to the home market.

Other competitors in the business are just beginning to reveal themselves. According to the *Electronics Letter,* a variety of new phases will appear in addition to the vertically integrated firms mentioned previously. The more likely new entrant groups will be the Hong Kong and Korean assemblers who are likely to duplicate the games in much the same fashion as they have done in the digital watch and hand-held calculator markets. Also, among the early entrants may be the nonintegrated calculator and watch companies. Ataria undoubtedly will enter the market with a home unit using a dedicated chip (a chip having only a single capability). In addition, as the pressures mount or as the odds tilt in favor of the semiconductor-based firms, the mechanical pinball producers such as Bally are likely to be stimulated to respond with some form of videogame.[2]

As the prices decline and the technology becomes resolved, it is only reasonable to expect that the more aggressive toy manufacturers will enter with products that will key into their traditional price line range ($20 to $30). Finally, at least for now, TV manufacturers presently are reluctant to do the obvious, that is, to incorporate the game capability into the TV set. The fear, and thus reluctance, is understandable. However, as explained by *Electronics Letter,* the TV manufacturers are "passing up a clear marketing advantage that they possess." [3]

Industry and Market Trends

With strong technology and marketing inputs from such firms, the videogame business is bound to experience rapid advancement in product capability and noticeable declines in business. In mid-1976, the average price for a videogame was $100 with prices reaching the $50 to $60 level by year's end. (J. C. Penny's *1976 Christmas Catalog* offers a four-game videogame for $59.88.) By the end of 1977, units should be in the $20 to $40 range depending on complexity. However, since only about 30 percent of the game cost is for chip and the rest is conventional and established items, shallower experience curves than for hand-held calculators are likely.

Estimates of market size vary widely because of incomplete estimates of production and market acceptance levels. *Electronics Letter* made the following estimates for videogame sales in its February 1976 issue:

> "Highly tentative estimates for 1976 range from 2 million units to 5 million units. Assuming a mid-point figure of 3.5 million units at an average retail price of $80 would imply a retail market of $280 million, or a manufacturer's market size of about $180 million. . . . By next Christmas, we expect every major retailer to be carrying at least one videogame and consumer demand to absorb every available set." [4]

As projected in *Electronics Letter,* Fairchild Camera and Instruments forecasts the 1977 market at 5 million units at an average retail price of $60 for total retail sales of $350 million. In 1980, the volume forecasted is 20 million units at $40 per unit retail for industry sales of $800 million.[5]

Product Development

Chip development is varied, to say the least. There are three chip technologies in competition: (1) dedicated chips, the most common and most replaceable; (2) game chip sets, a passing fancy; and (3) microprocessors. Given the trends in this area, it is possible, if not certain, that the microprocessor route will be the dominant basis for building videogames once the experimentation and shakeout stages of the life cycle have passed. Already, options exist for color, variable speeds, sound, on-screen scoring, variable paddle sizes, and "English" on the ball. Other programmable features are yet to hit the market, but there is no question there will be ample room for innovation for several years to come. The future of the games clearly is contingent upon the combined rates of development of the technology of semiconductors and the rate of consumer learning and acceptance of technology into their homes and life styles.

Future Developments and Marketing Strategies

There are as many product/market strategies in evidence as there are producers. For instance, the Fairchild Video Entertainment System is employing the "razor blade marketing approach." The system is based on the sale of a console unit retailing in the $100 to $150 range. Cartridges containing from two to four games may be plugged into the console. As consumers tire of one set of games, they simply purchase another cartridge for $15 to $20. With such an approach, a great deal of flexibility is possible. For instance, a "game-of-the-month" program and libraries offering loans of game cartridges are feasible. In addition to the videogame as a means of entertainment, there is an obvious application for educational purposes. Some authorities expect the educational uses would be at least equal to the entertainment applications. The acceptability of such innovation clearly is contingent upon how quickly consumers learn to use the game and how rapidly they seek variations in game content.

As the technology becomes resolved and as the market indicates its receptivity to the variety of applications possible for such devices, it is likely that the videogame will be among the more significant consumer applications of semiconductors yet to surface.

Most games on the market are mini-TV transmitters. There have been interference problems caused by the games to the point that the FCC has elected to test all new models appearing on the market. The interference problems and the slowing effect on the market entry of the FCC testing program has stimulated some game manufacturers to develop games that attach directly to the set. Heathkit, for one, has introduced a six-game Screensport kit which attaches directly to a Heathkit solid-state TV set. According to *Popular Mechanics,* some TV manufacturers are considering building receptacles into TV sets that will allow for direct connection not only of videogames but also quite possibly video tape/disk units, TV cameras, and at some point perhaps even home computers. Currently, Magnavox and Broadmoor/Olympics offer TV sets with totally integrated games.[6]

Unresolved Issues

There are many issues to be resolved, however. For instance, there currently are 125 million TV sets in use in the U.S. (about one-half are color) and a larger total number are in use throughout the world. Given this working inventory of sets, how many will be converted to video use? And at what rate of acceptance? For a TV set producer, what would be the cost/benefit analysis outcome from integrating videogame possibilities into the set? Is the razor blade product strategy sound given that fixed chip games may be profitably marketed in a couple of years at $19.95 each? What is the potential repair market associated with the games and who should take advantage of the opportunity?

Questions

1. What are some factors limiting the acceptance of videogames?

2. What can individual manufacturers or the industry do to accelerate the acceptance of the game concept?

3. If you were associated with a TV station or one of the networks, what kind of reaction would you have to the use of the videogame and what kind of action might you suggest to deal with the situation? (The average TV viewer spends over five hours per day in front of the set. How much of that time might be replaced by videogame use?)

4. In what ways might your knowledge of learning theory be applied to the development of marketing programs to stimulate rapid acceptance of videogames?

5. If you were a TV set manufacturer, what consideration would you make (a) about integrating a videogame directly into your TV sets, (b) about providing a receptacle for a videogame connection to your nonintegrated set?

6. Given the potential capability of videogame and related devices using semiconductors technology, what are some possible new product offers and what are the major consumer behavior issues associated with each offer?

Notes

[1] Al Bernsohn, "New Directions in Consumer Electronics," *Mainliner,* June 1976, p. 46. Coin-operated games attracted $250 million in coins in 1975.

[2] Benjamin M. Rosen, *Electronics Letter,* Morgan Stanley and Company, Inc., February 18, 1976, pp. 1-3.

[3] Ibid., p. 2.

[4] Ibid.

[5] Rosen, *op. cit.,* June 23, 1976, pp. 2-3

[6] Cindy Morgan, "Videogames: Put Your Backhand on TV," *Popular Mechanics,* October 1976, pp. 78-80.

Author's note: In developing this case, the author continued to receive information about the industry which made previous factors obsolete. The final touches to the case were made in October 1976.

chapter 3

Motivation and
Need Arousal

The Citizens and Southern National Bank of South Carolina (Part A)

This case was prepared by **Billy Silver,** vice-president of marketing communications, The Citizens and Southern National Bank of South Carolina, Columbia.

Historical Background

The Citizens and Southern National Bank of South Carolina was born in Charleston on March 19, 1928, when the Citizens and Southern Holding Company, a Georgia Corporation owned by the C&S Bank of Georgia, purchased the capital stock of the Atlantic Savings Bank and the Atlantic National Bank in Charleston. These two fine banks originally were organized as the Germania Savings Bank and the Germania National Bank. On becoming a national bank in 1940, the C&S Holding Company divested itself of control of the South Carolina operation.

C&S grew soundly from the start. When the Depression came and many banks failed, C&S remained strong. Every bank in the city of Spartanburg failed during the Depression, and in 1933, by request, C&S Bank established an office in Spartanburg. In 1934, the bank obtained permission to open in Columbia, the state's capital city. For the next twelve years, C&S confined its operations to these three cities, Charleston, Spartanburg, and Columbia.

As South Carolina began to recover from the Depression and to experience growth, C&S Bank, too, experienced growth in deposits and added new branches in the three cities. In 1944, Hugh C. Lane, son of the late Mills B. Lane, the founder, became president, and under his leadership, the bank was a pioneer in setting up a separate installment lending department and trust department. Moreover, he was responsible for developing the bank's reputation by giving the executive officers in each city the authority to make major decisions on loans and other matters without contacting the "home" office.

In 1956, C&S merged with the Growers Bank and Trust of Inman, and the following year the bank opened an office in Greenville.

In 1960, Hugh Lane was elected chairman of the board, and J. Willis Cantey was named president. That same year, the bank was one of the first four banks in the nation to begin using the IBM 1401 electronic computer system. The increased speed and efficiency of computer banking enabled the bank to eliminate all service charges on personal checking accounts of $100 minimum balances. While the competition followed suit in a few years, C&S was responsible for reducing checking account charges in South Carolina.

During the next few years, the bank experienced its most rapid growth and became known as the "Palmetto Pacesetter." (South Carolina is the Palmetto State.) Offices were established in Florence, Camden, Greer, Sumter, Darlington, Rock Hill, Anderson, Conway, Myrtle Beach, and Gaffney.

In 1966, C&S purchased the Jefferson Hotel property in Columbia for the establishment of a new headquarters office building. Today the C&S Bank Building towers twelve stories high at the corner of Main and Laurel Streets and houses not only the bank's executive officers, but also various other bank departments and offices.

In 1968, the Board of Directors of The Citizens and Southern National Bank of South Carolina became actively involved in establishing a one-bank holding company. On October 2, 1968, The Citizens and Southern Corporation was incorporated in the State of Delaware for the purpose of acquiring the stock of C&S Bank and investing in other financially related businesses. On June 30, 1969, stockholders of the bank became holders of corporation stock on a share-for-share basis.

From the beginning, the corporation was defined as a congeneric rather than a conglomerate (a congeneric corporation being one that is engaged in a number of related businesses). It was believed then that a one-bank holding company was the most logical structure to provide the financial services needed by the economic community.

In 1974, both Mr. Lane and Mr. Cantey retired. They were succeeded by Hugh M. Chapman as chairman of the board and Robert V. Royall Jr. as president. C&S has continued to grow under their leadership, and as of the end of 1975, C&S Bank operated seventy-four branch offices located across South Carolina, with total deposits of $521,607,000 and assets for the corporation totaling $657,436,000.

A Policy Statement from Management

The following report was recently issued by senior management to the bank's staff regarding its position on improving customer services.

"As bankers we are beginning to sense that we have long delayed in recognizing that the customer, or personal bank market, is evolving and changing rapidly. We are aware of continually rising personal incomes and affluence, and that the family unit has become an increasingly attractive source of deposit, loan, and profit growth. But banks have not dimensionalized this growth for their own purposes; nor have they fully anticipated the needs of this changing market. In addition, banks have, until recently, made little or no attempt to aggressively market what services they did have, but merely made them available if someone should want one.

"Most bank services do not play a significant or exciting role in the individual consumer's day-to-day decisions. In fact, most banks have not given enough attention to educating the customer to the services they offer or how they benefit him. However, today's household head is better educated, younger, and more susceptible to innovation and change than ever before. Research has pointed out that the traditional marketing and economic concepts no longer apply to today's market. Families live on a rental income with a prime consideration of how much something costs per month and not how much has been accumulated in assets.

"Banks can progress only by anticipating and satisfying the needs of their customers. Studies show that the history of the banking industry is filled with a tendency to plan ahead for what we would *like* to be, and not what our markets indicate we *must* be.

"To meet this challenge, banking must depend heavily on two-way communications between the customer and the bank. On the retail side of banking, this communications process is largely accomplished through advertising, promotion activities, public relations, point-of-sale displays, direct-mail campaigns, and contact between customers and bank employees. If we communicate effectively, the marketing function will be carried out properly, and we will serve our customers. If, on the other hand, we are unable to communicate effectively, our competition will be in a better position to satisfy the needs of our market.

"We must think of bank sales as nothing more than establishing the process of communication; or, to put it another way, selling is a process of communicating between a bank and a customer or prospective customer. This communication indicates unsatisfied needs, identifies how and why banks have the means to satisfy needs, causes another person to change his way of thinking, and stimulates action on the part of the customer.

"Profit is one of the key words of our industry and customer development programs should always be profit oriented. While not every sale should or must generate a profit, the sales concept used must be profit oriented."

Why Sales in Banking

As the report points out, many banks have come to the realization that they are not simply financial institutions, but are marketing institutions as well. However, there still are bankers who feel there is little justification for sales in their banks. When they are pinned down, it is usually found that they have personal reasons and frequently no sound or economic reasons for not having sales programs in their banks. However, there are some very sound reasons why banks should be involved in the selling of bank services to customers and noncustomers alike.

(1) A Changing Economy

Since World War II, average household holdings of financial assets have increased by approximately 250 percent. Unfortunately, banks' share of this growth has dropped from approximately 25 percent to 14 percent. Changes in the economic environment must be accompanied by changes in bank methods, and existing bank services probably will not continue to play as significant a role as before. Bank sales, however, can stimulate the customer. And the bank's sales management must assist the bank in evaluating present customers, their aspirations, expectations, and needs, and anticipate these for future satisfaction of customers.

(2) Increased Competition

The activities of bank competitors are changing and increasing as rapidly as the economy is. Banks are quickly being placed in a position of a retail merchant and must use every known technique to maintain and increase the level of growth and share of the market. A lion's share of expanded economic opportunity has gone to bank competitors in security markets, life insurance, savings and loans, and other associations or organizations principally in the business of extending credit. This is most striking in the mortgage field where statistics indicate that the bank share of the mortgage market has dropped from 40 percent to 23 percent. This statistic is in no way designed to indicate that banks have been in a position to satisfy all of these mortgage requirements, nor that it would have been desirable to do so. It merely helps to point out that banks do have increased competition from many sources, and the bank's ability to survive is going to depend, to a large degree, on the ability to communicate effectively with the customer. Another example is the tremendous growth of the small loan and finance companies. Still another indicator would be the growth of automobile financing by auto companies themselves and the increasing market share they have lured away from banks.

(3) Expanding Markets

Many banks have relied on traditional banking to cultivate expanding markets. The rapidly changing economy, increasing competition, rapid rise in population, and expansion of business is making it increasingly difficult to recognize and take advantage of opportunities to satisfy financial needs. The entire bank must present a unified front to build a bridge between the consumer and itself.

(4) Expansion of Existing Markets

Many studies have been conducted in service usage of present customers. A startling revelation is that the average bank customer uses only 2.1 services of the many available to satisfy his financial needs. It also has been shown that typical customers use approximately 4 to 10 banking services at any one point in their financial lives. If the entire staff were involved in selling additional banking services to present customers, it would help penetrate these existing market areas that might not otherwise be reached. Employees have their own sphere of influence in addition to the many customers and noncustomers that they see each day during regular banking hours. This sphere of influence includes business associates, club members, church members, doctors, dentists, and, of course, family and close friends who also are prospects for additional banking services.

(5) Deteriorating Customer Relations

In most cases the number of bank customers has increased in recent years. The increase is due to many reasons, but bankers frequently will attribute it to good customer relations. In most cases when banks analyze their growth, they find that they are only keeping pace with the growth in the total market. They are not capturing an increased share of the market and, in many cases, they find they are actually capturing a smaller share of the market.

Reducing loss of customers   A recent survey shows that bank customers close their accounts for the following reasons:

Noncontrollable Reasons	48 percent
Death	1%
No longer need it	29%
Move out of area	18%
Controllable Reasons	52 percent
Mistake made on account	8%
Turned down on loan	4%
Treatment by an employee	40%

When a customer leaves C&S for one of the above controllable reasons, it is extremely difficult to bring him back. For every customer lost, the bank must acquire a new customer just to break even, and the acquisition of this new customer costs the bank between $25 and $50 in advertising expenses alone just to attract him through the door. The new C&S customer is not as profitable to the bank as the lost customer because, on the average, the new customer does not use as many services or keep a balance as high as the average lost customer.

Expanding relationships with customers   Research points out that customers use an average of 2.1 services at each bank while the average number of services they use in the community jumps to 4.5 spread out over 2.3 financial institutions. The study further shows that the customer is, or could be, using from 4 to 10 services, many of which could be provided by C&S. The average customer using 2.1 services nets the bank an income of $50 per year. Therefore, the bank's best opportunities for sales lie in the area of expanding its relationships with present customers. This expansion could result in doubling the size of the bank, increasing the growth rate of each service, doubling the customer's value to the bank, and reducing the controllable loss rate.

Market research has shown that expanding our present relationship with customers would have a very heavy impact on both profits and customer retention. Obviously, the more services a customer uses, the greater our chances of keeping him at C&S.

By using an index of a one-to-one chance of losing a checking account, we can readily see how multiple accounts decrease our chances of losing valuable customers. The following study shows the dramatic influence that additional services have in cementing our relationship with our present customers.

Checking only	1-1
Savings only	10-1
Checking and savings	18-1
Checking, savings, and installment loan department or credit card	35-1
Checking, savings, loan, and safety deposit box	75-1
Checking and trust	200-1

Note that the mere addition of a savings account to a present checking account customer increases our chances of maintaining that customer 10 to 1. It becomes increasingly difficult for consumers to dissolve a banking relationship when they must close multiple accounts.

Acquiring new customers   The average customer uses 1.5 banks in his lifetime assuming he does not move out of the bank's service areas. This same customer during his lifetime will make between $400,000 and $500,000 which will flow through his checking account. This customer is worth $50 + per year to C&S, and assuming a banking relationship of thirty to forty years will be worth a total of $1,500 to $2,000 based on an average use of 2.1 services.

Sources of new customers   Potential bank customers come from several areas; however, the following four groups emerge as the principal sources:

1. Newcomers to the bank service area.

2. People emerging into the need for bank services.

3. People switching from competitors.

4. Other factors related to changes in household relationships (e.g. divorce), adding additional services, and cross-town moves (location convenience).

Reason for bank selection   Newcomers most often choose a bank based on recommendations from real estate salespeople or their new neighbors. Second in their priorities is location and convenience.

The emerging society is a broad spectrum of young people ranging from the high school junior or senior with a first job to the newlyweds beginning a new life pattern. This group of young people tends to lean towards recommendations from their friends in making their selections of banks.

Those persons making a switch from other banks with which they are dissatisfied are inclined toward choosing a bank that their friends and neighbors recommend.

Because all of the above groups tend to make their selection of a new bank on recommendations from other people, with convenience or location being the second factor, it is necessary that a bank provide for its present customers the best service available so that they will not only choose to remain with the bank, but not hesitate to recommend their bank to friends.

Since it has been established that those persons who already have made a commitment to a bank are difficult to dislodge, a bank must actively recruit new customers from the area of newcomers, the emerging society, and those persons who are considering making a change.

The Present Situation

A consultant was asked to attend a meeting of the bank's management and to listen to the group's discussion of the bank's current situation. At the end of the meeting, the consultant made the following statement:

"Gentlemen, I have enjoyed the opportunity today of listening to your concerns as to how C&S can improve its market position by better satisfying the needs of your present and potential customers. My research experience indicates to me that consumers perceive banks, and in fact all financial institutions, as a very unexciting business to deal with. Consumers basically feel today that one bank is pretty much like another. They feel that banks are places to put money for safekeeping, to facilitate their bill paying by way of check, and a place to go to borrow money for a car or boat. Banks have become commonplace and, frankly, quite boring In contrast, consider how consumers view cars, clothes, and personal grooming products. Cars fill more than a need for transportation, clothes are not purchased simply for warmth, and cosmetics are not purchased to cover blemishes but as a hope for beauty. Your bank must redesign its offerings to encompass something more than just meeting financial needs, much the same as a car is more to consumers than simply a mode of transportation.

"Your bank must consider what basic human needs you are satisfying and then develop a program to make consumers aware of their needs, the importance of their needs, and how your bank can best satisfy their needs. Do consumers want a boat loan or do they want an easy way to enjoy the adventure and excitement of sailing a boat? If you seriously consider what basic human needs you can best satisfy, you will have the key to motivating and exciting your consumers.

"I don't mean to make this sound like an easy task, but hopefully I have reoriented your thinking."

Questions

1. What do you feel are the human and consumer needs to which C&S should appeal? Explain.

2. Describe how you would make consumers aware of their needs for C&S bank services, intensify the importance of those needs, and show how C&S could best satisfy those needs.

3. Develop an advertising campaign which would appeal to the needs you cited above.

4. How can bank personnel who come into contact with present and prospective customers play a role in motivating present customers to use other bank services? What behavioral principles are you using?

chapter 4

Attitude Formation and Change

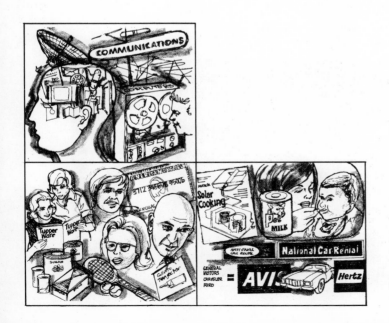

The Jenn-Air
Grill

This case was prepared by **Donald H. Granbois,** *School of Business, Indiana University.*

After many years of successfully producing and marketing ventilation equipment designed for industrial and commercial installations, the Jenn-Air Corporation of Indianapolis in 1967 developed its first consumer product. This product was an innovative grill for indoor countertop installation using electrically-heated permanent marble "rocks" which provided the same smoked flavor imparted by charcoal in outdoor grilling. The grill featured a highly efficient exhaust system consisting of a surface-level opening through which smoke and fumes were drawn by a fan and exhausted through a flexible hose leading through the wall to the outdoors. The exhaust system was far more effective and much more quiet than overhead hood fans commonly used with kitchen cooking equipment. With rotisserie, griddle, and shishkabob attachments, the grill retailed for approximately $270. The grill is pictured in Figure 1.

FIGURE 1   *Jenn-Air Grill*

Several fundamental issues in promotional strategy were especially troublesome, because of both the company's inexperience in consumer goods marketing and the innovative nature of the product prevented patterning its introductory promotion after that of existing successful products. A memo written by one member of the new product's marketing team summarized the issues and proposed an initial research effort as follows:

"Several aspects of consumer attitudes and reactions to the recent new Jean-Air grill need to be studied as a guide to future decisions on promotion. These decisions will affect the nature and content of consumer advertising undertaken directly by Jenn-Air, cooperative campaigns undertaken with dealers, advertising directed to builders and dealers, and the sales points emphasized by field men calling on dealers and builders and salespeople employed by dealers.

"At the present time, we have better knowledge of the attitudes of dealers and builders toward the product than we have of consumer relations. For example, we don't know how consumers perceive the grill, whether it is to be used primarily as a replacement for an outdoor grill or as a whole new system of cooking replacing the oven broiler. Presumably, the value of the product to the consumer might depend considerably upon this distinction; in the former case, the product might be seen as useful primarily for entertaining or for meal preparation when the husband is home and participating. In the latter case, the product could be used heavily in normal meal preparation.

"Second, attitudes toward installation need to be studied to assess possible negative feelings about the cost and inconvenience of installation, space required, and whether kitchen or family room locations are seen as appropriate.

"Third, consumer attitudes toward the product's functional performance need to be studied. In particular, the importance of the ventilation feature, actual use characteristics, and cleaning are of significance.

"Finally, reactions to price should be measured, perhaps by learning what consumers think might be a reasonable price for the various models and for installation.

"Although ideally a large-scale consumer attitude survey might eventually be used to study the topics discussed above, I recommend the use first of intensive group depth interviews to provide an initial "feel" for consumer responses. Fortunately, Walker Research, one of the most experienced and respected research organizations performing this service, is located in Indianapolis.

"I suggest that Walker Research be engaged to conduct two intensive group sessions, with the following characteristics:

1. An afternoon panel should consist of eight to ten housewives selected to represent the 35 to 45 year-old age group and to be owners of houses in the $25,000 to $40,000 range.

2. An evening panel should consist of five or six couples, representing the 45 to 55 year-old age group and owners of homes in the $40,000 and over range.

3. A Walker Research moderator (hopefully Mrs. Tommie Walker) will conduct both panels. A guide for the session should be provided by us for the moderator and will center around the four major attitude dimensions indicated above (product concept, installation, product function, and price).

4. An operational grill should be installed in the test kitchen area of Walker Research so that panel members can report their reactions to the grill in actual use.

5. The output of the panels will be a complete tape recording of all that takes place during the two sessions."

The proposal for the group depth sessions was approved and implemented resulting in the following report to the marketing team:

"On Wednesday, January 17, 1968, Mrs. Tommie Walker of Walker Research conducted two panel discussions with consumers invited to a model home in which there is a Jenn-Air installation. The afternoon group consisted of ten housewives, aged 35 to 45, representing ownership of homes in the $25,000 to $40,000 range. In the evening, a similar session was conducted with six married couples in the 45 to 55 age group representing ownership of homes in the $40,000 and over range. Both sessions were tape recorded.

"Although we will want to do a more detailed analysis of the tapes (and perhaps get exact quotations of some of the remarks offered by panel participants), the essence of the sessions hopefully will be captured in the following discussion."

Afternoon Panel

Following a brief warm-up discussion in which each woman related her present cooking equipment, the discussion turned to the cooking of meat, especially in terms of outdoor grills and broiling.

General Pattern of Outdoor Grilling

1. Every family represented cooked outdoors, several doing this year round.

2. It is common practice to bring the cooked meat back inside for eating.

Advantages of Outdoor Grilling

1. By far the strongest advantage is flavor.

2. Outdoor cooking also is seen as a way of reducing kitchen heat in the summer.

3. A less-strongly held advantage is the fact that husbands sometimes do the cooking outside.

Disadvantages of Outdoor Grilling

1. A strong disadvantage (on which there was general agreement) is the problem of coordinating outdoor cooking with the balance of the meal preparation which must take place in the kitchen.

2. The outdoor grill presents a cleaning problem.

3. Billowing smoke associated with outdoor cooking is disliked.

4. Outdoor cooking takes longer than conventional methods if fire preparation time is included.

5. A problem raised (but quickly dropped) was the question of health and the possibility that grilled meat causes cancer.

Conclusion

A means of cooking which captures the flavor of outdoor cooking without the problem of coordination and cleanup would seem to be highly desirable. A family room location of the unit would present the same coordination problem as outdoor grilling.

Nutrition

The moderator was unable to evoke much discussion of nutrition, not because it isn't important, but because it is *taken for granted* that every housewife (at least of the type represented in the panel) prepares nutritional meals routinely. Very little frying of meat was reported by the group except, for example, bacon, hamburgers, and sometimes pork chops.

Conclusion

Nutrition is not a strong appeal with this market group.

Rotisserie Cooking

Strong interest in rotisserie cooking was exhibited, with six of the ten women reporting this method as a common means of cooking meat. Several women use portable rotisserie units and talked at some length of the problem of cleaning these units.

Conclusion

The rotisserie attachment should be given some prominence in promotion. Not only is this a popular means for cooking chicken, roasts, etc., but its availability greatly expands the perceived usefulness of the product. (This point was strongly supported later in the session.)

Discussion of the Product Concept

Jenn-Air's home economist briefly explained the product concept after distributing the brochure. Her discussion included the ventilation concept; the removable grill feature; the availability of rotisserie, griddle, and shishkabob attachments; the preheating method of cooking meat; the principle of grease vaporization; and the grease-capture principle. A number of questions and comments were offered by panel members.

Questions

1. Is there ignited charcoal in the unit?
2. Is there a cover over the unit when it is not in use?
*3. Doesn't the preheat cycle create lots of heat in the kitchen?
4. Does the grill above the exhaust opening remove for cleaning?
*5. Is this intended to replace all present cooking equipment?
6. How effective is the fan? Are all fumes removed?
7. How about problem of flame-ups?
8. Is it designed only for new homes? Can venting be installed in existing homes?
9. What kind of wiring is required?
*10. How about popping and splattering of meat; doesn't this create a mess?
11. Can it be vented if you have no outside wall?

*Conclusion

The most serious objections raised in these questions deal with (1) heat generated during preheat cycle, and (2) soil caused by splattering meat.

Spontaneous comments   Spontaneous comments centered on the perceived heat problem, the recognition of the product as a *novelty* (perhaps for the family room), and concern over the unit's ability to ventilate effectively (although one or two women were quite sure the unit would be *more* effective than an overhead fan).

Further discussion of concept   At this point the moderator asked for a summary of the concept the panel members had of the product. At first there was some agreement that this was a novelty item, that one would get tired of charcoal flavor all the time, and that the unit definitely should not go in the kitchen. The rotisserie and griddle features were then brought up again (by panel members themselves), and it became apparent that the overall concept of the product began to change, as methods of cooking other than broiling came to mind.

The question of noise created by an overhead hood was raised by the moderator, and there was loud and general agreement that this problem was highly undesirable. The panel members could not respond to the question of cost, largely because of their unfamiliarity with the general price level of cooking equipment.

Conclusions

1. The product is considered far more attractive when the flexibility offered by the rotisserie and griddle are realized; most panel members initially thought of the product for broiling only, probably because of the nature of the information presented to them.

2. The low noise level of the unit is a strong product feature.

3. Women in this market group cannot compare the unit's price with that of other equipment because they don't have price information.

Demonstration of Unit

Although the tape is garbled at this point, three points came out of the attempt to demonstrate the physical product itself:

1. The grills were seen as easy to keep clean because of their black color.

2. Concern was shown for the problem of cleaning the heating element and the rocks.

3. The question of accuracy of heat control for the griddle was raised.

Conclusion

From the point of view of the research methodology, this was not a successful part of the session. Simply seeing the physical product did not overcome the previously stated objections, nor did it significantly clarify any previously poorly-understood product characteristics.

Kitchen Demonstration

Round steak was placed on the already-preheated grill as soon as everyone reached the kitchen. From this point on, most comments were very favorable. Illustrative comments follow:

*1. The idea of a single grill is great; it is much better to have this separate from the rest of the cooking equipment.

*2. It's a good idea to have the unit already installed in the house when you buy it.

3. It doesn't look like the meat is cooking fast enough; there's nowhere near the noise you associate with cooking meat.

4. The grill over the vent would have to be washed each time you cook.

5. Can the grill be full and still function properly?

*6. (General favorable comment on quiet operation.)

7. How much space is required under the counter? General agreement: no more than required by a disposer.

8. Are rocks permanent?

9. Why isn't there more grease? Is it because meat is seared?

*10. (General agreement the unit required less space than had been thought; one woman compared it favorably with the size of a built-in cutting board.)

*11. (General agreement that there was remarkably little splatter.)

*12. (General agreement that the heat level was very low; many held a hand over the unit and expressed surprise.)

*Conclusions

1. The most serious objections raised earlier were overcome by the kitchen demonstration. Panel members agreed that a kitchen location would be preferable, were convinced that the unit would not heat up the kitchen, and were agreeably surprised at the low level of splattering.

2. All were impressed with the flavor of the meat, but no one seemed overly *surprised;* they had been led to *expect* charcoal flavor. The flavor

concept is more believable than other aspects of the unit's functioning and probably requires less promotional push in order to achieve believability.

3. The venting efficiency of the unit was rated very high.

Final Comments

1. Picture is deceiving; unit appears slimmer and less space consuming than in picture.

2. Meat doesn't curl around the edges as it does in oven broiler, an advantage of the unit.

3. Steak was thought to cook more quickly than in oven broiler.

4. Suggested cover so that space can be used when unit is not in operation.

Evening Panel

Overall, the evening panel produced much less direct questioning and commenting on the part of the panel members. In general, many of the same topics were brought up and detailed analysis is not called for.

Questions

1. What does the attitudinal information from the research suggest to Jenn-Air management? That is, how might they develop a marketing program for their range based on this survey?

2. How would you evaluate and critique the use of the group depth interview in this situation? Explain.

3. Develop several hypotheses for further research concerning coding behavior, criteria consumers use in evaluating cooking equipment, and their probable acceptance of new grills. What other attitudes would you examine in cooking behavior? Explain.

4. How might research in cooking behavior create new product opportunities (or product modifications)? Explain.

5. Assuming the findings of later surveys substantiated the conclusion drawn from the reported group interviews, prepare detailed recommendations for promotional strategy for the new grill, including suggestions for target audience definition, message content, and media strategy.

Sears:
Merchant to the Masses

This case was prepared by **Denis F. Healy,** *College of Business and Economics, University of Delaware.*

Sears is still growing but has moved into an era in which it is increasingly difficult for it to maneuver easily in established or emerging markets, while other major chains have established themselves in most major markets. In addition, the growth of massive shopping centers has peaked, and newer competitive forms such as specialty mass merchandisers are becoming visible. Finally, consumption patterns appear to be changing.

The world's largest retailer is constantly faced with the task of obtaining information about its many markets and of adapting marketing strategies to respond creatively to market opportunities. With changes in consumer lifestyles, increasing affluence, shifting attitudes toward consumption, and new modes of retail distribution such as specialty mass merchandisers, it is extremely important that Sears monitor its environment. The tracking of consumer behavior and attitudes becomes a key step in the formulation and control of its marketing programs.

Company History [1]

The Sears story is truly fascinating and one without parallel in the history of distribution. Sears was founded in 1886 by Richard W. Sears who left home at the age of 16 to raise money to support his family. Sears learned telegraphy and eventually landed a job as agent for the Minneapolis and St. Louis Railway in a station in North Redwood, Minnesota. To supplement his income, Sears took up a variety of odd jobs and one day purchased a shipment of watches that the local jewelry store refused. Watches, of course, were the symbol of railroading and he was able to sell these and many other subsequent shipments to railroad employees at a handsome profit. This marked the beginnings of the R. W. Sears Watch Company.

Watches, being delicate and temperamental items, eventually require service. It was the repair aspect of the business that provided Sears with a

67

follow-up trade. To meet the demands for repair service, it became necessary in 1887 to run the following advertisement in the *Chicago Daily News:*

> Wanted: Watchmaker with reference who can furnish tools. State age, experience, and salary required. Address T39, Daily News.

The ad was answered by Alvan C. Roebuck who signed on for $3.50 a week plus room and board.

Because of physical distribution advantages, the company, now called Sears, Roebuck, and Company, moved to Chicago and by 1895 had published its first catalog of 507 pages. Sears, Roebuck, and Company prospered and grew rapidly and by early 1906 had invested $5 million in a 50-acre site and a 3 million square foot mail order plant. This building, which has an all-wood frame, is still one of the largest in the world.

It wasn't long before Sears decided to branch out, and by 1925 mail order branches were open in Dallas, Seattle, Philadelphia, and Kansas City.

With growth and the pressure to change and to be efficient, the company devised ingenious mail order scheduling processes and opened a sophisticated testing laboratory in 1911 to establish performance standards and to control quality of incoming goods. Today, the laboratory employs over 200 professionals who test thousands of products annually against Sears standards.

The mail order business was well underway before Sears decided to enter the retail field. In 1906, Richard Sears wrote:

> "We do comparatively little business in cities, and we assume the cities are not at all our field—maybe they are not—but I think it is our duty to prove they are not . . ." [2]

It took until 1925 for these words to be put into action. Under the direction of General Robert E. Wood, the company decided to open an experimental retail outlet in the Chicago area. By the end of the year seven more stores were opened, four in existing mail order facilities. Although many events occurred to prompt Wood's decision, perhaps the most significant was the rapid growth of chain stores (which cut into the mail order business Sears had enjoyed) and the rapid shift in demographic characteristics of the country. People began to move toward the cities in large numbers.

The growth of the retail end of the business has been dazzling. Sears expanded from eight stores in 1925 to 192 stores in 1928, to 324 in 1929, and to 400 in 1930. The company grew to its 1975 level, having 858 retail stores, 13 catalog distribution centers, and 2,918 other selling facilities and independent catalog merchants. Today the company has over 110 million square feet of retail space. This impressive record of physical growth is paralleled by Sears' financial growth record. During the company's history sales have grown from $750,000 in 1895 to $13.6 billion in 1975. Earnings for the same period have spiralled to $523 million in 1975. [3]

Sears
Today

Sears, the world's largest retailer of general merchandise, sells broad lines of private brand name goods through approximately 3,800 selling outlets, 1,300 of which are independent catalog dealers. Sears realized $13.6 billion in net sales for 1975, with 81.2 percent coming from retail units, 9.3 percent from catalog orders outside of the retail unit, and 9.5 percent through repair services, finance charges, and industrial sales.

Sears has nearly 22 million credit customers with credit sales accounting for 52.9 percent of total sales. The company has forty-nine buying departments which buy from over 12,000 domestic suppliers. About 6 percent of Sears' purchases come from foreign suppliers.[4]

In 1976 the company planned to open twenty-eight retail stores including thirteen in new markets. The total gross additional square footage is 4 million, and, after adjustments for relocated stores, the new addition is 2.9 million square feet. The total planned capital expenditures for 1976 were $275 million.

Over the past five years, Sears invested $1.8 billion for new and improved facilities and for normal replacement items. The investment portion for the retail operations was $1.2 billion and was used to add 19.2 million square feet to gross retail space. The expansion was for 89 complete line department stores, 63 medium-sized units, and 11 hard-lines stores. In addition, 29 existing stores were enlarged. Of the 163 new units, 86 were placed in new market areas and the remaining 77 replaced older stores in established markets.

The investment in catalog operations over the past five years was $243 million. Expenditures were made to build new catalog distribution centers in Columbus, Ohio, and Jacksonville, Florida; for enlargement of existing centers; and for the construction of the new national catalog fashion merchandising center in Elk Grove, Illinois.[5]

Changes in Retailing

There are numerous factors contributing to changes in the retail market and for Sears in particular. On the one hand are positive forces for change such as the absolute growth in numbers of consumers. The geographic mobility rate of nearly 20 percent per year for U.S. families contributes to the need for merchandise, and the growth of planned towns and communities continues to offer merchandising opportunities for a company such as Sears.

On the other hand, there are factors that some observers believe contribute to a slowdown in growth opportunities for Sears and similar operations. *Business Week* has reported that uncertain economic conditions and soaring prices resulted in increased consumer conservatism and a temporary shrinkage of total retail sales in 1974-1975. The effects of this are evident in several areas. For instance, the growth of the suburbs has slowed considerably since the 1960s. Inflation rates have been high over the first half of the 1970s, thus limiting opportunities for many to purchase homes as quickly or as large as desired. Also, there has been a shift in automobile purchase patterns. This may be a mixed blessing for Sears since it has a substantial automotive operation.[6]

In addition to these shifts in the market are changes in the composition and style of merchants. Traditional competition between the chain department and discount stores today must recognize a new form of retailer, namely the specialty mass merchandiser as exemplified by such firms as Levitz Furniture Co., Wickes Lumber, Radio Shack, Toys "R" Us, and The Gap, to name a few. These outlets offer a wide selection of products in their respective product classes. In some areas, specialty mass merchants are clustering together, thus offering consumers all of the locational advantages of a department store operation with the product offering of the specialist. From the specialists' standpoint, such an approach increases the amount of potential traffic over an isolated store location. However, many of these specialized mass merchants have enjoyed short-term successes and are finding it difficult in the cycling economy of the mid 1970s.

Other market forces and competitive actions present challenges to Sears and other large-scale merchants. For example, the mass market of the 1950s and 1960s has become increasingly prone to segmentation strategies by retailers due to its size and the impact of sophisticated survey capabilities and computer resources. The impact has been to identify highly demanding and well defined local markets. Although this presents opportunities, such a phenomenon also obliges merchants to attain extraordinary levels of flexibility and responsiveness.[7] It is alleged that the larger chains find such requirements extremely demanding on their operating structures and marketing prowess.

Growth comes from increasing the volume through existing stores and from expansion to new markets. For Sears and many of its rivals saturation has been reached in the prime markets, and high store productivity levels have been achieved. To extract more volume and profits from the market, therefore, firms are obliged to increase productivity of existing facilities or to consider expansion into new or less saturated areas. Some impediments to this are soaring energy, construction, and real estate costs, as well as pressures from environmentalists.

Responding to the Changing Environment

In addition to the conditions and measures already mentioned, merchants are moving in several new directions in order to cope with the pressures. They are as follows:

1. Increased merchandising speed and flexibility, achieved by developing the ability to move into new lines of merchandise and to rearrange display areas to meet new product needs.

2. More intensive utilization of existing space by more dense and concentrated use of display areas thus increasing selling floor capacity by 20

to 40 percent, reducing merchandise handling and storage costs by as much as 50 percent, all with an emphasis on creating more excitement.

3. Computerized point of sale registers to increase productivity and provide more and better information about activity levels.

4. Increased attention to store productivity with careful consideration being given to marginal units, the development of smaller stores in smaller markets, and cautiousness with respect to further development of giant stores.[8]

Industry authorities are reported to believe that Sears has lost market position over the past few years. They further indicate that as Sears attempted to offer products to more affluent and sophisticated market segments, it lost a more than equivalent share of its traditional markets in the lower income brackets.[9]

Sears officials, on the other hand, indicate they have gained market share in areas of greatest opportunity and that they have foregone share in less attractive segments and product lines. In a sort of cascading fashion, Sears officials report that new Sears customers normally come from department stores. And the customers Sears loses are existing cash customers who move on to discount stores. On balance, they claim to have a net increase in penetration in markets where increased shares are targeted.[10]

Sears Market Position and Competitive Response

Many believe that the major competitors of Sears are such firms as J. C. Penney, Montgomery Ward, and the like. In fact, Sears competes with hundreds of thousands of retailers of all sizes and in every community in which it operates either a retail store or a catalog outlet.

Against the large retail chain stores Sears enjoys a commanding position. It is nearly twice the size of J. C. Penney ($13.1 billion vs. $6.9 billion in sales for fiscal 1975). According to *Business Week,* Sears is ". . . a merchandising colossus that accounts for just under half of all catalog sales, 3.5 percent of total nonfood retail sales, and fully 1 percent of the country's gross national product. One out of every three American families now carries a Sears credit card." [11]

Obviously, a company of the size and diversity of Sears runs the risk of becoming unwieldy to manage. Also, it may lose touch with its markets if it does not monitor its position and adapt to market demands. Under the pressure of increased competition and more conservative and selective consumers, Sears has taken major steps to reinforce its position in its target markets. Some of the marketing-related considerations are:

1. Increased attention to store efficiency resulting in tighter control of merchandising, sales personnel, and store costs.

2. Greater development of smaller stores in contrast to the giant stores of the 1960s.

3. More utilization of pricing and promotional techniques to maintain or improve market shares.[12]

Sears' Short-Term
Outlook

In its *1975 Annual Report,* Sears discussed issues which undoubtedly bear on the directions and commitments the company will make in the near future. Sears believes the economy is recovering and that the trend will be sustained. With the consumer leading the recovery and unemployment declining, Sears projects that consumers' real disposable income will increase at a rate between 4.5 and 5 percent. The implication is that the economy and Sears will greatly benefit from increased consumer demand.

The Sears report notes that expected demographic changes in the near future will strongly affect consumer spending behavior. The report cites statistics revealing that in the past ten years there was an increase of 12.5 million people in the 20 to 44 year-old age bracket, whereas there will be a 19 million increase in the same age bracket over the next ten years. Since this age bracket encompasses the group of people who form the vast majority of new households, there will be a sharp increase in demand for home-oriented products, and Sears feels certain it can meet the increased demand "with quality merchandise at competitive prices." [13]

Sears' Merchandising Objectives

It is apparent that Sears is committed to more intensified marketing efforts in both established and emerging markets. In interviews with James W. Button, senior executive vice-president of merchandising for Sears, two major marketing committments were expressed as follows:

1. Sears is dedicated to identifying and developing significant marketing opportunities in which the company is or can achieve a position as a leading supplier at price points above the market average.

2. Sears is concentrating on more intensive and extensive use of retail space. [14]

Achieving these objectives requires great coordination of effort among stores and departments, a reverse from the operating mode in recent times. To achieve the coordination, a more centralized management structure is required. This will result in less autonomy being allowed at the store level and more control being exerted by the Chicago and New York based parent organization.

Organizational
Structure

The Sears organization, including its Allstate subsidiary, employs over 400,000 persons. [15] The organizational structure consists of the "parent organization," or headquarters, which is concentrated in Chicago and New York and at successively lower levels, territories, groups, and zones.

The parent organization is responsible for the strategic moves of the company and for providing a variety of expert services in the financial, technical, real estate, strategic planning, general and consumer research areas. In addition, the parent is the sole buyer of merchandise. Rather, buying is concentrated in the hands of fifty parent merchandising departments. The merchandising departments contain world-reknown experts in their respective lines of merchandise. As a result, they are able to specify precisely the product attributes desired and to maintain quality control over the products supplied. Store level executives, however, do have the option not to stock many of the nonbasic items purchased through the parent merchandising departments.

The next layer of the organization is the territorial level. Currently there are five: Los Angeles, Dallas, Chicago, Atlanta, and Philadelphia, each headed by a vice-president. The territorial organization is organized along the same lines as the parent organization except the departments are smaller and have only territorial responsibility. Within a territory, stores are organized into groups for big-city stores and zones for stores not contained in groups.

A typical group organization is headed by a group general manager who has a staff consisting of sales promotion and merchandising managers. In addition, the group manager has his own expert staff in such fields as personnel, display, credit, operating, and auditing. The thirteen catalog merchandise distribution centers report to the territorial vice-presidents and are provided with a support organization at the territorial level.

The Merchandising Commitment

Sears indicates there are four major responsibilities assigned to the merchandising level of the organization.[16] They are to:

1. Develop and select the merchandise to be sold in Sears retail stores and from catalogs.

2. Choose manufacturers to produce this merchandise.

3. Formulate selling plans, including advertising and sales promotion, for both retail and catalog operations.

4. Establish catalog selling prices and suggested selling prices for retail.

Over the years Sears has elected to use its own set of brand names rather than those of its suppliers. It has sought to use the mass media as effectively as possible. In conjunction with its extensive product testing laboratory, Sears has developed its own product specifications and performance standards. In addition, it has made major strides in developing new or improved products and markets as may be witnessed by its great success with Tuf-Skin Jeans, radial tires, and the Die-Hard battery. Its commitment to excellence in this area is contained in the following statement:

> Sears' *total marketing* strategy is a strategy to define the
> wants and needs of customers and respond to them through

responsible, creative product development. Under the company's total marketing concept, products are evaluated in terms of raw materials, form, shape, function, styling, safety, quality, and serviceability.[17]

Consumer Research at Sears

Until 1964, Sears had no formal consumer research organization. Today the group employs about forty professionals and makes extensive use of outside consumer research services. It is reputed to be one of the largest such groups in the country devoted exclusively to consumer studies. Studies are conducted in the areas of store location, market profile, segmentation, attitudes, consumer motivation, product preference, marketing strategy, consumer satisfaction and end use, communication, weather patterns, and economic trends. These studies, in conjunction with information obtained at the retail store and from product suppliers, provide a comprehensive basis for merchandising decisions.[18]

Questions

1. Describe the influences that consumer attitudes may have on the decision to purchase such items as jewelry, hand tools, women's clothing, and kitchen appliances at Sears.

2. What, if anything, might Sears do to shape attitudes toward it as a store and toward the items listed in question 1.

3. Comment on the value of consumer attitude research to Sears and indicate specific attitude areas where such studies might be conducted.

4. Discuss the possibilities for market segmentation for Sears using consumer life styles as segmenting variables.

5. Competitive merchants such as J. C. Penney and K-Mart may be perceived as occupying different market positions from Sears and each other. What kind of information would you seek to verify this and how would you use the information to create competitive strategies?

6. To what extent are there likely to be inconsistencies in the attitudes various members of the family have toward Sears? What might Sears do to resolve the inconsistencies?

Notes

[1] The material presented in this section has been obtained from *Merchant to the Millions: A Brief History of the Origin and Development of Sears, Roebuck, and Co.* (Chicago: Sears, Roebuck, and Co., 1974); and B. Emmet, and J. E. Jeuck, *Catalogues and Counters* (Chicago: University of Chicago Press, 1950).

[2] Ibid., p. 10.

[3] *Merchant to the Millions,* pp. 10-11; Sears, Roebuck, and Company, *1975 Annual Report,* pp. 10-12, 22-23.

[4] *1975 Annual Report.*

[5] Ibid.

[6] A synthesis of information from "J. C. Penney: Getting More From the Same Space," *Business Week,* August 18, 1975, pp. 80-88; and "Sears' Identity Crisis," *Business Week,* December 8, 1975, pp. 52-58.

[7] *Business Week,* August 18, 1975, pp. 80-81.

[8] Ibid.

[9] *Business Week,* December 8, 1975.

[10] J. W. Button, Sears senior executive vice-president of merchandising, in an interview conducted September 28, 1976.

[11] *Business Week,* December 8, 1975, p. 52.

[12] Ibid., p. 53.

[13] *1975 Annual Report,* p. 3.

[14] J. W. Button in interviews conducted August 18, 1976, and September 29, 1976.

[15] The material in this section was obtained from *Merchant to the Millions,* pp. 14-18.

[16] Ibid.

[17] Ibid., p. 24.

[18] "The Use of Market Research by Sears, Roebuck, and Company," Sears undated memorandum.

part 3

Influence of the
Total Individual

This section examines the "total" individual consumer from three
viewpoints: personality, self concept, and life style. Each case allows the
student the opportunity to consider the relationships among these
views of the "total" individual and his or her consumption behavior.

chapter 5

Personality
Traits

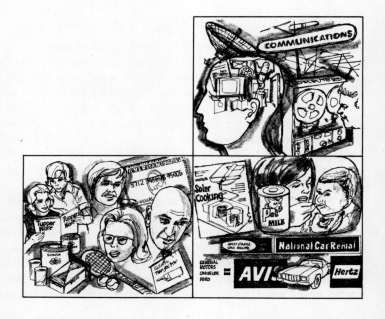

Lionel
Electronics, Inc.

This case was prepared by **M. Wayne DeLozier**, *College of Business Administration, University of South Carolina. Copyright* © *1976. Permission granted by the author.*

With the boom in citizen band (CB) radios, Lionel Electronics had increased sales from approximately $1 million in 1970 to nearly $24 million by 1975. Sales for the first six months of 1976 were $32 million and Lionel expected total year-end sales of $67 million. Lionel has been operating twenty-four hours a day, seven days a week for the past fourteen months and has experienced problems in obtaining supplies and labor. However, because of stepped-up production by suppliers and the influx of workers into the small town of Walnut Grove, Minnesota, these problems were being alleviated.

Background on Lionel

Charles Kane started Lionel as Kane's Electronic Repairs in 1963 after receiving his B.S. degree in electrical engineering. Although not formally trained in business, Kane had always wanted a business of his own, influenced primarily by his father who had owned a TV and appliance store.

Initially, Kane's business came from repair work on televisions, radios, and stereo equipment. In his spare time, Kane rebuilt "worn-out" radios and sold them to customers and friends at a very low price. Mostly due to his fascination with ham radios (his hobby) and CB radios, Kane began to stock and sell both kinds of radios in his store in order to increase his business and his income.

By 1966, his small retail and repair business had sales of $122,000 and employed three workers. With the death of his grandmother, Kane inherited over $250,000 and decided to use the money to invest in the expansion of his business. Because of the small size of Walnut Grove, Kane realized that the potential of the repair and sales business for electronic equipment was very limited. So in 1967 Kane decided to begin limited production of ham radio equipment, something he already knew a great deal about. With the help of friends, some of whom he had met in college, Kane was able to set up channels of distribution throughout the southern part of Minnesota and into parts of South Dakota, Iowa, Wisconsin, and Illinois.

Through the urgings of his college roommate, Larry Armstrong, Kane began to produce a line of citizen band radios in 1969. By 1970, sales had reached $985,000, primarily from sales of base station CBs. In that year, Kane changed the name of his business to Lionel Electronics, Inc., because he felt that his interest in engineering, and electronics in particular, stemmed from his early childhood interest in running his Lionel train.

In early 1971, Kane recognized that he could not continue to coordinate both the production and marketing efforts of the firm. Although he had hired a sales manager, a production supervisor, and a finance officer, Kane realized he was devoting too much time to *managing* parts of the business and not giving enough of his time to problems of growth and corporate planning. In June of that year, Kane hired his long-time friend, Frank Putnam, who had recently received a master's degree in business administration. Frank had met Charlie in undergraduate days, after which he spent six years as a civil engineer with state government.

Putnam took the job as vice-president of marketing which allowed Kane to devote more time to company planning and production. Putnam immediately recognized the growth potential of the business as well as expanding market opportunities.

By 1974, Lionel had achieved national distribution of its products, primarily in the CB line. Putnam was amazed at Lionel's progress but also was concerned over competition in the expanding CB market as well as the potential problems inherent in reaching the peak and eventual decline in CB sales which constituted 85 percent of Lionel's business.

Current Situation

Putnam began to feel that Lionel must develop new products for new markets, not only to grow but also to weather the entry of competition from such powerful companies as RCA, GE, and Westinghouse, among others.

Because Lionel had developed a strong reputation for superiority in electronics and because consumers associated Lionel with quality, Putnam began to explore the possibilities of developing products which present Lionel customers might purchase. Since 85 percent of Lionel's business came from CB sales, Putnam decided to survey the personality traits of CB owners to determine how they differ from nonowners. The idea to study personalities arose from his conversations with dealers who believed CB purchasers were interested in gadgetry and tended to be extroverted and outdoor types. Putnam believed that if he could identify the CB personality that he would know into which product lines to expand and also how to promote them.

In early 1976, Putnam met with ICON Associates, a market research firm, to discuss his concerns and his thoughts. ICON specialized in the use of personality traits to describe and predict consumer purchase behavior, and Putnam was aware of their success.

ICON had developed and tested a unique consumer personality inventory test based primarily upon the California Personality Inventory, the Gordon Personal Profile, the Edwards Personal Preference Schedule, the Thurstone Temperament Schedule, and the theories of such theorists as Jung, Adler, Fromm, and Rogers. ICON's CPIT (California Personality Inventory Test) has proven to be effective for some products, but not for others. In particular, it has been very successful for consumer durables, but less so for nondurables.

The Markey Survey

ICON was hired by Putnam with the approval of Kane to determine the personality characteristics of CB owners and to determine whether their personalities differed from those who had not purchased a CB and from those who were not interested in purchasing a CB. Furthermore, ICON was commissioned to ascertain whether CB owners differed significantly in the kinds of products they were or might be interested in purchasing.

A personal interview was conducted by ICON in five major cities and eight rural areas to collect data which would answer some of Lionel's questions. The following report was submitted to Frank Putnam by the ICON research staff:

"Our research into the personality characteristics of CB owners and potential owners (potential owners defined as those showing a strong interest to purchase a CB within the next twelve months) versus nonowners reveals the following:

1. CB owners are very extroverted, where nonowners tend to be slightly introverted.

2. Those who own CBs tend to be highly achievement oriented. Nonowners were significantly less achievement oriented.

3. There were no significant differences in authoritarianism, dogmatism, responsibility, and detachment between owners and nonowners.

4. Although there were no apparent differences between owners and nonowners along the aggressiveness dimension, a follow-up, in-depth study revealed that owners desired to be more aggressive than they were and than nonowners were or wished to be.

5. CB owners tended to be more competitive than nonowners.

6. CB owners were significantly more risk averse than nonowners.

7. CB owners were much more conservative than nonowners of CBs.

8. Along the dimension of persuasibility, CB owners were found to be more persuasible on issues of security, family, national issues, and business practices, but less persuasible on dress fashions and social change.

9. Although less sociable in large groups, CB owners tended to desire close relationships with a few people and to socialize in small groups.

10. Other results of the test showed a strong desire for dominance, great self control, and a fascination with gadgetry among CB owners. Moreover, CB owners showed a strong desire for acceptance and approval seeking. CB owners exhibit a need for independence, yet show strong signs of dependence on others. They are very sympathetic, yet intolerant of others' imperfections."

Frank Putnam contemplated the report he had received and wondered how he should proceed in the development of new product lines with the Lionel name. He felt sure that there was a commonality between the type of people who owned or desired to own CBs and other similar products. He wasn't sure which product line to pursue, but "Fuzz Busters" (devices that detect police radar), stereo components, electric pencil sharpeners, and similar products entered his mind.

Questions

1. Based upon the personality traits of CB owners and potential owners described in the case, what product line extension alternatives would you recommend to Frank Putnam? Upon what do you base your recommendations? Which would you choose and why?

2. In what way would you promote Lionel CBs to potential CB owners? How would you promote your proposed product line(s) to present and potential CB owners? Explain.

3. What are the implications of product line extension for Lionel? Explain.

4. What other product purchase decisions might be associated with CB owner personalities? Defend.

5. Are there any implications for product modifications for CB owners? If so, what? Explain.

chapter 6

Self
Concept

Puriteen
Cosmetics, Inc.

This case was prepared by **M. Wayne DeLozier,** *College of Business Administration, University of South Carolina. Copyright* © *1976. Permission granted by the author.*

Puriteen, a cosmetics company based in Atlanta, recently acquired a faltering perfume and cologne company located in Orangedale, Florida (a suburb of Jacksonville). The small producer, Henri's, was started by Henri and Marie Depuy in 1972, but local and area business was not enough to keep alive the dreams of the married couple to develop their own perfume and cologne business.

Background on Henri's

Henri and Marie came to the United States in 1965 from Grasse, France, the world's chief center of perfume manufacture. Having become naturalized U.S. citizens, the well-educated Depuys decided to sink their life savings, if necessary, into their new business venture. Both had worked in a Grasse perfume company and had gained the necessary technology and skills to manufacture perfume.

The Depuys began in their garage producing two fragrances, "Henri's" and "Marie," named after themselves. Henri's was a special formulation handed down from generation to generation through the Depuy family in France. (Such practices are quite common among the French.)

However, after struggling for four years producing and selling the two fragrances, the Depuys realized the coming demise of their business and decided to seek a buyer for their family-heirloom formula.

Raymond L. "Pete" Dozier, vice-president of marketing at Puriteen, learned of the Depuys' situation through a friend, Mitchell R. Morris, while in Jacksonville on a business trip. Morris, a district sales manager for Puriteen, had bought a bottle of Henri's for his wife Jil and was recently made aware of the Depuys' situation. Jil and Mitch were impressed with the fragrance of Henri's and were saddened that the Depuys were planning to sell their business.

Speaking with Dozier, Morris learned of Puriteen's interest to expand into the perfume and cologne business to complement its cosmetic lines. During the conversation, Morris told Dozier of the Depuys' business and strongly urged Dozier to discuss a business deal with Henri.

After six weeks of negotiations with the Depuys, the Puriteen Company agreed to pay Henri and Marie a 10 percent royalty on the net sales of the two perfumes and to hire the Depuys to supervise the manufacture of the perfumes. The success of the negotiations for the Depuys was largely due to Marie's idea of sending a bottle of each fragrance to the wives of Puriteen's top management.

Background on Puriteen

Puriteen was founded in 1946 by William D. "Son" Grimsley and Raymond L. "Pete" Dozier. Son and Pete met in the Navy during World War II and found that they had a mutual interest in developing a business at the war's end. Son, who had earned a B.S. degree in chemistry at Georgia Tech, took his first job in a cosmetics firm before the war. During his three years with the cosmetics company, Son advanced to assistant director of research before volunteering for military service.

Pete received a degree in economics at a well known northeastern university and after graduation spent four years in the sales division of a regional pharmaceutical company.

Before the war's end, Son had received legal notice that his Aunt Jeanette had died and left him $26,000 in cash, seventy-five acres of land near Covington, Georgia, and forty hogs, ten horses, and twenty-five milk-producing cows. His inheritance provided the major portion of capital for starting up a business, and in 1946 Son and Pete created Puriteen.

Son took on the responsibilities of production and development of several cosmetic lines, while Pete handled sales and finance.

By year-end 1975, Puriteen had become a leader in cosmetics in the Southeast with $125 million in sales. Distribution of Puriteen products stretched from Virginia south to Florida and west to the Mississippi River.

The New Product

In mid-1975, Puriteen's top management had decided to expand their lines by entering the perfume and cologne market. Long-range plans were to enter the shaving cream and deodorant markets as well. Dozier had defined their business as a personal care business and believed that these and other products were essential to long-term growth.

In February 1976, Puriteen acquired Henri's, and Dozier began to consider plans for marketing the two newly acquired perfumes.

Henri's and Marie perfumes were fresh, new fragrances to the market. Both rated very high in consumer smell preference tests and certainly had tremendous potential. However, Dozier knew from his experiences and those of other companies that the success of such products depended upon the creation of an appealing image for the brand.

The Generic Product

Perfume is a fragrant substance which has been used since prehistoric times. The essence of many fragrances comes from the oils in the petals of fresh flowers, such as the rose, carnation, and orange blossom. However, fragrances are not limited to the petal, but can come from the leaves of lavendar, peppermint, and geranium. Also, the oils of cinnamon and balsam are derived from bark, while the oils of cedar come from its wood. The fragrance of ginger and sassafras comes from roots, whereas that of orange, lemon, and nutmeg comes from fruits and seeds. Thus, there are many sources from which to derive fragrances for perfume.

Certain materials must be added to the perfume fragrances to prevent evaporation by a process called *fixation.* Ambergris, musk, and castor are fixatives which are often used in the production of perfumes.

Artificial perfumes have been created at a lower cost through the use of synthetics and semisynthetics. They generally are classified under the categories of aldehydes, esters, and ethers, and are rapidly growing in use.

Henri's and Marie are produced with natural ingredients and are therefore more expensive to produce and higher priced than many of the more popular brands of perfume on the U.S. market.

Entering the Perfume Market

Pete Dozier had recently taken several evening courses in marketing at Georgia State in Atlanta to keep track of the current developments in marketing. One of the courses he took was Consumer Behavior. He became very interested in the notion of developing brands which were based upon consumer self concepts.

In March of 1976, Dozier decided to use his understanding of self theory to develop a marketing program for Henri's. By June he had developed a semantic differential to measure the self and self-ideal images of female consumers and the images they held for three unfamiliar perfume brands (the brand names were fictitious).

The tests were conducted in New Orleans, Tallahassee, Atlanta, Raleigh, and Memphis. Four hundred ninety-six personal interviews were conducted (approximately 100 interviews per city). Subjects were given a semantic differential scale on which to describe their self and self-ideal concepts, and their perceptions of each of three perfume advertisements presented them. Each perfume advertisement was a video-taped version of a proposed Henri's advertisement. However, fictional names were used in each case. The order of presentations of the ads and self concepts were random-ized. Subjects were asked at the end of the session to select which of the brands they preferred. They were offered the brand they selected as a prize if their numbers were selected at a later drawing.

The advertised "brands" were given three different themes. One used a sensual theme, the second a romantic theme, and the third a prestigious, regal theme. The following is a partial reproduction of each theme:

> *Nakū.* "Nakū—the naked scent. Unadorned, primitive, sensuous Naku. Nakū is for the woman who has a mind of her own; for the woman who goes her own free and feminine way. It's for the woman who understands that perfume is feminine power! Nakū—the naked scent. It is the essential you!" (Sensual theme)

> *Rumäns.* "Fragrance admittedly triggers emotions, but science doesn't know why. The whole wide world of scents is full of mysteries. However, Rumäns has captured the one scent that can make your world come alive with excitement and romance.

> "Rumäns is a word of endearment, full of affection. Like dew sparkling, brooks babbling, stars smiling, lovers meeting, Rumäns goes about its business of making its wearer feel spirited, airy, romantic.

> "Wear Rumäns day and night. Because love comes without warning!" (Romantic theme)

> *El Primo.* "Once she was the *only* woman in the world allowed to wear this perfume. The Queen of Navarre commissioned the most famed alchemist in Paris to create a perfume of magical potency and bewitching powers. A perfume so irresistable, it disarmed her competitors. A perfume so feminine, it intensified her legendary appeal, drawing the great and the glorious to her court. This magical perfume was El Primo. Unchanged since 1572, it casts its spell for great women today. El Primo, the perfume made for a queen!" (Prestigious, regal theme)

Each script was provided with an appropriate model and picture sequence to match the theme.

The results of the test are presented in Tables 1 through 4.

Developing the Marketing Program

Dozier feels sure that the quality of the two perfumes is the best on the market. But he also knows that product quality alone does not sell a product. It requires a sound communications program. He feels that matching brand image to consumer self image is a sound approach. He must recommend a plan to the Puriteen board next week.

TABLE 1   *Perfume images*

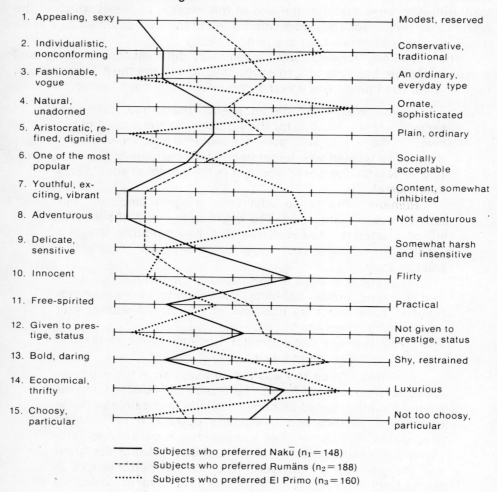

1. Appealing, sexy / Modest, reserved
2. Individualistic, nonconforming / Conservative, traditional
3. Fashionable, vogue / An ordinary, everyday type
4. Natural, unadorned / Ornate, sophisticated
5. Aristocratic, refined, dignified / Plain, ordinary
6. One of the most popular / Socially acceptable
7. Youthful, exciting, vibrant / Content, somewhat inhibited
8. Adventurous / Not adventurous
9. Delicate, sensitive / Somewhat harsh and insensitive
10. Innocent / Flirty
11. Free-spirited / Practical
12. Given to prestige, status / Not given to prestige, status
13. Bold, daring / Shy, restrained
14. Economical, thrifty / Luxurious
15. Choosy, particular / Not too choosy, particular

——— Subjects who preferred Nakū (n₁ = 148)

- - - - Subjects who preferred Rumäns (n₂ = 188)

········ Subjects who preferred El Primo (n₃ = 160)

TABLE 2   *Self concepts*

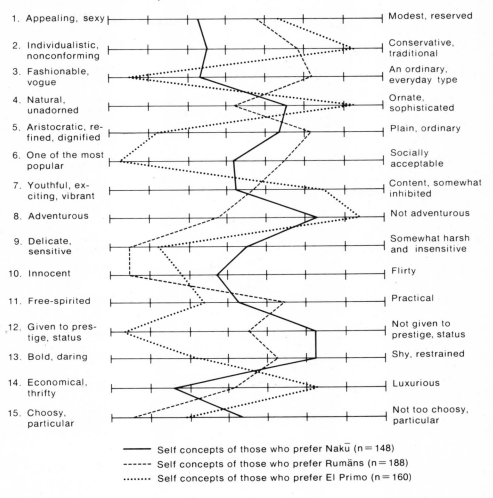

1. Appealing, sexy — Modest, reserved
2. Individualistic, nonconforming — Conservative, traditional
3. Fashionable, vogue — An ordinary, everyday type
4. Natural, unadorned — Ornate, sophisticated
5. Aristocratic, refined, dignified — Plain, ordinary
6. One of the most popular — Socially acceptable
7. Youthful, exciting, vibrant — Content, somewhat inhibited
8. Adventurous — Not adventurous
9. Delicate, sensitive — Somewhat harsh and insensitive
10. Innocent — Flirty
11. Free-spirited — Practical
12. Given to prestige, status — Not given to prestige, status
13. Bold, daring — Shy, restrained
14. Economical, thrifty — Luxurious
15. Choosy, particular — Not too choosy, particular

——— Self concepts of those who prefer Nakū (n = 148)
----- Self concepts of those who prefer Rumäns (n = 188)
········ Self concepts of those who prefer El Primo (n = 160)

TABLE 3   *Self-ideal concepts*

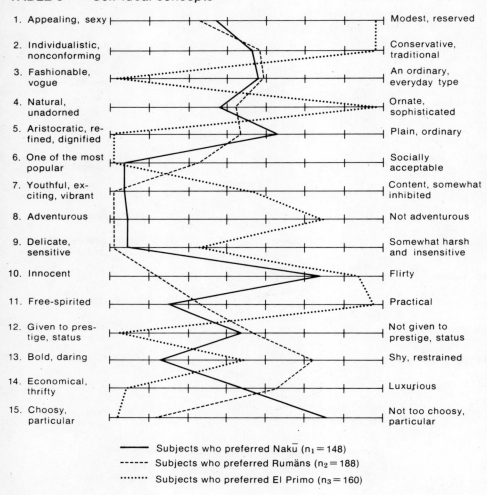

1. Appealing, sexy	Modest, reserved
2. Individualistic, nonconforming	Conservative, traditional
3. Fashionable, vogue	An ordinary, everyday type
4. Natural, unadorned	Ornate, sophisticated
5. Aristocratic, refined, dignified	Plain, ordinary
6. One of the most popular	Socially acceptable
7. Youthful, exciting, vibrant	Content, somewhat inhibited
8. Adventurous	Not adventurous
9. Delicate, sensitive	Somewhat harsh and insensitive
10. Innocent	Flirty
11. Free-spirited	Practical
12. Given to prestige, status	Not given to prestige, status
13. Bold, daring	Shy, restrained
14. Economical, thrifty	Luxurious
15. Choosy, particular	Not too choosy, particular

—————— Subjects who preferred Nakū (n₁ = 148)

------------ Subjects who preferred Rumäns (n₂ = 188)

·············· Subjects who preferred El Primo (n₃ = 160)

TABLE 4   *Ages and family incomes of subjects preferring each brand*

Family Income	Nakū Age Categories				Rumäns Age Categories				El Primo Age Categories				Totals
	18-25	26-35	36-49	50 and over	18-25	26-35	36-49	50 and over	18-25	26-35	36-49	50 and over	
$6,000-9,999	2	22	2	—	18	12	1	—	3	—	—	1	61
$10,000-14,999	5	30	15	—	33	8	15	1	2	6	2	4	121
$15,000-19,999	3	15	17	4	29	14	14	3	18	6	14	22	159
$20,000 and over	1	27	2	3	15	6	13	6	19	8	19	36	155
Totals	11	94	36	7	95	40	43	10	42	20	35	63	
Grand Total		148				188				160			496

91

Questions

1. Self theory holds that individuals try to protect or enhance self concept, that is, they make decisions which are most consistent with their self or self-ideal images. Given this theory, what marketing plan should Dozier recommend to the Board of Directors of Puriteen?

2. What kinds of analyses might you perform on the data?

3. What additional information would you want in developing a program for Puriteen?

4. Evaluate the dimensions used in Dozier's semantic differential. How would you improve it?

5. Are there certain products which lend themselves to self-theory congruence? If so, what are the characteristics of those products?

6. Which self concept is most useful—self or self-ideal concept—in developing marketing programs? Defend your answer.

7. How does the use of consumer self concept differ from the use of consumer personality traits as a basis for developing brand images? Explain.

chapter 7

Life
Style

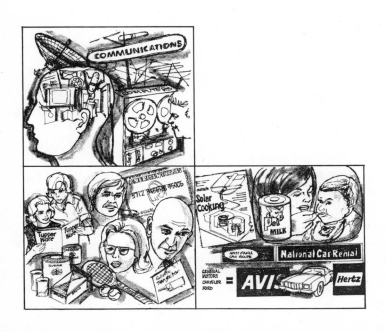

Avon Products, Inc.:
For Whom the Belles Toll

This case was prepared by **Denis F. Healy,** *College of Business and Economics, University of Delaware. The material in this case has been obtained from a variety of published sources. The case has been prepared for teaching purposes only and is not intended to be evaluative of industry or company structure or performance.*

"Our growth only emphasizes what energy and fair dealings with everyone can accomplish. We propose first to be fair with our customers by giving them the very best goods that can be made for the money; we propose to be fair and just, even liberal, with those who form the sinew of our business.

"*As we have grown in the past, so shall we grow in the future;* the limit in this business is measured only by the amount of hard work and energy that is put into it. While we have worked faithfully and loyally in this field, yet if we stop and look over the past and then into the future, we can see that the possibilities are growing greater and greater every day; that we have scarcely begun to reach the proper results from the field we have before us. The millions and millions of people in this country of ours today who are not using our goods are the losers, and it is our place and our purpose to see that at least they must be made acquainted with the merits of the goods, the honesty with which they are made and delivered direct from the laboratory to the consumer." [1]

With these words, the founder of Avon products, David H. McConnell, commented on the promise and future of Avon Products. In the *1975 Annual Report,* Fred G. Fusee, chairman of the board, and David W. Mitchell, president and chief executive officer commented:

"Although we recognize that it is most hazardous to forecast the future and we have no intention to do so, we will repeat as an *objective* the statement made at our annual meeting in 1974: 'The company continues to believe that, given relatively stable economic conditions, its sales and earnings can grow at an average annual rate of 12-15 percent over the long term.' "

Without a doubt, Avon has been a stalwart company in spite of a radically changed and turbulent marketplace. It claims to be the world's largest manufacturer and distributor of cosmetics, toiletries, and costume jewelry.[2] Avon has managed to respond to changing life styles and shifting markets through well-organized and orchestrated managerial systems and marketing approaches.

Commenting on Avon's success, *Forbes* reported in 1973:

> "Avon's explosive growth took place after World War II, with the growth of disposable income, the spread of suburbanization and the increase in the proportion of large families tending to keep women confined to their homes. Prior to this, Avon was just getting by. As recently as 1946, the company's sales were only $17 million—small progress indeed for a company already 60 years old. The economic and sociological trends in the late forties, fifties, and sixties were just right for Avon." [3]

Recent changes in life styles, the emergence of the liberated and career-oriented woman, consumerism, competitive threats, and so on, pose challenges and opportunities to Avon's vitality and growth potential. With the resource base and distribution capabilities of Avon, creative responses are possible and even likely. Historically, Avon's marketing costs have been lower than competitors. And through the use of direct sales representatives and modest advertising, Avon has been able to obtain very high gross margins. But with changing times and costs, Avon realizes that it must consider new alternatives.

The Company and Its History

David H. McConnell, a door-to-door book salesman, founded Avon in 1886 as the California Perfume Company. To stimulate interest, he adopted the practice of giving small vials of perfume to housewives who listened to his sales pitch. Over time he recognized the nature of the product he was offering and recruited Mrs. P. F. E. Albee as the first Avon lady. Mrs. Albee, who was 50 at the time, developed the Avon selling program and was given the honorary title Mother of the California Perfume Company by Mr. McConnell. Under her direction, she "made door-to-door selling respectable. Unlike many door-to-door salesmen, the Avon lady was considered neither a drifter nor a pest. She was a neighbor come calling." [4]

Avon has come a long way since Mrs. Albee. The *1975 Annual Report* shows that Avon has 800,000 active representatives, operating in nineteen countries, selling to 50 million consumers. Total population of these countries is approximately 870 million people. Sales in 1975 were $1.3 billion representing an increase of 3 percent over 1974. The U.S. and Canadian portion of sales in 1975 was $755 million, a 2 percent decrease over 1974.

International subsidiary sales amounted to $526 million for an increase of 9 percent over 1974. Tables 1 and 2 present financial and growth information.

The *1973 Annual Report* commented on the growth record as follows:

> "In the 1950s sales in the U.S. and Canada increased at an annual rate of 18 percent while earnings grew 22 percent annually.
>
> "Not unexpectedly, the annual rates of gain in sales and earnings in the U.S. and Canada slowed somewhat during the period from 1960-1973, to 13 percent and 14 percent, respectively. During this same period, international sales and earnings increased very rapidly as we developed existing markets and entered additional countries. As a result the annual rates of gain in consolidated sales and earnings during this period were 16 percent and 17 percent respectively." [5]

Present
Operations and Products

Not counting makeup shades, Avon offers 700 products to its markets. Although it is a comparatively recent entrant into the costume jewelry business, it has the distinction of being the world's largest marketer of such products —testimony to the distribution strength of the firm. In 1974, Avon claimed to have 15 percent of the $5 billion U.S. cosmetics and toiletries market. In foreign markets, it estimates having a 25 percent share in several countries.[6] Table 3 shows the distribution of recent revenues by product class.

In addition to the direct sales of cosmetics, Avon has diversified into the costume jewelry business, the operation of beauty salons, mail order sales of men's and women's apparel under the "Family Fashions" name, and the sale of glass and plastic housewares in Canada under the name "Geni" using the party plan method. These activities (excluding costume jewelry) are operated under the Corporate Development group. In 1975, sales of $14.1 million were realized, representing a growth of 35 percent over 1974 levels.[7]

The cornerstone of the Avon operation is its worldwide network of 800,000 Avon ladies. This field sales system has evolved over the past ninety years and today involves five levels of management. The senior position is given the title of general manager.

The general manager is responsible for one of seven branches in the U.S. and has two regional managers reporting to him. Each regional manager assumes responsibility for eight divisional managers. Divisional managers direct eighteen district managers who in turn have recruiting, training, and supervisory responsibilities for about 100 Avon representatives. Avon ladies are given sales territories of between 100 and 200 households in their own neighborhoods and typically are able to cover between twenty to thirty households every two weeks for twenty-six sales compaigns a year.[8]

TABLE 1   Ten-year review (Dollar figures in thousands)

	1975	1974	1973	1972
Net sales	$1,295,062	$1,260,292	$1,150,659	$1,005,316
Cost of goods sold	473,756	499,821	414,106	356,086
Selling and administrative expenses	540,312	521,733	470,005	394,603
Earnings before taxes	280,994	238,738	266,548	254,627
% to net sales	21.7%	18.9%	23.1%	25.3%
Taxes on earnings	141,990	126,983	131,398	129,798
Net earnings	$139,004	$111,755	$135,150	$124,829
% to net sales	10.7%	8.9%	11.7%	12.4%
Number of employees				
U.S. and Canada	11,700	13,000	13,200	12,200
International	13,300	13,900	14,000	12,900
Total	25,000	26,900	27,200	25,100

	1971	1970	1969	1968	1967	1966
Net sales	$873,158	$759,171	$656,660	$558,587	$474,814	$408,178
Cost of goods sold	315,848	270,672	230,379	194,956	166,244	143,358
Selling and administrative expenses	336,011	291,955	251,123	210,997	180,160	155,674
Earnings before taxes	221,294	196,544	175,158	152,634	128,410	109,146
% to net sales	25.3%	25.9%	26.7%	27.3%	27.0%	26.7%
Taxes on earnings	112,107	97,856	90,915	81,374	63,027	53,868
Net earnings	$109,187	$98,688	$84,243	$71,260	$65,383	$55,278
% to net sales	12.5%	13.0%	12.8%	12.8%	13.8%	13.5%
Number of employees						
U.S. and Canada	10,900	10,600	10,000	9,200	8,400	7,800
International	12,400	11,500	10,800	9,100	7,300	6,100
Total	23,300	22,100	20,800	18,300	15,700	13,900

International operations are found in eighteen countries outside the U.S. In 1976, Avon entered the Hong Kong market and plans to enter the Phillipines in 1977. The possibility of entering countries in the Far East and Africa also is being considered. In terms of population, the foreign areas have about 600 million people compared to the 250 million residents of the U.S. and Canada. Serving the foreign markets requires 500,000 representatives compared to 300,000 for the U.S. and Canada.[9] The foreign markets, at this stage of their development, are considerably less productive than the

TABLE 2   *Sales and earnings trends*
SOURCE: *1974-1975 Annual Report*

	1974-1975	1973-1974	Percent Change ( ) = Loss 1960-1973	1950s
Consolidated sales	3	10	16	N/A
U.S. and Canada	(2)	5	13	18
International	9	16	N/A	N/A
Consolidated earnings	24	(17)	17	N/A
U.S. and Canada	6	(8)	14	22
International	76	(30)	N/A	N/A

TABLE 3   *Sales revenue distribution 1973-1975*
SOURCE: *1973-1975 Annual Report*

	% 1975	% 1973-1974
Fragrance and bath products for women	35-40	40-45
Makeup, skin care, and other women's products	25-30	25-30
Men's products	10-15	10-15
Other cosmetics and toiletry items for children and family use	15-20	15-20
Costume jewelry	7	—

TABLE 4   *Sales summary 1975*

	Dollars 1975	% Avg. Increase 1974
U.S. and Canada	755	(2)
International	526	9
Europe	274	2
Latin America and the Pacific	252	17

TABLE 5   *International operations 1975*
SOURCE: *1975 Annual Report*

Argentina	England	Italy	Puerto Rico
Australia	France	Japan	Spain
Belgium	Germany	Mexico	Sweden
Brazil	Guatemala	The Netherlands	Venezuela
Canada	Ireland		

domestic operations. However, Avon feels that "With the increasing prosperity of foreign nations, we have major opportunities to improve the overall sales and earnings of our business." [10] Tables 4 and 5 depict information about the international operations of Avon.

Company
Objectives and Commitments

A company of the size and diversity of Avon justifiably must recognize multiple commitments and must have a series of underlying objectives for its business. In the early '70s, Avon began to give explicit recognition to the notion of social responsibility. This resulted in a "Statement of Corporate Responsibility" which deals with the consumer, discrimination, and the environment. The written commitment to the consumer says:

> "We seek to assure complete customer satisfaction by offering quality and safe merchandise through prompt and courteous service, using the most ethical marketing methods. We subscribe to the principle that all consumers should be informed. Therefore, we shall take further steps to communicate to them information about our company and our products, and to encourage their inquiries and comments." [11]

In responding to this statement the *1974 Annual Report* noted:

> "We were among the first in the cosmetics industry to join in a three-part self-regulation program. This involves filing lists of formula ingredients with the Food and Drug Administration, registering plant locations and reporting consumer experience with our products.
>
> "As the sales leader in the U.S. direct selling industry, we have a special interest in protecting the consumer from unethical door-to-door selling practices and actively support the Code of Ethics of the Direct Selling Association with its self-regulatory guidelines." [12]

In terms of economic objectives, the following two were presented in 1973:

> "First—to achieve greater penetration of the United States market, with special emphasis on improving the effectiveness of our field organization. It is our goal through better training and new programs for our District Managers to increase the number of customers served by Representatives and thus expand coverage of the country's households.
>
> "Second—to pursue the fine potential in foreign markets, which in total are several times larger than the United States. In so doing, it is our objective to improve the marketing programs and operating efficiency of our international operations and to raise their level of profitability to a point comparable with that of the United States." [13]

In 1975, David W. Mitchell, president of Avon Products, Inc., said, "My primary objective is to put Avon into the sales and profit patterns of the 1960s . . . I think that is a realistic and achievable goal." [14]

The Business Environment and
Avon's Position

As with virtually every other company in its industry, the impact of spiraling costs, shortages of raw materials, and the energy crisis has had a damaging effect on Avon. Furthermore, the inflation of the first half of the '70s retarded consumer interest in cosmetic and personal care and related products.

FIGURE 1   *Avon's door-to-door sales*

The sensitivity of Avon to business cycle fluctuations, some speculate, is amplified by the character of its customers who usually are members of blue-collar families. Avon, on the other hand, indicates that the demographic characteristics and trends of its market will help it grow through the balance of the 1970s and early 1980s. David W. Mitchell commented before a group of West Coast Analysts that the fastest growing segment of the U.S. female population is the 25-44 age group. This group accounts for 60 percent of total Avon sales. Also, about 60 percent of sales comes from those in the $15,000 to $20,000 income group. About 50 percent of U.S. families are expected to be in this group by 1980.[15]

In 1974, sales and earnings dropped markedly during the period of high inflation. The rebound for 1975, according to *Fortune* occurred, "only after draconian cost controls were imposed." But, as the article continued, "no amount of cost cutting will solve Avon's basic problem—it needs to increase sales."[16] Recent favorable trends in sales productivity through increased advertising, reorganization of the selling organization, and product line revisions have contributed to increased sales. The sales growth of 10 percent through mid-1976 is attributed to more favorable economic conditions and more aggressive marketing programs.

One of the most pressing and unique challenges confronting the company is the changing life style of its customers and representatives. The same inflationary pressures that precipitated a general decline in sales also has a hidden impact. With increased costs of living, more and more women are finding it necessary to work part- or full-time to supplement the family income. Currently, more than two out of five women of working age are employed. As a result, it has become more difficult to find potential customers at home. In addition, women have become quite mobile and less home-bound in the last decade. For those women not working, "tennis fever," volunteer work, and other diversions tend to pull them away from home during the prime selling hours. This forces the Avon representative to work in the evening and Saturday, to be much more active on the phone, to call on women at their place of work, and to use other indirect selling methods.[17] Regarding working women, David W. Mitchell said ". . . 42 percent of our customers are working women—the same percentage as the national average, and they account for 50 percent of our total U.S. sales." [18]

On the other side of the coin, however, Avon feels it might benefit by having access to a larger potential market of representatives, although many are finding other work more satisfying and profitable.

As if these pressures were not enough, Avon faces a challenge from a growing number of powerful and sophisticated marketers. *Business Week* made the following observations on the competitive situation:

> "To add to the challenge, the cosmetics industry itself is changing complexion. Starting ten or fifteen years ago, major outside companies began buying dozens of small independent cosmetics houses. Now, many of the larger houses are being gobbled up. Among the latest: Max Factor (Norton Simon), Helena Rubinstein (Colgate-Palmolive), Elizabeth Arden (Eli Lilly), and Lanvin-Charles of the Ritz (Squibb).
> "On the door-to-door side of the business, Dart Industries added Vanda Beauty Counselor (along with Tupperware), Bristol Myer bought Luzier cosmetics, and giant General Foods acquired Diviane Woodward cosmetics." [19]

It should be noted, however, that the performance of some firms in the cosmetics industry is yet to be assessed. The selling power of Avon is demonstrated by the four-week sales record of The Betsy Ross Figurine, Cologne Decanter in which about 1.5 million units were sold at $6.99 each for total sales of over $10 million.[20]

The Industry

In 1973, *Forbes* reported that Avon had captured 80 percent to 90 percent of the domestic, direct sales market for cosmetics. There were no competitors with more than 4 percent of the door-to-door market. Moreover, Avon was reported to hold approximately 20 percent of the total U.S. cosmetic market of $5 billion.[21]

Presently, Avon estimates it has about 25 percent of the foreign market.[22] In its mode of distribution, Avon has a virtual monopoly with its most staunch competitor reported to be Mary Kay Cosmetics. Mary Kay was founded in 1963 and in 1972 had sales of $17.6 million. The firm has somewhat different selling styles and philosophies from Avon. It calls its salespersons "consultants" and uses home demonstrations for groups rather than for individuals. In 1973, Mary Kay had 340 field managers and about 16,000 consultants, all on straight commission. The commission structure is higher than Avon's, and movement to the field manager position is earned by sales performance as a consultant and is retained subsequently by territorial productivity.[23]

The Marketplace

As mentioned previously, there have been dramatic changes in the consumption patterns and life styles of consumers. The influence of rapid inflation, changing orientations to work, and the change in the family unit and leisure activity have challenged the creativity of Avon and others in the industry. Consumers most affected economically and psychically tend to be those in Avon's prime market. The "Squeeze on the Middle Class" is taking its toll by making it more difficult to purchase a single family home, to afford education for one's family, and to purchase discretionary, nondurable items such as those offered by Avon. The prolonged inflationary and unemployment period of the middle '70s has caused uncertainty in the minds of all but the most secure consumer. Although the impact of the squeeze is visible mostly in a slow-down of consumer durable purchases, a prolonged period such as this one also has a profound effect on consumer purchasing patterns and attitudes toward nondurable goods.[24]

The Avon Product Line

Cosmetics

The market for cosmetic products is segmented readily into a number of classifications based on age and sex. For Avon, the primary market is women in the 18-55 year-old group. In addition, they have developed a line of products for men which constitutes between ten and fifteen percent of net sales. For the teens market, Avon offers a line of fragrances called Sweet Honesty, introduced in 1973, which quickly became one of its top three fragrances. Overall the teen market for cosmetics is estimated to purchase over $40 per capita a year. The baby market also is served by Avon through its Clearly Gentle line of ointments and lotions. Also, soaps, shampoos, and hair care products are offered. Finally, there is the black market. In mid-1975, Avon began marketing a line of makeup, Shades of Beauty, designed for and marketed to black consumers.[25] Also available to the black market are hair care and skin care products.

Noncosmetic Items

In addition to the door-to-door sales of cosmetics, Avon engages in direct selling activities in two other major product areas, clothing (Family Fashion) using mail order methods, and housewares (Geni) using the party plan approach. During 1975, Avon reported on these areas:

> "Last year Family Fashions increased its customer base to 575,000 and expanded sales to all fifty states. Other 1975 developments included centralization of all operations in Newport News, Virginia . . . issuance of our first complete product catalogs . . . and introduction of a new home furnishings category, such as sheets, bedspreads, and draperies. Family Fashions products are sold by mail order and not through Avon representatives.
>
> "Two years after acquisition of Geni Company, about 2,000 Geni representatives now sell plastic and glass housewares through the party plan across Canada. Products include decorative servingware, saladware, thermal containers, and such items as terrariams, cigarette boxes, and bathware. There are some seventy-five products in the line with prices ranging from $1.75 to $15.95. The most popular products are in the $10 to $11 bracket." [26]

For the Family Fashion line, a sales increase of 40 percent was reported representing a 50 percent growth in unit sales with 1.5 million pieces. There were over 600 items in the line.[27]

Another major market served by the representatives is in jewelry and gift items. Avon, after only four years in the business, is the nation's largest distributor of costume jewelry. Sales for 1975 are estimated at over $225 million for a 15 percent gain over 1974. Jewelry sales represented 7 percent of total corporate sales in 1975. In the jewelry portion of the business, prices range from $4 to $14 with women's items accounting for most of the business. About fifty new designs, mainly suited to the younger working woman, were introduced in 1975. The other part of the line, gifts, is principally in the form of decanters. In this area, 122 new items were introduced in 1975 compared to 179 in 1974.[28]

Questions

1. In what ways have consumer life styles changed? How have these recent changes affected Avon's marketing approach?

2. How should Avon adapt its marketing program to the changing consumer life styles you have identified?

3. What are the international implications for Avon?

4. Identify the threats and opportunities that the change in consumer life styles has for Avon. Discuss how Avon should minimize the threats and take advantage of the opportunities.

5. Are there particular segments in which life styles are changing more rapidly than others? If so, describe these segments.

Notes

¹ Taken from "Great Oak" as it appeared on the cover of Avon's *1972 Annual Report* and written by Avon's founder, David H. McConnell, in 1903.

² Avon Products, Inc., *1975 Annual Report*, p. 1.

³ "Avon Products: Is Its Beauty Only Skin Deep?," *Forbes*, July 1, 1973, p. 22.

⁴ Ibid., p. 20.

⁵ Avon Products, Inc., *1973 Annual Report*, p. 9.

⁶ Avon Products, Inc., *1974 Annual Report*, p. 12.

⁷ *1975 Annual Report*, p. 3.

⁸ "Troubled Avon," *Business Week*, May 11, 1974, p. 100.

⁹ *1975 Annual Report*, p. 4.

¹⁰ *1973 Annual Report*, p. 4.

¹¹ "The Avon Commitment," Harvard Business School Case No. 9-375-165, p. 14.

¹² *1974 Annual Report*, p. 16.

¹³ *1973 Annual Report*, p. 6.

¹⁴ "In Quest of that Old Glamour," *Fortune*, January 1976, p. 28.

¹⁵ David W. Mitchell, "Speech Before West Coast Analysts' Meeting," June 14, 1976, pp. 4-5.

¹⁶ *Fortune*, January 1976, p. 28.

¹⁷ "Avon Calling—Is Anyone Home?" *Finance World*, October 30, 1974, p. 37; See also *Business Week*, May 11, 1974, pp. 98-106.

¹⁸ "Speech Before West Coast Analysts' Meeting," pp. 5-6.

¹⁹ *Business Week*, May 11, 1974, p. 98.

²⁰ Letter to Avon Shareholders, July 23, 1976, p. 2.

²¹ *Forbes*, July 1, 1973, p. 20.

²² *1974 Annual Report*, p. 12.

²³ *Forbes*, July 1, 1973, p. 20.

²⁴ "The Squeeze on the Middle Class," *Business Week*, March 10, 1975, pp. 52-60.

²⁵ *1974 Annual Report*, p. 12; *1972 Annual Report*, p. 7.

²⁶ *1975 Annual Report*, p. 18.

²⁷ Ibid.

²⁸ Ibid.

part 4

Social Influence on Consumer Behavior

The previous sections viewed the consumer in a "vacuum," isolated from the influence of others. This section looks at the consumer within the context of the important groups that affect his entire life, and at their influence upon his consumption behavior in particular. The groups considered most important in the influence of buyer behavior are cultural, subcultural, social class, family, and reference groups.

Two cases are included on the diffusion and adoption processes that illustrate the influence of groups on the purchase of new products.

chapter 8

Cultural and
Subcultural Influence

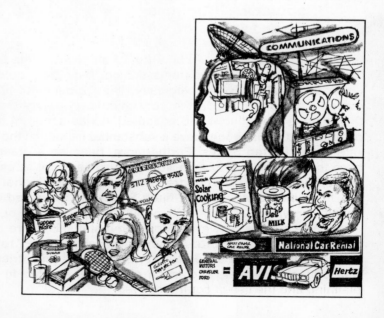

Population
Services, Inc.

In late December 1970, Mr. Philip Harvey and Dr. T. R. L. Black were attempting to finalize plans for their new nonprofit organization, Population Services, Inc., in Chapel Hill, North Carolina. Mr. Harvey and Dr. Black strongly believed that the current methods of disseminating birth control information and marketing birth control materials was inadequate. Population Services, Inc. (PSI) was being formed in an attempt to improve these methods.

Population Problems:
Domestic and International

It was estimated that about one-fifth of all births in the United States were "unwanted," that is, the parents did not feel they could afford the child, either financially or psychologically. The incidence of unwanted births occurred more often among the poor, the near-poor, and the least educated than among the affluent and educated. It was apparent that the prevention of unwanted births would have a substantial impact on the population growth rate in the United States. Furthermore, because a drastic situation would have to exist before a woman would report her child as unwanted, the actual proportion of undesired children was considerably higher than reported.

In countries other than United States the unwanted child problem was equally prevalent. The overall population problem around the world was even more serious, however. Most often statistics were presented on such countries as India or Brazil where overpopulation in relation to food and other resources were especially serious. In other countries the situation also was critical, however, and much effort was needed in developing family planning and the use of contraceptives.

Family planning programs had been undertaken all over the world with some success, especially considering the magnitude of the problem. However, it was clear that continuing population growth was outstripping the work of the family planning agencies. More effort, probably of several types, was needed to overcome the persistent tendency for population to grow faster than the world's ability to provide food, clothing, housing, and other goods.

Teenagers Most Affected

The rate of illegitimate births in the United States nearly doubled during the 1960s. Adult American women actually had a decline in illegitimate births during this period, but this decline was more than offset by a tremendous increase in illegitimacy among the nation's teenagers. Apparently many teenagers did not realize how easy it was to become pregnant, and those who did realize did not have medically prescribed contraceptives available to them. Although contraceptives were becoming increasingly available to older women, they were not easily available to teenagers who comprised 70 percent of the unmarried women population.

The Tip of the Iceberg

The established doctrine, particularly among hard-headed businessmen, was that if the poor would stop conceiving so many children, the population problem would go away. "After all," it was said, "isn't it in the ghettos where people are crowded together and where the riots start?" This was just the "tip of the iceberg," however. In fact, fewer than one-third of all babies born in the U.S. each year were born to the poor, fewer than 20 percent to the nonwhite population.[1]

The majority of U.S. population growth came not from the poor and nonwhite, but rather from the relatively affluent and middle-class Americans who believed they could "afford" the third or fourth child. The cost of an additional child, it was increasingly recognized, must be measured by more than just the effect on the family's income. Cost would have to be measured as well by the effect on already overcrowded institutions, on scarce, non-renewable resources, and on the physical and social environment in which the extra child must live.

To be sure, poorer people had higher birth rates than did more affluent ones. This was true not only of blacks, Chicanos, and American Indians, however, but also of the so-called white Anglo-Saxon Protestants. As all citizens became more affluent, a likely outcome of economic growth, indications were that the differences in birth rates among U.S. citizens would diminish. Under the growth conditions present, however, the world would still produce more new babies than the planet could provide for.

Answers to Population Problems

It would have seemed possible to solve some of the problems of population growth by encouraging people, with subsidies and retraining, to migrate to areas where there were still needs for people, both in the U.S. and abroad. Because of the homing instinct of most people on the earth, this was a vain hope. Similar with the other proposals made, there was little hope that they could ever be implemented, and if they were, there was little hope that they could be effective. For example, a proposal was made to pay a bonus to families limiting themselves to a certain number of children by way of tax incentives. It seemed unlikely that these schemes in themselves would have enough effect to slow down the rate of population growth to the point where the earth's resources would not be overtaxed.

It was necessary to make contraceptive devices, both medical and non-medical, more available to all people, married and single.

Objectives of
PSI

Both Mr. Harvey and Dr. Black were well aware of the world-wide population situation. Mr. Harvey had worked for CARE for five years in India, and Dr. Black had practiced medicine in Australia and New Guinea, specializing in obstetrics, marital counselling and family planning, and midwife training. They had met while studying population and family planning at the School of Public Health at the University of North Carolina at Chapel Hill.

Mr. Harvey and Dr. Black were concerned that the dissemination of birth control and family planning information and the marketing of birth control material had too long been the domain of medical people. Because there were not enough world-wide medical resources to cope with sickness, let alone population control, the medical profession had skills which were too scarce to effectively implement population control without help. The birth control situation was seen as a selling or marketing job in which modern effective marketing techniques would supplement the scarce medical skills.

The PSI experience was also seen as a useful way for Mr. Harvey and Dr. Black to fulfill the field work requirements of the Master of Science in Public Health degrees on which they were both working.

In looking at population control, they divided the problem into two segments: less developed countries (LDCs) and the U.S. Mr. Harvey felt that the solutions in the U.S. and LDCs were similar but that the problems were different. In the LDCs the problem was economic while in the U.S. it was social.

Mr. Harvey and Dr. Black felt that if birth control were to be promoted to the LDCs and the lower-income segment of the United States, it also would have to be promoted to the mass middle-income segment. Otherwise, the poor would reject a "Do as I say, not as I do" philosophy. PSI thus had many options open to it in its efforts to improve the promotion of birth control. It also had a great deal of information on the current markets for birth control materials.

Birth Control
U.S. and World-Wide

The Medical Approach

Nearly all family planning activities centered around having the woman who sought not to conceive visit her family doctor or a clinic and, after counselling by a physician (or, in some case, a paramedical person), have a contraceptive prescribed to be purchased at a pharmacy. A number of problems existed with regard to this system. For one thing, it was relatively expensive. Families in the United States found it difficult to pay for such care; those in other countries found it impossible to do so.

Where family planning clinics were public agencies and free, a trip to such a place was very intimidating to many women. Around the world an ethic had grown up, fostered by most religions, that a woman's major reason for being was to bear children. Many women felt embarrassed to admit that they did not want to carry out what they were "brought into the world to do."

The most important problem with regard to what has been termed *the medical approach* was simply the lack of facilities. Virtually no country in the world had enough medical personnel to treat the many diseases existing. To divert a significant number of these to birth control work was impossible.

This was the basic reason for the growth of nonmedical contraceptives, and the reason for the development of Population Services, Inc.

Nonmedical Approaches

Into the gap between the need to provide means of controlling births and the services available from family planning agencies around the world had stepped the producers of contraceptives of various types.[2] In many countries the so-called commercial sector was much larger than the nonprofit (government distribution) sector. Table 1 presents the users of each type of contraceptive world-wide.

Although it was difficult to determine accurate figures for population, not to mention for contraceptive use, three things were clear from Table 1:

1. Much less than 20 percent of families world-wide used any form of contraceptive.

2. Condoms (latex and other materials) and birth control pills were by far the most widely used contraceptives.

3. In the United States the pill had a much larger market than any other birth control method.

The Condom

The major nonmedical contraceptive, as revealed in Table 1, was the condom; also, it was the only contraceptive device used by the male. It was estimated that 1968 world condom production was slightly less than 16 million gross.

TABLE 1   *Estimated users of contraceptives 1968* [a] *(in millions)*
SOURCE: Sollins and Belsky

Type of Contraceptive	World [b]	United States
Aerosol foam	1-2	1-2
Condom	17-19	4-5
Diaphragm	2-3	2-3
Intrauterine device	5-6 [c]	1-2
Oral contraceptive	17-19	7-8
All specified types	42-49	15-20

[a] The estimates of users given in Table 1 are derived from distributors' information according to the following assumptions and should be regarded as a rough approximation:

Each cycle of oral contraceptives is sufficient for the average menstrual cycle of twenty-eight days. The number of users is then 12/13 or 92 percent of the number of cycles distributed per month, where "user" is construed as woman-year of protection.

For condoms, studies in the United States and other countries indicate an average of 100 to 130 coital experiences per couple per year; assuming that not all condoms purchased are utilized, we have elected to use 1.1 to convert "gross of condoms per year" to "users."

Foam users may be calculated from the same coital experience rate. At a dosage of 1 gm per application, a factor of 0.4 will serve to convert "cans sold per year" to "users."

For diaphragms, used mainly in the United States, users have been estimated by extrapolation from studies by Charles F. Westoff and Normal B. Ryder ("Reproduction in the United States, 1965," forthcoming).

[b] Including the United States but excluding Mainland China and Eastern European countries with centrally planned economies.

[c] This includes four million users in developing countries through national programs.

Current capacity plus expansion definitely programmed (not including new investment) was estimated to be between 19 and 20 million gross. New private investment was unlikely to be drawn into the condom producing business, not because of low profits—they were adequate. The reason was the apparent low growth in demand. To meet current prices, a plant built to produce at least two million gross per year was required. Markets to absorb such additional capacity were not numerous at that time.

Despite the "scare tactic" efforts of the military to convince American men to use condoms and the apparent failure of such tactics, Mr. Harvey and Dr. Black felt that the condom had never been properly marketed in the United States, and that aggressive marketing of condoms and other non-prescription birth control products could pay high dividends, both commercial and social.

Condom types and packaging   Condom manufacturers in the United States were not generally innovative, perhaps because of the oligopolistic nature of the market. Primary variations were in material, lubrication, and transparency.

Materials. The vast majority of condoms were made of latex, both hand and machine dipped. A small portion were of sheep and lamb caecum. Although the latter were much more sensitive in intercourse, they did not stretch as readily as latex and were much more expensive. In the late 1960s, plastic condoms were in the experimental stage but had not been developed commercially.

Lubrication. Condoms were available in both lubricated and non-lubricated types. The nonlubricated ones were generally less expensive. The lubrication was of two types, silicone and moist. There were several degrees of lubrication; some users preferred condoms which were more lubricated than others.

Transparency. Some condoms were transparent; others, opaque; others, somewhere between these extremes. In part, transparency was a function of lubrication; silicone lubrication normally was used with transparent condoms, moist lubrication with opaque ones.

Most U.S. manufactured condoms were white, the natural color of the latex, with rather drab packaging. Some European and Japanese manufacturers had produced condoms in many bright colors and with attractive packaging. These colored and better packaged condoms generally cost a little more than the others.

Condom distribution   There were three major condom distributors in the United States, Young Drug Products Corporation, Julius Schmid Company, and Akwell Industries, Inc. Together they marketed almost all of the condoms sold in the U.S.

Young Drug Products Corporation and Julius Schmid Company relied heavily on salespeople and sold primarily to wholesale and retail druggists. They attempted to promulgate a "white coat" image, a feeling of medical approval and legitimacy. Akwell Industries, on the other hand, marketed most of the vending-machine-sold condoms and sold to a large number of small drug, service station, and other retail outlets. Akwell, it was observed, seemed to be looked upon by Young and Schmid as a maverick, as not upholding the ethical practices of the condom industry. If true, perhaps it was because the vending-machine-sold condoms were found in the rest rooms of taverns, bars, and other public places, and thus gained a disreputable image. This image may have been looked upon as unwise in light of the legal history of condom selling.

A federal statute from 1872 had effectively prohibited mail order selling or advertising of birth control devices. Indications were that this statute came about because of Puritan thinking and because of the large number of fradulent devices being promoted by mail at that time. A number of firms had challenged the law in the 1960s, and although it was still in effect in

1970, PSI had obtained unofficial clearance from the Post Office Department to send literature and birth control devices by mail.

Another effect of the uncertain legal situation, however, had been to eliminate effectively foreign competition from the market. PSI had made contacts in both the United Kingdom and Japan and had excellent possibilities of obtaining high quality, lower priced condoms from manufacturers in these two countries.

Several states had laws in effect concerning the promotion and selling of contraceptive devices. For example, California and Kentucky required state licenses for selling contraceptives. Other states specified that advertising and display of contraceptives were not allowed. Many media were wary of accepting advertisements for any product or service even remotely illegal, although PSI had found that more and more newspapers over the period of months it had been in operation seemed willing to accept ads. Harvey and Black felt it would be "an uphill battle" to have advertising accepted by some newspapers, but that ultimately PSI could be successful.

In general, drug and other retail outlets did not have countertop displays of contraceptive devices. A few druggists displayed vaginal foams near the prescription department, but only a relative handful were willing to display condoms. These were almost always kept under the counter. Reports were that those few retailers who had the courage to display condoms increased sales on this very profitable item by 300 percent to 400 percent.

Overseas distribution of condoms was much more open than in the United States. In Great Britain and other countries throughout the world, condoms were sold over the counter in barber shops, "hygiene" shops, and other types of outlets. At least 10 percent of the British market was reported to be sold by mail. In Germany, catalogs illustrating a multitude of sex-related products were widely distributed, and reports were that an extensive mail order business was done through them.

At one time, Harvey and Black had considered opening a retail shop for the display and promotion of contraceptive devices, primarily condoms. Their idea had come from the Swedish "Birds and Bees" shops which sold, in addition to contraceptives and birth control information, mod clothes and soda fountain items. Some street-located vending machines for condoms had been seen in Sweden as well. Because of the major expense involved in this retail type of operation, they temporarily abandoned the idea.

Condoms were sold also in vending machines which were generally located in the men's rooms of bars and taverns. These machines sold mostly second grade products (nonlubricated, matchbook type packaging, selling for about 25¢ each) and cost about $50 each.

There were reported to be 80 to 100 private brands of condoms sold in the United States, many of them manufactured by Akwell Industries. Indications were that consumers were not particularly sensitive to condom brand names, probably because condoms had received so little marketing effort.

Condom promotion   In general, condoms had not been advertised in the

United States until 1970, and then only by Julius Schmid Company in a few national magazines such as *Playboy.* Apparently condom manufacturers believed that their products were, in general, inappropriate for advertising.

PSI's advertising to date consisted of classified or small display ads, primarily in college and so-called "underground" newspapers. Although response to the advertising had been encouraging, sales were not in sufficient volume to break even in the mail order operation.

The Current Situation

In late December, Mr. Harvey and Dr. Black were developing plans for PSI. They knew that their financial resources were limited to between $5,000 and $10,000. Their objective was simple—to develop better methods of delivering contraceptive information and materials to relevant segments of the American populace, especially to prevent unwanted first pregnancies, and, more especially, to prevent unwanted premarital conception. On the one hand, they knew that their venture was involved with a stable, well developed marketing situation, fraught with delicate social traditions and complex distribution and buying patterns. On the other hand, they felt sure that a great need was not being met and that a potentially profitable market was going untapped.

Questions

1. Identify the cultural differences toward contraceptive practices, attitudes, and purchasing behavior between the United States and foreign countries. How do the marketing efforts differ?

2. How would you develop a marketing program to disseminate contraceptive information and provide contraceptive products to various LDCs such as India? What information would you want and why?

3. Describe the approaches you would use to disseminate contraceptive information to the various subcultures within the United States. How do the approaches differ? Explain.

4. What are the public policy implications suggested in this case? What role should PSI play in developing public policy on population control? How should they go about it?

5. How would you handle the potential social and religious repercussions of your dissemination of contraceptive information to unmarrieds?

Notes

[1] Paul R. Ehrlich and John P. Holdren, "Who Makes the Babies?" *Saturday Review,* February 6, 1971, p. 60.

[2] Alfred D. Sollins and Raymond L. Belsky, "Commercial Production and Distribution of Contraceptives," *Reports on Population/Family Planning,* the Population Council, June 1970. This section of the case is heavily based on this article.

Johnson
Products Company

This case was prepared by **Denis F. Healy,** *College of Business and Economics, University of Delaware. The material in this case has been obtained from a variety of published sources. The case has been prepared for teaching purposes only and is not intended to be evaluative of industry or company structure, conduct, or performance.*

Johnson Products Company (JPC) has enjoyed great success in the sale of hair care products to the black consumer market. In fact, Johnson Products is one of the largest predominantly black-managed and owned enterprises in the United States. JPC has between 45 and 50 percent market share of the ethnic market and less than a 1 percent share of the total personal care market in the U.S. Growing cultural awareness by blacks and other groups continues to provide new product and market segmenting opportunities for the firm. However, the profit potential of ethnic markets has become sufficiently attractive to major producers such as Revlon, Avon Products, Inc., and Clairol that they also have developed several lines of products for these markets.

Johnson Products is faced with an increasingly competitive market, growing opportunities to market internationally, and growing opportunities to expand into nonethnic lines of toiletries and cosmetics. Management currently is trying to decide which of these directions to take. Furthermore, JPC is confronted with a need for additional information about its existing markets, distribution systems, and the behavioral characteristics of nonethnic markets.

The Company

George E. Johnson founded Johnson Products Company in 1954 with $250 of borrowed capital. While continuing to work full time as a compounder for a black-owned cosmetic company (Fuller Products), Mr. Johnson and his wife developed and produced Ultra-Wave Hair Culture, a chemical hair straightener for men. Johnson's nine years of experience with Fuller Products had provided him with considerable knowledge about the chemistry of cosmetic products.

115

From 1954 to 1964, Johnson Products grew from a single-product operation to one of multiple products (the Ultra Sheen line) with multiple channels of distribution (professional barbers, beauticians, and the retail market). Sales grew to over $1 million in 1964. A summary of JPC's growth is shown in Table 1. In late 1964, a major fire virtually destroyed Johnson's production facilities. Without the help of his former employer, his suppliers, and his friends, Johnson Products, as it is known today, probably would not exist.

TABLE 1   *Summary of JPC's growth*
SOURCE: Brochure prepared by Johnson Products Company, July 1975.

Year	Sales	Employees	Products
1955	$ 18,000	4	1
1962	$ 629,000	26	12
1965	$ 1,500,000	47	15
1967	$ 4,000,000	117	19
1969	$10,500,000	156	23
1972	$18,000,000	257	37
1974	$31,585,000	410	44

In 1965, JPC introduced Ultra Sheen No Base Creme Relaxer, the first product of its kind to remedy the black woman's problem of relaxing curly hair (a form of straightener) so that she could choose the hair style that best suited her. This innovation opened the door for other products which made hair and skin treatment easy and effective. The introduction of these products occurred almost simultaneously with the emergence of the national revolution in individual freedom, black pride, and more natural life styles.

In 1968, Afro Sheen was introduced to meet black consumer needs. By 1970, Johnson Products Company was associated with black fashion and recognized as a leader in black enterprise. For JPC, this period was characterized by dramatic growth in existing lines and in the introduction of new products. The highlight of 1970 was the company's introduction of Ultra Sheen Cosmetics. This move rounded out its product line, making it an active marketer in every major category of personal care products.

In 1971, two major events occurred. First, the company became the first predominantly black-owned company to be traded over a major stock exchange, which gave Johnson's a high degree of visibility among investors. Since equity capital had been the basis of financing Johnson's growth, this event was very significant. The second development was the introduction of the nationally syndicated weekly television show, "Soul Train," which appeals primarily to black youth and appears in over 100 markets weekly. The program is sponsored by Johnson Products Company.

The marketing thrust of the personal care products business is based heavily on promotion and strong ties with the channels of distribution. Johnson's has developed several channels for its products through barbers, beauticians, and rack jobbers to retail outlets. In addition, it has developed a unique point of purchase display, the "modular merchandiser" which allows the merchant to cluster his stock of Johnson Products in an attractive, easy-to-use display.

FIGURE 1   *Modular merchandiser*

In 1975, the company entered the men's fragrance market with Black Tie Cologne and Splash-On, and entered nonU.S. markets (Africa, Canada, the Bahamas, Puerto Rico, and several other Caribbean countries) with 1975 sales of $1.1 million. Table 2 provides the major events in JPC's history and Table 3 shows a financial summary for JPC from 1971 to 1975.

New product development is a major activity at JPC. During the past two years, several products were released to the professional (barbers/ beauticians) and retail markets. Currently, JPC is considering the development of new product lines for nonethnic markets. Table 4 summarizes JPC's new product releases.

The Industry

The personal care products industry is dominated by such firms as Avon Products, Inc., Alberto Culver, Gillette, Clairol, and Revlon. These five collectively account for over $5 billion in the personal care market. The 1975 U.S. total for cosmetics and toiletries was $6.7 billion.[1] Market entry and success is governed by access to channels of distribution and by the size and effectiveness of promotional efforts.

TABLE 2   *Historical highlights of Johnson Products Company*
SOURCE: Brochure prepared by Johnson Products Company, July 1975.

1954	Company founded.
1957	Ultra Sheen Conditioner and Hair Dress introduced.
1958	Ultra Sheen line entered professional beauticians' market.
1960	Ultra Sheen line introduced in retail market.
1965	Ultra Sheen No Base Creme Relaxer introduced.
1966	Completed first phase of new headquarters.
1968	Afro Sheen products introduced.
1968	Established the George E. Johnson Foundation.
1969	Sponsored its first nationwide TV special ". . . & Beautiful."
1969	Completed second phase of new headquarters.
1969	Company made its first public stock offering.
1970	Ultra Sheen cosmetics introduced.
1971	Began sponsorship of "Soul Train," nationally syndicated TV show.
1971	Johnson Products Company listed on American Stock Exchange.
1972	Established the George E. Johnson Education Fund.
1973	Completed third phase of new headquarters.
1974	Purchased eleven adjoining acres with building.
1975	Entered men's fragrance market with Black Tie Cologne and Splash-On.

TABLE 3   *Financial review (in thousands)*
SOURCE: Johnson Products Company, *1975 Annual Report*, p. 2.

Years Ended August 31,	1975	1974	1973	1972	1971
Summary of operations					
Net sales					
Hair care	$33,556	$28,829	$22,273	$16,746	$14,212
Other	4,104	2,756	1,967	822	244
Total	37,660	31,585	24,240	17,568	14,456
Cost of sales	13,330	10,133	7,575	5,224	4,308
Selling, General, and Administrative (exclusive of Advertising and Promotion)	9,094	7,661	5,795	4,177	3,886
Advertising and Promotion	4,498	4,202	3,733	3,097	2,830
Interest income	(372)	(404)	(168)	(106)	(81)
Income taxes	5,460	4,991	3,614	2,566	1,712
Net income	$ 5,650	$ 5,002	$ 3,691	$ 2,610	$ 1,801

The drug and cosmetic industry historically has been among the largest advertisers in the country. Normally, 20 of the top 100 advertisers are from drugs and cosmetics.

In the past few years, the major marketers of personal care products have adopted a market segmentation philosophy and have developed lines of products tailored to blacks. Although their current share of the ethnic market is comparatively small, they pose significant competition to JPC and its strategy of market concentration.

TABLE 4   *New product releases*
SOURCE: Brochure prepared by Johnson Products Company, July 1975.

New products for the professional division are:
Ultra Sheen Hold-N-Sheen, a nonaerosol product that allows a soft hold, high sheen hair style. It is the first product on the market designed for both hold and sheen.
Ultra Sheen Hair Color Lotion, the first semipermanent hair color that can be applied directly after hair has been chemically relaxed.

New product for both the professional and retail divisions:
Ultra Sheen Super No Base Creme Relaxer, for hair difficult to relax.

New to the retail division:
Ultra Sheen Nail Polish in fifteen shades.
Ultra Sheen Lip Gloss Pots in six shades to complement the lipstick line.
Ultra Sheen Conditioner and Hair Dress for Extra Dry Hair, developed for the consumer who wants to relieve and control excessive dryness.
Black Tie Cologne and Splash-On, elegant products for the men's fragrance market.

The Black American Market

The black population of the United States is substantially larger than most people think. There were 24.4 million black Americans as of April 1975. Two characteristics of this population segment are of particular importance to Johnson Products. First, the black American population is younger (median age 23.1 years) than white Americans (median age 29.3 years). Since younger consumers tend to be heavier users of personal care products, the black American market is highly lucrative. Also, because a higher proportion of black than white consumers (44 vs. 34 percent) will be growing into the prime consumer age range (18 to 35 years) over the next twenty years, this market segment also has long-range profit potential.[2]

Second, the geographic distribution of blacks is much more concentrated in the central cities than their white counterparts. In 1975, approximately 58 percent of the black population lived inside central cities, whereas only 26 percent of the white population lived there. This concentration tends to make the black market more accessible to mass media and retail distribution, thus making the marketing effort to this segment more efficient. Finally, it is important to note that the black population in the United States is growing more rapidly than the white population (1.6 percent per year vs. 0.9 percent for whites).[3]

To understand the size of the black market, imagine a country with a per capita income which is slightly more than that of Western Europe and considerably higher than the per capita income of Asia, Africa, and Latin America. Further, imagine this country with 6 million families or households of which more than half own automobiles. Incidentally, this imaginary country has thirty times as many passenger cars as there are in the Soviet Union and more than in all of Asia, Africa, and Latin America. One family in sixteen has two cars and one in every 100 has three or more autos. Forty percent of these families own homes and 75 percent of the homes have televisions. This figure represents twice as many TVs as in all of France or Italy and four times as many as in East Germany or Sweden. These families have more of their members studying in colleges than the total college enrollment in Great Britain or Italy and slightly less than in West Germany or France. This country really is not imaginery. It does exist. It is the black market in the United States.

As a group, blacks have tended to become acculturalized, accepting the values of the majority, the white middle-class culture. But they are at a disadvantage in their ability to acquire the goods associated with some of these values. The basic economic and cultural dilemma of blacks is whether to strive against the odds to attain these middle-class symbolic goods and services or to give in and live without them. In this regard, the market tends to be divisible into two segments labeled "Strivers" and "Nonstrivers." Strivers tend to defer immediate personal gratification and achievement of majority goals. Nonstrivers are oriented to today and immediate gratification even at the sacrifice of achieving the social status associated with the white majority.[4]

As might be expected, the buying patterns and preferences of these subdivisions are quite different and require different marketing strategies. In the future, as acculturalization continues, one might expect that the nonstriver segment will diminish in size and buying power. Should the striver segment continue to grow, ethnically-oriented products such as those produced by Johnson Products Company may have to be adapted or be replaced by products which are more congruent with the white subculture.

A variety of studies over the past decade concerning the buying and consumption behavior of blacks suggest several tentative conclusions.

1. Blacks appear to be more brand loyal than equivalent whites.

2. Blacks spend more for clothing and nonautomobile transportation; less for food, housing, medical care, and automobile transportation; and equivalent amounts for recreation and leisure, home furnishings, and equipment than comparable levels of whites.

3. Blacks spend more on maintaining appearances and on immediate gratification.

4. For products appealing to both blacks and whites, the general media has the greatest reach. For products with unique appeal to blacks, the black-oriented media has better reach.

5. The use of black models or integrated models is more appealing to blacks than all-white models, although for blacks under 30, the use of integrated models evokes unfavorable reactions.

6. The responsiveness of blacks to advertising appears to be more positive than for whites. Responsiveness is defined in terms of recall and attitude change.

7. Blacks tend to be more aware of both private label and national brands and to have higher levels of price awareness than equivalent whites.

8. White consumers shop by phone and mail more than black consumers.

9. Discount stores are chosen over department stores for shopping more often by blacks than by whites.[5]

Managerial Philosophy and Practices

Johnson Products is committed to further development of the black personal care products market through product improvement, line extension programs, and identification and satisfaction of unfulfilled consumer needs. The company plans to move into nonethnic markets, but Johnson approaches this move with caution. "Until such time as I develop the depth and number of management personnel which I would need to turn my attention in some other direction, I'll concentrate strictly on the black consumer market. Ultimately, we will enter the general market, but not until we've got a stronger company based more solidly in the black community, which will take time." [6]

More recent moves by the company suggest that at least part of the management development process is over. In late 1975, Johnson announced that JPC would begin franchising beauty salons called Ultra Sheen Beauty Boutiques. According to the *1975 Annual Report,* ". . . they will revolutionalize the black beauty industry. They will be outlets for total beauty care and personal care products, and gifts and related items. They will be staffed by people who meet the high standards of our franchising agreement." [7] The initial part of the program involves the opening of several company-owned operations in the Chicago market. Johnson, in expressing his excitement over the prospects, said, "I see this as an avenue of major growth for our company. I also see it doing something else for all of us. This program has the potential of offering the structure that is essential for development of a solid economic base for the industry and benefiting the entire black community of America." [8]

In the past couple of years, JPC has moved into new product and market areas. The introduction of the Black Tie line of fragrances for men is the beginning of a series of new products for men and for the general market. These products will include fragrances and related items for facial treatment and beautification. Finally, in the area of new markets, Johnson expresses a continuing interest in developing foreign markets. Sales in its newest market, Nigeria, are very encouraging but fluctuations in government policies raise concerns about the ultimate sales growth of Johnson Products. In spite of such problems, Johnson gives recognition to the potential of foreign markets with the comment, "It is important to remember that there are far more people of color abroad than in the United States. As economic development continues in these areas, the potential for sales also increases." [9]

In addition to the widely recognized financial success of JPC is recognition of the commitment of Mr. Johnson to social issues. Over the years, George E. Johnson has been an advocate of black capitalism and a leader on matters relating to the social responsibility of business.

In 1972, Mr. Johnson established the George E. Johnson Foundation which is dedicated to ". . . improving the quality of life for Black America in jobs, housing, health, education, youth services, legal justice, and family planning." In starting the fund, he made a gift of $1.5 million of his personal funds.[10] Subsequently, he has continued significant contributions to the fund.

The Marketing Emphasis

The principal geographic markets for the company have been major population centers. The biggest market is New York City followed by Chicago and Los Angeles. Distribution outlets have been high volume drug and discount stores, variety stores, and supermarket outlets. The firm has tended to avoid distribution through department stores as is the case with many other black-managed companies.

In reaching mass retailers, the company has employed rack jobbers who normally specialize in the distribution of ethnic products. The jobber determines the most appropriate product mix and space allocation for Johnson Products and competitive items and is a vital information link to headquarters. The company prides itself on the strength and durability of its independent distributors. Johnson observed, "It would take a long time and much money for another company to duplicate this organization, and the likelihood of its success is small, considering our market position." [11]

At the retail level, JPC has faced unique problems in displaying its products. Research conducted by the company indicated that its products sell substantially better when they are grouped together or "clustered" than when they are dispersed throughout other products in the same category. Getting retailers to arrange shelving space to accommodate this finding was difficult until Johnson created the "modular merchandiser." The unit consists of a number of Plexiglass elements of various sizes which can be assembled into a wide variety of sizes and shapes. Johnson provides these displays, costing about $400 each, to volume retailers. The use of the modular merchandiser guarantees a home for the entire line and effectively employs the clustering principle. By mid-1975, over 1,000 units were in use. The success of the unit was demonstrated in Los Angeles recently. Sales of hair care items increased one-third in six months using traditional shelf patterns, whereas sales of Ultra Sheen cosmetics surged to six times the base volume.[12]

Advertising and promotion costs were $4.5 million in 1975 compared to $4.2 million in 1974 for an increase of 7 percent. As a ratio to sales, however, the percentage dropped to 11.9 percent in 1974 from 13.3 percent in 1974. This decrease is similar to previous years (1973, 15.4 percent; 1972, 17.6 percent; 1971, 19.6 percent) as the impact of wider markets and more effective distribution takes hold. Johnson, however, expects a turnaround as the need grows to introduce new products and to develop new markets. In 1975, for example, sales of Black Tie were $850,000 with development and introduction costs of $245,000.[13]

In the advertising area, one cannot overlook the TV program, "Soul Train," which represents the largest individual item in the budget. The balance is spent on spot radio and TV, billboard space in black residential neighborhoods, and on space in black-oriented publications. Interestingly, JPC advertises on a limited basis in *Ebony* and *Jet,* publications owned by the Johnson Publishing Company. Johnson Publishing is not related to JPC, but does make a competitive line of hair care products.

The marketing function is organized in a product management system headed by the director of products. In addition, there is an advertising manager and a director of marketing services. The marketing organization is headed by the senior vice-president of marketing.

Market research is conducted regularly to aid in tailoring product concept, fragrance, function, and package to consumer tastes. A major study of consumer attitudes and product usage was completed in 1975. The study involved in-depth interviews with 2,000 black consumers. One of the more important findings in the study was that brand loyalty, measured by uninterrupted usage of product, was much greater for Johnson products than for all other competitive brands. Among women, the loyalty was 71 percent for Ultra Sheen Conditioner and Hair Dress compared to a 50 percent rating for competitive products. For men, 78 percent used Afro Sheen Conditioner and Hair Dress exclusively as compared to 63 percent for competitive products.[14]

Questions

1. What are some major trends in the black American subculture which are likely to present opportunities and threats to Johnson Products? Explain.

2. What behavioral issues should Johnson Products address as it moves into the general market and into international markets? How would these behavioral factors affect its domestic marketing strategy? Its international marketing strategy?

3. Describe how you would evaluate the effectiveness of "Soul Train" and the "modular merchandiser." What behavioral concepts are pertinent to your appraisal?

4. Developing strong, loyal, distribution channels is essential to the success of the JPC program. What are some key areas of channel management and distributor behavior that Johnson should track?

5. Suggest approaches for Johnson to study:
a. existing market coverage
b. new market potential (diversification possibilities)
c. new product concepts (unsolved black consumer needs)
d. the competitive effects of market encroachment by firms such as Clairol, Avon, etc.

6. With Johnson's limited advertising dollars, what promotional strategies might be used to counteract the heavy budgets of its competitors?

Notes

[1] "What the Public Spent for Drugs, Cosmetrics, and Toiletries in 1975," *Product Management,* August 1976, pp. 25-31.

[2] Johnson Products Company, *1975 Annual Report,* p. 4.

[3] *1975 Annual Report.*

[4] Kollat, David T., Roger W. Blackwell, and James F. Robeson, *Strategic Marketing* (New York: Holt, Rinehart & Winston, 1972), Ch. 9; R. A. Bauer, S. M. Cunningham, and L. H. Wortzel, "The Marketing Dilemma of Negroes," *Journal of Marketing,* July 1965; Donald Sexton, "Black Buyer Behavior," *Journal of Marketing,* October 1972.

[5] Engel, James F. David T. Kollat, and Roger W. Blackwell, *Consumer Behavior,* 2nd ed. (New York: Holt, Rinehart & Winston, 1973), pp. 69-109, 176-189.

[6] "The New Black Cosmetics Magnate," *Black Enterprise,* June 1973, p. 73.

[7] *1975 Annual Report,* p. 1.

[8] Ibid.

[9] Ibid.

[10] "Johnson Products Company, Inc.," Johnson Product Company, July 1975.

[11] *1975 Annual Report,* p. 4.

[12] Ibid., p. 6.

[13] Ibid., p. 10. The 1976 advertising to sales ratio is between 13 percent and 14 percent because of Black Tie promotion.

[14] Ibid., p. 6.

chapter 9

Social Class
Influence

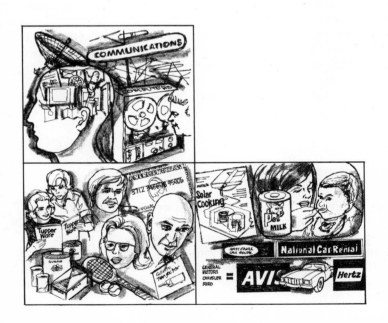

Bailey
Cab Company

This case was prepared by **Andrew C. Ruppel,** *McIntire School of Commerce, University of Virginia.*

A loan to buy some new cars and to set up a radio dispatch operation was all William Bailey was seeking to resurrect his defunct taxi business. He approached the Forsyth County Economic Development Corporation (FCEDC) for loan assistance. The corporation had been established to foster economic growth in the county and its major city, Winston-Salem, with a particular emphasis in assisting minority-owned enterprise.

FCEDC worked out a financing package to provide the necessary equipment to re-establish the Bailey Cab Company. What concerned the FCEDC director, however, was the revenue outlook. Bailey assured her that the demand was there; the two existing cab companies had plenty of business. But the director wanted more objective estimates of the taxi demand situation. She obtained the services of a graduate business student on a part-time basis to research the demand question for her. The student did two things: (1) extracted data on taxi activity from a consulting traffic engineer's study of the Winston-Salem transportation situation, and (2) supervised a field survey of potential taxi riders. Summaries of these two investigations follow.

Analysis of Taxi Traffic
Data in Transportation Study

An extensive study of the Winston-Salem transportation situation, with recommendations for a program to keep pace with future developments, had been performed five years earlier by a consulting engineering firm. The greater Winston-Salem area was partitioned into thirty areas or districts for the purposes of traffic flow analysis. Data on taxi activity was obtained as one part of that study by means of household and cab driver interviews. The following is analysis of that data.

Who Uses Taxis?

Answer: only slightly more than 1 percent of the population. On an average weekday approximately 1,810 taxi rides were taken. (Most cabs are obtained via phone calls; few are hailed.) Population of the study area (the thirty traffic districts) was 157,630 persons. Assuming no taxi rider took more than one trip, the usage percentage actually was 1.15. If we assume the rides were taken by residents of municipal Winston-Salem only (population at time of study: 140,250) rather than of the larger study area, the usage percentage rises to 1.29.

As a portion of total trips (382,000) taken in a 24-hour period in the study area using all forms of vehicular transportation, taxi rides accounted for less than 0.5 percent of total trips.

While the dwelling unit survey portion of the consulting engineer's study gathered socioeconomic and demographic data, the published reports did not provide a breakdown of taxi trips by such dimensions. (One can roughly infer these patterns, however, by noting the reasons for riding a taxi.)

Why Are Taxis Used?

Table 1 displays the trip purposes of taxi riders as determined by the dwelling unit interviews. We see that almost one out of every five trips (352/1,810) involves a passenger going from home to work and almost one out of six is a trip back home from work. Disregarding the direction of flow, just over one-third of all taxi rides on an average day involve movement between home and work. (See Table 2.) In fact, 90 percent of all rides were associated with the home, either as an origin or as a destination. As seen from Table 2, after trips between home and work are accounted for, trips for the purposes of handling personal business (doctor visits, paying bills, etc.) and for convenience goods (including food) shopping were the most frequent.

Where Does Taxi Traffic Arise?

Separation of trip origins from destinations was not made in the published engineer's report. Hence we must work with *trip ends*—an origin or a termination—two trip ends per trip. Since there were some 1,810 taxi trips, there are 3,620 trip ends to be classified by the thirty areas. Area 1, the central business district (CBD), is the most active taxi traffic area, with 21 percent of the trip ends. Areas 1, 3, and 4 combined involve 42 percent trip ends generated. The main characteristics as related to taxi usage of the seven top areas of trip end activity (involving 66 percent of trip ends) are as follows:

Area 1: CBD, prime employment and shopping section. R. J. Reynolds cigarette plant.

Area 3: Dense residential zone, with some industrial activity near the railroad. Model Cities neighborhood covers a major portion.

TABLE 1   Weekday trip purpose

From \ To	Home	Work	Personal Business	Recreation	School	Social	Change Travel Mode	Convenience Shopping	Goods, Apparel, and Furnishings Shopping	Unclassified	Total trips	Percent
Home	—	352	217	20	83	82		88			842	47
Work	290	—	10					21			321	18
Personal business	165		31			11	10	10			227	13
Recreation	10			—							10	—
School	62			10	—						72	4
Social	94					—			9		103	6
Change travel mode		11					—				11	—
Convenience shopping	151							—			151	8
Goods, apparel, and furnishings shopping	32		10			21			—		63	3
Unclassified										10	10	—
Total trips	804	363	268	30	83	114	10	119	9	10	1810	100
Percent	44	20	15	2	5	6	—	7	—	—	100	

TABLE 2   *Taxi usage—typical weekday*
SOURCE: Derived from Table 1.

End Point Categories *	No of Trips	Percent	Cumul. Pct.
Home—Work	642	35	35
Home—Personal business	382	21	56
Home—Convenience shopping	239	13	69
Home—Social	176	10	79
Home—School	145	8	87
Home—Shopping (Goods, Apparel, and Furnishings)	32	2	89
Personal business—Personal business	31	2	91
Work—Convenience shopping	21	1	92
Other	142	8	100
Total	1,810	100	—

* i.e., trip nodes, disregarding direction of movement.

Area 4: Densest residential area in the city; largely black; 250-bed hospital in southern portion. Has lowest auto ownership rate of any district.

Area 17: Residential section, however, prime facilities are Western Electric manufacturing, Southern Bell, Southern Box Corp., and Winston-Salem's second largest shopping center.

Area 6: Mixed residential and industrial area. Winston-Salem State College.

Area 18: Site of the two major hospitals (over 1,000 beds combined) and several medical centers. Largest shopping center in Winston-Salem and Hanes' Knitting Division.

Area 7: Contains Old Salem historic restoration. Residential area with some commercial facilities including large discount store.

Field Survey of Potential Taxi Riders

Limited resources were available for conducting a survey. In order to maximize their effectiveness, it was decided to concentrate the survey effort in an area that most likely would reflect the present state of taxi service utilization. Since the engineer's study revealed that 90 percent of all taxi trips in a typical day were involved with the home, a dense residential area was selected, namely Area 4. In fact, this sector is the densest residential area in the city. Predominately black, the residents have the lowest car-ownership rate of the thirty districts. At the same time, the area is interlaced with bus routes, and these routes are some of the more profitable for the city's sole bus line, Safe Bus Company. Table 3 gives further details on this area of the city.

TABLE 3   *Characteristics of Area 4*
SOURCE: *Winston-Salem Area Transportation Study,* Vol. I: Travel Demands and Recommended Transportation Plan, Ch. 5.

Land use: Primarily residential with some public and semipublic space. Vacant land anticipated to be put to industrial and commercial use.

Population: 12,100 persons, mostly black.

Persons per dwelling unit: approx. 3.45

Number of dwelling units: 3,500

Persons per gross acre: 14.86 (highest in the greater Winston-Salem region).

Persons employed within the district: 1,730 (includes people who live outside district).

% of district population in labor force: 30%

White collar/blue collar composition: 88%/12%

Median income: $3,930

Autos per 1,000 persons: 172

Autos per dwelling unit: 0.59

Daily taxi trips per dwelling unit: 0.05

Two young black male college students canvassed the area during the last two weeks in July asking the occupants of every tenth dwelling unit the questions listed in the Appendix. One surveyor moved along all the numbered streets (which ran east-west), while the other covered the name streets (generally north-south in direction). Because of budget constraints no callbacks were made; the interviewers were asked to inquire at neighboring units when no interview could be carried out at the predesignated places. Some 252 interviews were actually made, representing about 7.2 percent of the estimated total number of dwelling units in the area. Table 4 gives the main results of the field survey, and Table 5 shows the trip rate for each day of the week covered by the survey.

The high value for Sunday in Table 5 is in part explained by two facts: (1) the buses do not run on Sundays (nor after 9 p.m.); and (2) cabs are used by some to get to and from church. It is apparent from the survey that people who reported they used cabs did so frequently. The eighty-seven reported trips were taken by members of sixty dwelling units, or 1.45 trips per dwelling unit per day. The unsolicited comments of some respondents (see Table 6) tend to support this intensity of use.

As the comments in Table 7 indicate, there are people who would like to see improvements in the bus system as well as in taxi operations.

Trip purpose data obtained via the survey essentially confirmed earlier results. More than 90 percent of trips were connected with the home. Three-fourths of the reported trips began at home. The home-to-work proportion was nowhere near the figure found five years earlier. The discrepancy can be attributed mainly to the inability to classify fully all the answers given to Question 3 on the interview sheet (found in the Appendix). In most cases, the "where to" but not the "why" was obtained. This gap was due largely to

TABLE 4   *Results of Area 4 field survey*

Dwelling Units (DU) Surveyed: 252

"Did anybody in this household ride a cab yesterday?"
    YES: 60 (24%)   NO: 192 (76%)

"How many different times?"
    87 trips or 0.345 trip per DU

"Does anybody living here own a car?"
    YES: 147 (58%)   NO: 105 (42%)

"How many?"
    204 cars or 0.81 car per DU or 1.4 cars per *car-owning* DU

	Dwelling Units		
Cross-tabulation	*With Cars*	*Without Cars*	Totals
Took taxi ride(s)	9 (6%)	51 (48%)	60
Did not take any	138 (94%)	54 (52%)	192
Totals	147 (100%)	105 (100%)	252

DUs responding "YES" to taxi-ridership owned, on the average, 0.17 car per DU.
DUs responding "NO" to taxi-ridership owned, on the average, 1.0 car per DU.

TABLE 5   *Taxi trip rates by day of week*

Day	DUs Sampled	Trips Reported	Trip Rate
Monday	40	16	0.40
Tuesday*	40	14	0.35
Wednesday	40	12	0.30
Thursday*	36	11	0.31
Friday	20	6	0.30
Sunday	36	19	0.53
Wednesday	20	7	0.35
Thursday	20	2	0.10
Total	252	87	0.34 Avg.

* Rained on these survey days.

TABLE 6   *Unsolicited comments by taxi-using survey respondents*

22nd Street: "Really need cab service, especially for going to work."
Jackson Avenue: "Use cab three or four times a week."
Claremont Avenue: "Use taxi a lot on Friday and Saturday."
Lafayette Avenue: "(Use cabs) always on Mondays and Friday."
Graham Avenue: "Use cabs all the time."
19th Street: "Use a lot during weekends."
Gray Avenue: "Use taxis often."
12th Street: "Use taxis occasionally."
Cameron Avenue: "Taxis used frequently."
14th Street: "Ride taxis, but didn't ride one yesterday."
16th Street: "Lots of people on 16th Street use cabs."
Woodland Avenue: "Rode cab this morning to town."

TABLE 7   *Unsolicited comments by survey respondents on bus and taxi transportation*

22nd Street: "Taxis or more buses (are needed)."
Jackson Avenue: "Taxi here a long time coming."
Locust Avenue: "Better service from taxis needed."
Cameron Avenue: "When taxis (are) used, it's hard to get one."
18th Street: ". . . bus lines (should) run on Sundays so people can get to and from church."
Woodland Avenue: "Another company needed."
14th Street: "Need more taxis and buses."
8th Street: "Hard to get a cab; usually I ride the bus."
13th Street: "Need some taxis."
15th Street: "Need more buses."
Claremont Avenue: "Need service on Sunday because buses don't run."

TABLE 8   *Taxi trip purposes of July survey respondents*

From \ To	Home	Work	Shopping	Personal Business	Various	Completely Unspecified	Total	%
Home		9	7	13	37*		66	76
Work	4						4	5
Shopping	1						1	1
Personal business							0	0
Various	9						9	10
Completely unspecified						7	7	8
Total	14	9	7	13	37*	7	87	100%
%	16	10	8	15	43	8	100%	

* Largest single subcategory is simply "downtown."

the poor wording of the question itself. Table 8 displays the trip purpose data as gathered by the field survey. As seen, failure to separate the various purposes for going "downtown" hampers an analysis of trip purpose.

As one would suspect, "downtown" is a major destination for many taxi trips. It was named specifically in 50 percent of the classifiable cases. In 11 percent of classifiable responses, the downtown area was designated as a taxi trip starting point. Table 9 summarizes the obtained responses concerning geographic movement patterns. Comparison of these figures with those found in the consulting engineer's report (after appropriate aggregation of districts) is really not appropriate. The former refer only to trips by survey

TABLE 9   *Origin-destination patterns*

From \ To	Survey Area	Downtown	East	West	Southside	Unclassified	Total	Pct.
Survey area	8	31	2	6	6	13	66	76
Downtown	7						7	8
East							0	0
West	1						1	1
Southside	1						1	1
Unclassified	5					7	12	14
Total	22	31	2	6	6	20	87	100
Pct.	25	36	2	7	7	23	100	

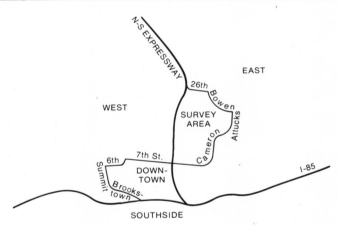

area residents, while the latter cover movements made by all residents into and out of each of the thirty traffic districts.

Questions

1. What do you conclude about the use of taxi cabs by various social classes? In what terms do you define these social classes?

2. How would you estimate Bailey's most likely market share? What consumer behavioral factors would shape Bailey's market share?

3. What kind of advertising, if any, would be most appropriate for Bailey Cab?

4. What other marketing mix variables should Bailey consider? Explain.

5. Do you feel FCEDC should make the loan to Bailey? Why or why not?

Appendix

FCEDC Special Survey

Day and date _____   Interview no. _____

Address _____

          Number   Street

1. Did anybody in this household ride in a cab yester-day?

          YES   NO

2. How many different times? _____

3. Would you please give us the reason and the di-rection for each cab ride?

Example: "I went from home to work; starting here and ending on the southside."

RIDE 1

    From _____to _____

    Starting at _____ending at _____

RIDE 2

    From _____to _____

    Starting at _____ending at _____

RIDE 3

    From _____to _____

    Starting at _____ending at _____

(Use another sheet if there are more)

4. Does anybody living here own a car?   YES   NO

5. How many? _____

6. May we have your phone number? _____

Thank you   Surveyor's initials: _____

(Comments by respondents Checker's initials: _____

    written here.)

chapter 10

Reference
Group Influence

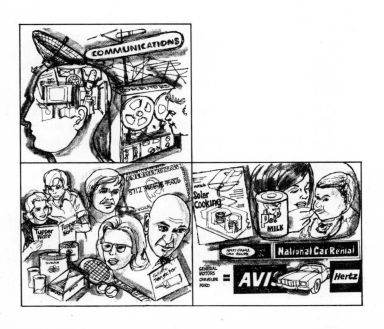

Mueller
Brewery, Inc.

This case was prepared by **M. Wayne DeLozier,** *College of Business Administration, University of South Carolina. Copyright © 1976. Permission granted by the author.*

Mueller's, a large mideast regional brewery, was established in 1826 by Dale M. Mueller. By 1950, the company had expanded its market to an eight-state area. By 1972, Mueller's began to experience a leveling of sales in some states with declines in others. Competition from the national breweries was a major problem, but a regional competitor, Strickland Breweries also was making inroads into Mueller's markets. Mueller's had fallen from the number two position in the region in 1952 to number four by year-end 1971 (in terms of market share), and it appeared to top management that Mueller's could slip to number five by 1972 or 1973.

Background on the Company

Mueller's early success in the beer market can be attributed to the low level of competition it had faced in early years and a build-up of consumer loyalty for a regionally produced beer. Moreover, Mueller's had developed strong loyalty among its distributors who vigorously placed Mueller's into every potential outlet in the region.

Mueller's management is and always has been very conservative and very cautious. It wasn't until 1968 that they decided to introduce a second brand of beer, Little Queen, which was a 7-ounce bottle aimed at the female market.

Mueller's management did not believe it was necessary to conduct consumer research, since they felt that all consumers who drank beer wanted a good-tasting beer and that's what Mueller's was. Management had concentrated much of its promotional effort in the sales promotion area, providing supermarkets with banners and taverns with clocks, lighting fixtures, and other sales promotional materials. Until 1958, advertising had been restricted mostly to billboards with some radio and newspaper ads.

In 1958, the impact of television advertising had become evident to Mueller's management, so a local advertising agency was hired to handle all corporate advertising, including television. A typical Mueller television commercial in 1968 showed people sitting around a table laughing and talking with the men drinking Mueller's and the women drinking Little Queen. Because of Mueller's cost consciousness, most television ads were shown at late hours when rates were lowest.

By 1972, Mueller's management began to feel that their marketing effort needed to be re-examined. Distributor loyalty had declined, largely because they were unable to push Mueller's into the outlets. Sam Jones, a distributor in Dayton, described his situation this way:

"We're pushing as hard as we ever have, but the bars, the supermarkets, the convenience stores, and others just simply don't need it. They're still stocked from the last time we were there. The beer ain't moving off the shelves. It ain't worth our time no more when we can sell them Schlitz, Bud, Pabst, and Strickland's."

Mueller management concluded from information from their distributors that the problem was at the consumer level and that a greater promotional effort toward the consumer was needed. Advertising, they believed, held the key, and their current agency must not be getting the job done.

In 1972, Mueller's invited advertising agencies to submit proposals for their account. Six regional agencies presented proposals and Mueller's decided on the McClinton, Sharpe, and Kirkpatrick Advertising Agency. Charles Kirkpatrick, one of three partners of the Dayton, Ohio agency, was in charge of the account.

The Agency
Proposal

Kirkpatrick outlined the agency's proposal for Mueller's in the following oral report:

"First, gentlemen, we must recognize that 72 percent of the beer consumed in your eight-state region is purchased by 28 percent of the beer drinking population. And do you know who that 28 percent is? Blue-collar workers—the factory worker and the construction worker. That's who we must persuade to drink Mueller's. In that connection, we propose an advertising campaign which shows the typical blue-collar worker on the job with his hard hat on, and after work stopping off at the local tavern to have a Mueller's. In addition, because of the blue-collar, hard-hat patriotism for country, we'll show the American flag at the end of each commercial and say 'Mueller's—an all American beer.' The blue-collar worker can identify with that kind of commercial. Mueller's will become the blue-collar beer. Of course, we won't say its a blue-collar beer; we'll refer to it by showing ads with their kind of people drinking Mueller's.

"Now, we can't forget about the future. The young people of America are the future beer drinkers. College and high school beer consumers constitute a significant market, but more importantly the beer consumers of the future. I propose, gentlemen, that we aim a portion of our campaign at the college scene. High schoolers look up to college students, identify with them, and wish to emulate them. Thus, part of our commercials will depict the college crowd drinking Mueller's.

"We get the best of both worlds. We attract the blue-collar worker with the 'hard-hat, American' ad and the future beer drinkers with identification with 'Mr. Joe College.' It can't miss."

After Kirkpatrick's presentation, several TV commercials that the agency had already taped were shown. Mueller executives were impressed with the commercials and the logic of Kirkpatrick's presentation. A one-year contract was signed and the McClinton, Sharpe, and Kirkpatrick Advertising Agency gained the Mueller account.

Through 1973 the new advertising campaign was aired on television and radio and the print media presented the same appeals. By year-end 1973, Mueller sales had declined and top management demanded an explanation from Kirkpatrick and reason to renew the contract. Kirkpatrick explained that the company was in a period of transition and that one more year was needed.

Rather than "change horses in mid-stream" Mueller's renewed the contract, but by year-end 1974, sales had slipped further and Mueller's had dropped to fifth position in market share. Moreover, the growth rate of the beer market had slowed primarily due to increased consumer interest in wine.

Mueller's executives convened to consider the next step. They placed blame on the agency and considered alternative approaches for the 1976 market effort.

Questions

1. The advertising agency described in the case was attempting to use reference groups to sell its client's beer. What is your assessment of the reference groups selected and what problem(s) is inherent in the strategy?

2. If Mueller's management decides that using a reference group in its advertising campaign is a sound approach, what reference group would you recommend? Why?

3. Do you feel the use of reference groups is a good approach in advertising a brand of beer? Why or why not?

4. For what products is reference group influence strongest on consumer purchase behavior? Explain.

chapter 11

Family
Influence

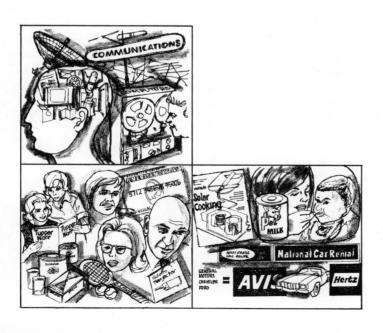

Lindbeck Laboratories, Food Products Division: Analyzing the Family Market for a New Breakfast Substitute

*This case was prepared by **Paul S. Hugstad,** School of Business Administration and Economics, California State University at Fullerton.*

In 1974, Lindbeck Laboratories entered the market for a cholesterol-free egg substitute with the introduction of its Yolkers. Standard Brands, Inc. and Miles Laboratories had pioneered this product market several years before with their Fleishmann's Egg Beaters and Morning Star Farm's Scramblers.

Because of Fleishmann's strong name identification with low cholesterol (margarine as well as egg substitute) and also the present limited size of the cholesterol-sensitive market, Lindbeck Laboratories was very interested in the possibility of widening the market for Yolkers to include more families from the middle and blue collar class, the majority of which presently did not use egg substitutes.

Background of the Egg Substitute Market

During the middle and late 1960s a number of studies reporting a link between high cholesterol diets and the incidence of heart attack were published. Both doctors and nutritionists began publicizing the need for consumers to cut back on foods rich in cholesterol such as bacon, eggs, and a number of dairy products.

This concern over diet opened up a new market for cholesterol-free substitutes that was especially noticeable in the breakfast food group.

Lindbeck Laboratories began product development of a cholesterol-free egg substitute in 1973 and in the fall of 1974 rushed its initial formulation of Yolkers to the market. Initial sales were disappointing and work was begun on an improved version of the product which more closely resembled the look and taste of real scrambled eggs.

After extensive re-engineering and product preference testing, the new version of Yolkers was improved to the point where it was equally preferred to real scrambled eggs in consumer blind taste tests.

This improved version of Yolkers was placed on the market in the summer of 1975. Although sales levels increased somewhat, they still lagged behind projections. The 1975 Yolkers sales fell just short of $10 million a year. While egg sales were temporarily impacted during this period, by 1976, egg sales had returned to nearly their 1972 level. Sales figures for the five-year period beginning in 1972 are shown in Table 1.

With the introduction of Yolkers in 1975, the sales of competitors began gradually falling off until mid-1976 when the market share of the new entrant appeared to be stabilizing at its present market share of 15 percent.

TABLE 1   Annual sales volume (in millions)

Year	Egg Substitutes	Eggs
1972	55.3	1112.3
1973	77.8	988.4
1974	89.6	990.7
1975	110.2	1050.6
1976	110.4	1109.0

The
Products

Yolkers and other egg substitute products were made basically of the same formulation. Their major ingredients included egg white (82 percent), liquid corn oil (10 percent), and nonfat dry milk (7 percent). These ingredients were frozen and packaged in individual cartons of four to eight fluid ounces each, and bundled together with an outer cardboard wrapper. Yolkers came in three, four-ounce cartons, bound together with a foil wrapper.

Instructions on the Yolkers package stated that each four-ounce carton was equivalent to two large eggs. The Yolkers package of three, four-ounce cartons sold for 75¢ with most other brands being competitively priced.

Instructions called for the product to be moved from the freezer to the refrigerator for defrosting twelve hours before use, or to be run under hot water for quicker defrosting. Once defrosted, the cartons needed to be used within seven days and could not be refrozen. Cooking Yolkers was done in the same manner as preparing scrambled eggs.

Egg substitutes were being distributed through the frozen foods section of most grocery stores, displayed alongside other breakfast substitutes such as frozen waffles and bacon substitute.

Yolkers recently had begun a store coupon promotion offering a 10¢ reduction on the next purchase of Yolkers in an attempt to induce brand switching.

Market Analysis of Family Purchases

Lindbeck Laboratories had been subscribing to National Grocers panel data since the introduction of Yolkers in September 1974. Analysis of over twelve periods of brand purchase data revealed no significant differences in the type of purchasers of various brands of egg substitutes, but did show purchasers of egg substitutes to have definite demographic characteristics. Table 2 presents a summary breakdown of National Grocers purchase profile data representing the preceding six months time period.

Interviews with repeat purchasers confirmed expectations that Yolkers were being purchased as a health food primarily by wives with husbands under doctor's orders to restrict cholesterol intake.

Younger couples who were using egg substitutes commented that they had both become aware of the need to prevent cholesterol build-up before they became older, but when asked, commented that they saw no need to so restrict their children's diet. Several of these couples also mentioned the convenience aspect of preparing Yolkers but complained that they sometimes forgot to defrost them in advance.

Most of the couples interviewed were satisfied with the taste of the product although several husbands mentioned that the artificial taste still

TABLE 2   *Profile of the Yolkers buyer*

Age of wife	Yolkers Purchase Data (In packages/month)
18-21	.14
22-27	1.89
28-34	.23
35-45	1.93
46-55	2.34
56 and over	.21
Educational level (wife)	
Less than high school	.10
High school	.89
College graduate	1.3
Post graduate	2.02
Family income	
0-$8,000	.13
$8,000-$14,000	.28
$14,000-$20,000	.72
$20,000-$35,000	1.83
$35,000 and over	2.31
Family size	
2	1.49
3-4	1.12
5-6	.31
7 or more	.08
Occupation of head of household	
Professional	2.11
Managerial	2.33
Clerical and sales	1.09
Skilled	.26
Semiskilled and laborer	.22
Unskilled	.08

was noticeable. When asked if they still ate eggs sometimes, the frequent reply was "only on special occasions, when baking, or with the kids."

Tables 3 and 4, respectively, present a summary of the motives and roles of various family types who are users of egg substitutes.

TABLE 3   Analysis of egg substitute user buying motives

| | Primary Buying Motive | | | |
Age of wife	Ease of Preparation	Taste	Low Cholesterol	Other*
18-21	18%	56%	4%	30%
22-27	53	32	12	25
28-34	8	6	4	5
35-45	6	2	40	5
46-55	5	0	38	5
55 and over	10	4	2	30
	100%	100%	100%	100%
Wife's education level				
Less than high school	0%	20%	5%	5%
High school graduate	10	60	10	40
College graduate	50	15	55	40
Post graduate	40	5	30	15
	100%	100%	100%	100%
Family size				
2	90%	50%	20%	70%
3-4	10	35	70	20
5-6	0	10	10	5
7 or more	0	5	0	5
	100%	100%	100%	100%
Total family income				
0-$8,000	5%	0%	0%	5%
$8,000-$14,000	5	10	15	15
$14,000-$20,000	10	25	30	20
$20,000-$35,000	45	50	45	20
$35,000 and over	35	15	10	40
	100%	100%	100%	100%

*Included such things as easily stored, new, and innovative.

Proposed Change in Market Orientation

Presently, Lindbeck Laboratories was dissatisfied with its restricted market position and was discussing ways of breaking out of its follower role in the egg substitute market. It was noted that presently few lower-middle class and blue collar families were using the product, and since these families also tended to be larger than those from the upper-middle class, a concerted effort should be made to make the product more appealing to them.

Plans were being formulated to re-orient their efforts away from the already saturated market toward this new family market which comprised 70 percent of the total breakfast food products market. The key to the de-

TABLE 4   *Family roles in buying egg substitutes (Husband (H), Wife (W), Children (C))*

Age of wife	Purchaser(s)	Major Purchase Influencer(s)	Major User(s)
18-21	H or W	H, W	H
22-27	H or W	H, W	H, W, C
28-34	W	W	H, W, C
35-45	W	H, C	H
46-55	W	H, C	H
55 and over	H or W	H, W	H, W
Wife's education level			
Less than high school	W	H,C	H
High school graduate	W	C	H
College graduate	W	H	H, W, C
Post graduate	H or W	W	H, W, C
Family size			
2	H, W	H	H, W
3-4	H, W	C	H, W, C
5-6	W	H	H
7 or more	W	H	H
Total family income			
0-$8,000	W	W	H
$8,000-$14,000	W	C	H, W
$14,000-$20,000	W	W	H
$20,000-$35,000	H or W	H	H, W, C
$35,000 and over	H or W	H	H, W, C

velopment of this new market was an understanding of how the family buying process operated for different types of families. The feasibility of effectively reaching this new market was questioned by some members of management.

A second important decision revolved around which family member(s) a new or revised strategy should be aimed. While there was general agreement that the mother was the most obvious target, the purchase influence pattern was seen as potentially different depending upon the social class and stage of the family life cycle of the families concerned.

The strength of various buying motives also was felt to differ depending upon a family's social class background.

Before proceeding further with a complete reformulation of the Yolkers marketing strategy, it was felt that the roles of various family members in purchasing a product such as Yolkers must be more clearly delineated for both lower-middle class and blue collar families.

Questions

1. Characterize the family purchase-decision process for Yolkers. How might the role of the husband, wife, and children change depending upon their social class background?

2. What are some of the barriers to reaching the traditional "28-45 year-old housewife" market?

3. Should the stage in the family's life cycle be considered in developing a marketing strategy for breakfast food substitutes? If so, how?

4. Suggest a marketing strategy to more successfully penetrate the lower-middle class and blue collar market for breakfast food substitutes. What will be key to the success of such a program?

chapter 12

The Spread of Influence:
The Diffusion-Adoption Processes

Prince
Tennis Racquet

This case was prepared by **Andrew C. Ruppel,** *McIntire School of Commerce, University of Virginia.*

"You could play at Wimbledon with a card table mounted on a handle, if you wanted," Howard Head is quoted as saying. He obviously was dramatizing that there are no official rules, specifications, or regulations concerning tennis racquet shapes, length, or size. It is not clear why this condition exists, but perhaps it derives from the social etiquette—fair play spirit—that devotees attribute to the game. (Surprisingly, therefore, tennis ball specifications, set by the International Lawn Tennis Association, do exist and govern ball weight, diameter, and rebound properties.)

But the desire to "play fair" was not the sole reason why tennis players did not come to the courts armed with oversize racquets, which presumably would give them a shot-making advantage. Oversize wood racquets simply would be too heavy to swing for an entire match (the typical racquet weighs less than one pound) and the strings, being stretched over a longer distance, might provide a "mushy" response. In other words, the technology of wood tennis racquets did not favor oversize racquets. (See Appendix 1 for tennis racquet terminology.)

But racquet technology has changed dramatically, as indeed has the technology of sporting equipment in general. Essentially that change has been one of a shift from the organic technology of wood, animal hides, and grass to a synthetics technology of alloys, plastics, and artificial surfaces.

One of the pioneers in the sporting equipment materials revolution has been Howard Head. It was Head who conceived, designed, and developed the metal ski. Lighter than a comparable wood pair, but more rigid, a pair of aluminum alloy, sandwich construction, Head skis enhanced the performance of all the skiers who used them. It would not be at all inaccurate to say that Head skis contributed to the dramatic interest in skiing that has been a major component of the leisure boom of the past two decades.

Head Ski Company, Inc., formed in the early 1950s, prospered in the 1960s as it began marketing metal and fiberglass tennis racquets. The company became an appealing venture for conglomerates, and in 1971, AMF, Inc., a producer of bowling equipment among other things, acquired approximately 90 percent of the shares of Head Ski for $14.5 million in cash.[1] In April of that year, AMF's directors approved the merger of Head Ski with AMF. Now known as the AMF Head Division, the unit is part of AMF's Sports Product Group, and a leading producer of metal and composite material tennis racquets as well as skis. A wholly-owned subsidiary, AMF Head Sportswear, produces tennis shoes and accessories. In 1974, leisure time products were responsible for 64 percent of AMF's revenues.

Ostensibly retired from business then, Head increased his personal participation in the sports for which he had developed revolutionary equipment. He did more skiing, played more tennis. However, he was annoyed with a ball-tossing machine he had bought for tennis practice at home because of its poor performance. Being a design engineer, Head modified the device so it would fire up a variety of tennis shots to challenge the practicer. Thus, he became sufficiently involved with the machine's producer, Prince Manufacturing, and is now chairman of its board of directors.

Head now began to look more closely at tennis racquets, wondering why the materials explosion that hit tennis racquet construction had not triggered some different designs especially since one of the key properties of the aluminum alloys, stainless steels, fiberglass laminates, and graphite composites being used to fabricate racquets was a high strength-to-weight ratio.

When metal racquets were first introduced in the 1950s, players looked upon them with disdain. But by the late 1960s, sales of metal racquets had increased to such a point that some predicted the demise of the wood racquet. This has not been the case, but the respective merits of metal vs. wood, and now metal vs. wood vs. composite materials are a source of continuous discussion among players. Compare various racquets in Table 1.

TABLE 1   *Tennis racquet manufacturers*

SOURCE: Derived, with additions, from Jeffrey Bairstow, "Which Racquet is Right for Your Game," TENNIS, January 1976, pp. 19-23. Copyright © TENNIS Features, Inc. Racquet manufactures producing solely for the under-$25 market not listed. Median price of the racquets listed in the Bairstow article is $40, unstrung.

Manufacturer	MTLS	$	Endorsements, *Autographs
Acro	M	I, II	—
Adidas	W, C	I, II	—
Aldila	C	III	—
AMF-Head	M, C	I, II	*Ashe
Araya	M	I	—
Bagherra	C	II, III	—
Bancroft	W	I	*Borg, *King
Century	W	I	—
Chemold	W, M	n/d	Court, Emerson, Laver
Concept Sports	W	I	—
Cortland	M	n/d	—
Dayton	M	I, II	—
Dunlop	W, M	I	Goolagong

TABLE 1   *Tennic racquet manufacturers—continued*

Manufacturer	MTLS	$	Endorsements, *Autographs
Dura-Fiber	C	II, III	—
Fischer	M, C	I, II	—
Fred Perry	W, M	n/d	—
Frederick-Willys	M, C	II	—
Futabaya	W	I	—
Garcia	W	I	—
General Tire (Penn)	W	I	—
Genesis	C	n/d	—
Goodwin	W	n/d	—
Jason-Empire	M	I	—
JMI Sports	W	n/d	—
Kawasaki	W	n/d	*Drysdale
Leach	C	n/d	—
MacGregor	W, M	n/d	—
Marcraft	W	n/d	—
Net Products	W	I, II	—
PDP Sports	M, C	I, II	Tanner
Prince	M	II	—
Pro-Am	M	n/d	—
Pro Group	C	III	*Trabert
Rawlings	W, M	I	*Newcomb
Seamco	W, M	I	*Rosewall
Skyline	C	III	—
Slazenger	W, M, C	I, II, III	—
Spalding	W, M	I, II	*Gonzalez, *Casals, *Gorman, Navratilova
Tensor	M	I	—
Tremont Research	C	II	—
Victor (Davis)	W	I, II	—
Volkl	C	III	—
Wilson	W, M	I, II	*Kramer, *Evert, *Smith, *King, *Connors
WIP	W	n/d	—
Yamaha	C	I, III	Court, Stolle
Yoneyama	M	n/d	—
Yonex	W, M	I, II	Roche

Key:
MTLS = Material, W = Wood, M = Metal, C = Composite
$ = Price Class (unstrung), I = $25-50, II = $50-$100, III = $100-200, n/d = not determined

As budding players soon learn, there is an optimum spot on the strings of the racquet to strike the ball called the *sweet spot.* Its location generally is below the geometric center of the face, down closer to the racquet's throat. Trying to meet the ball with the sweet spot can result in "wood shots"— hitting the ball with the frame or neck. Head sought a racquet design that would reduce this problem; one that would move the sweet spot up, away from the throat, and at the same time make it larger. The design, however, had to yield a racquet whose weight and balance were similar to racquets in use. The result was an aluminum alloy and plastic oversize racquet, one some two inches wider and three and one-half inches longer than standard racquets. (Bear in mind that there are, in fact, no standards governing tennis racquets.) Head's racquet design after development and testing was quickly introduced to the market in 1976 as the Prince Tennis Racquet (see Exhibit 1).

The following is a collection of comments about the Prince Tennis Racquet, obtained in early June 1976.

Salesman, Irving Sport Shops (eleven stores; two in D.C., remaining nine in Virginia and Maryland suburbs.): "No, we don't have it (the Prince Tennis Racquet). I believe it's available only by mail order, like the (Wilson) T-2000 when it first came out."

Salesman, Herman's World of Sporting Goods (seven stores; one in D.C., remaining six in neighboring Maryland and Virginia.): "Prince racquet? Right over here. (Hands customer one from several on a peg-board wall display featuring a large number of racquets. Price tag reads $64.99.) Must have sold two dozen since February—that's when we got 'em in stock. Believe it first came out in October. . . . Yes, it's a bit on the expensive side. It'd cost about $10 to $14 to string it. . . . No, it's not really for the pro—hasn't been used in tournaments yet. It's better for the beginner or intermediate, gives them better control—less likely to miss the ball. A guy could feel self-conscious, I guess, coming on the court with a Prince. If he wins, the other guy could blame it on the racquet. . . . How do people hear about it? Well, they see others on the court with a Prince—it stands out. And there have been some articles in the tennis mags (see Appendix B), yeah, and in the *(Washington) Post,* too."

Letter to TENNIS magazine (June 1976) from a Minnesota reader: ". . . I think the (Prince Tennis) racquet would be very useful in teaching beginners to hit fewer off-center shots, but I don't think it is fair to the more advanced player who has a hard time beating the beginner with the jumbo racquet. To me, it would be just as illegal for someone to use the jumbo as it would for someone to go out on the golf course with a driver that has a 12-inch face. I know that I will never use the jumbo racquet." [2]

Washington Star tennis columnist in an article (May 30, 1976) about the comeback of white tennis outfits: "Players are also going back to basics as far as costs are concerned. Status is measured by Yonex and Prince racquets rather than Lacoste shirts."

Avid amateur tennis player: "Guess I first heard about the Prince racquet three months ago. Saw the ads and went to one of the tennis shops that I buy from a lot. Guy said they were on order. I put my name down for one. When the racquet came in, I was real eager to try it. Took some courage to walk out on the court, though. I mean people would say 'Hey, Benton, where'd you get that mongoloid racquet?' or 'Here comes Benton with his 'Jesus

Saves' sign.' Carrying it is an admission to people that you've got a problem with your game. But I tell you, it improved mine. I'm hitting better overheads and volleys. It's great in doubles play and serves surprisingly well. It's not so hot from the backcourt or for driving the ball.

"I've been so successful with it I've sold at least eight others on buying a Prince. Six like it, two gave 'em up—one guy had his probably strung too tight, too much vibration. You shouldn't go over seventy pounds.

"I think anybody off the tour could benefit (from using a Prince.) However, it might not be a bad racquet for (Harold) Solomon, not for Ashe, though. Definitely not for Ashe. Not for the flat, power hitters. The racquet should be good for beginners and intermediates. But the hot shots won't like it because of the image problem.

"If the USLTA doesn't set any size restrictions then I think there'll be a proliferation of racquet sizes. Prince is a hot seller. The competition is bound to move in. They'll start tailoring racquets to a specific situation. We'll have serving racquets, doubles racquets—if no restrictions are set. Frankly, I'd like to see it a little smaller, more like the Wilson T-4000. They should stay with the metal frame though."

Player who gave up playing with a Prince racquet: "Well, I've got a tennis elbow. And the Prince gives you more opportunity to hit off-center shots—there's more area. . . . I saw the ads and a friend on the court with it. You could see the improvement in his game. He plays with more confidence, better at overheads and volleys. . . . Sure it's on the expensive side, but look at the price of golf equipment. How will it sell? Well, that's a legal issue. I

FIGURE 1   *Cartoon. Reprinted by permission of Newspaper Enterprises Association.*

Berry's World

© 1976 by NEA, Inc.   Jim Berry

"I know there's nothing illegal about that new racket of yours but don't you feel a wee bit guilty using it?"

mean the Association could rule it out. I don't think any of the stars will use it; they don't need it. Their eye-hand coordination is so good they always get the sweet spot."

Questions

1. What conceptual framework would be useful to Prince in developing a marketing strategy for its new tennis racquet? In what ways can this framework be useful to Prince?

2. What risks face adopters of an innovation? What are these risks in the case of Prince? How might they be overcome?

3. How would you segment the market for Prince Tennis Racquets? Explain.

4. How should Prince promote the new racquet? What appeal(s) would you suggest? Why? How should the promotional strategy change over time? Explain.

5. Into what adopter categories would you place (a) Benton, (b) the player with tennis elbow, (c) the letter writer from Minnesota, (d) Bairstow, (e) the cartoon character on right, and (f) the cartoon character on left? Why?

Notes

[1] *Moody's Industrial Manual,* Vol. 1. (New York: Moody's Investors Service, Inc., 1975) p. 1426.

[2] Letters to the editor, TENNIS, June 1976. Copyright © TENNIS Features, Inc.

Appendix 1: Tennis Racquet Terminology

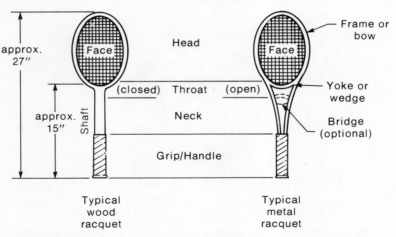

Typical wood racquet

Typical metal racquet

Balance: Weight distribution in the racquet. A balanced 27-inch racquet balances at the 13½-inch point. If the racquet tips to the head, it is called *head heavy* or *whippy.*

Feel: Sum total of physical and psychological impressions of a racquet.

Grip: Circumference around the wrapped portion of the handle. Ranges from 4⅛ to 5 inches. Relates to size of person's hand. Material of grip, usually leather, is a consideration.

Laminations: Number of layers of wood in a wood racquet; the higher the better.

Stiffness: Rigidity of the racquet and its ability to absorb ball impact. Largely dependent on design of the throat and neck and the materials used. Opposite of stiffness is *flex* (flexibility). Four grades of stiffness are recognized.

Weight: Ranges from 12 to just under 15 ounces. With a higher strength-to-weight ratio, metal makes lighter racquets, generally, than does wood. Light, medium, and heavy is often used to describe racquet weight classes, however, these are rather "loose" labels.

Appendix 2: An Evaluation of the Prince Tennis Racquet

Excerpts from Jeffrey Bairstow, "Will the New Jumbo Racquet Help Your Game?" TENNIS, April 1976, pp. 58-59. (1976 TENNIS Features, Inc.)

Ordinarily, I have a very useful forehand, a so-so backhand, a serve that I've learned to live with and a net game that makes even my mother laugh. Well, after one set wielding the monster racquet, my usual doubles opponents were learning to take cover behind the net whenever I prepared to hit a forehand and my partner was pleading with me to stop putting away so many volleys! Believe me, I had fun—even if the other guys thought that the huge racquet was a trifle unsporting.

For me, the prototypical hacker, the racquet did at least three things. First, it helped me hit volleys more easily and with much better direction; that is to say, most went over instead of into the net. Secondly, it added so much zip to my ground strokes that I thought I might actually drill a tennis ball-sized hole in the opposing net person. And, thirdly, it boosted my confidence to the point where I was taking shots that, ordinarily, I would have whiffed completely. The differences in performances were significantly greater than I've ever noted before when trying out a new racquet.

I loaned the racquet to a beginners' clinic at an indoor club. On collecting the racquet, I was bombarded with requests for the name of the nearest store stocking the racquet. Several members of the clinic were amazed at their new-found ability to hit powerful ground strokes. "This thing turns a klutz like me into a tennis player," marveled one novice.

There's one drawback I can tell you about already, though. My wife doesn't like the Prince because its head is so large it won't fit into the racquet pocket of her new tennis bag.

EXHIBIT 1 *Two-page advertisement for the Prince Tennis Racquet.*

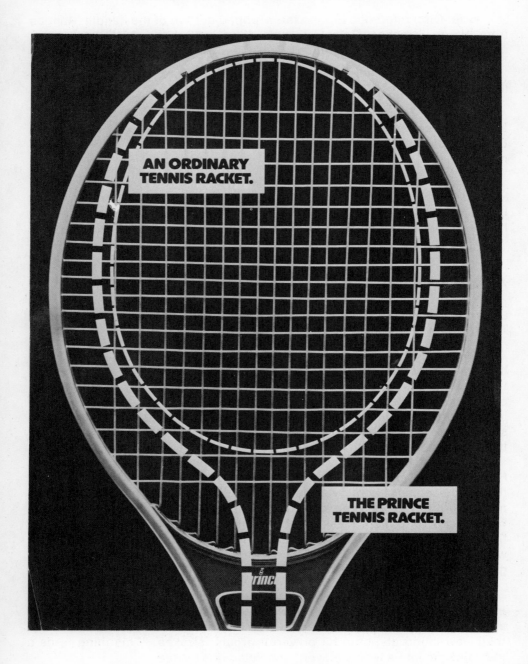

EXHIBIT 1   *Continued.*

WITHOUT BREAKING ANY RULES, WE BROKE ALL THE RULES.

With the help of Howard Head, we've created a tennis racket with a 50% larger hitting area. This new racket weighs no more and offers no more wind resistance than an ordinary racket. What's more it is entirely acceptable to both the USPTA and USTA.

This ingenious new racket is called the Prince. Here are just a few of its advantages:

A LARGER SWEET SPOT.

A sweet spot, as if you didn't know, is the high response zone of the strings. A sweet spot 3½ times as large as that of an ordinary racket has an obvious and enormous benefit for any player—from a rank beginner to a Wimbledon champion.

MORE ACCURACY. LESS EFFORT.

The shape of the Prince racket places more of the head's mass further from the center of the racket. This makes the racket less vulnerable to twisting in a player's hand. Which in turn leads to truer, more controlled shots with less effort.

MORE UNIFORM BALL RESPONSE.

The cross strings and the main strings of the Prince have much less proportionate variation than a conventional racket. This consistency of length, offers a more consistent ball response off the strings.

IT'S EASIER TO HIT THE BALL HARDER.

Because there's a much larger high velocity zone on the strings you nat-

urally hit more high velocity shots. In short, you'll find you get more pace on the ball, more often.

GUT-LIKE RESPONSE WITH NYLON.

Conventionally, nylon strings are less responsive than gut. But by stringing nylon over greater lengths at slightly higher tensions, it becomes a different animal. The increased stretch allows the strings to bend back like a drum head and offers better contact with the ball—which means better control.

THE IDEAL RACKET HAS AN IDEAL PRICE.

Not only will the Prince give you a competitive advantage, it's also competitively priced. It sells for $65; a price no higher than that of some ordinary rackets. And now that we've told you a little about the Prince you probably want to see our amazing new tennis racket for yourself.

Toll free, call (800) 257-9480 or, in New Jersey, (800) 792-8697, for the pro shop or tennis shop nearest you.

Discover the many advantages of the Prince racket—before your opponent does.

prince TENNIS RACKET

Litton Industries: The Adoption and Diffusion of Microwave Technology

This case was prepared by **Paul S. Hugstad,** *School of Business Administration and Economics, California State University at Fullerton.*

In the fall of 1976, Litton's Microwave Cooking Products Division was involved in reviewing and modifying its entire marketing program for expanding sales of microwave ovens in its consumer markets. Because of recent dramatic increases in industry sales of microwave ovens, steepening competition from both domestic and foreign competitors, and the evolution of microwave technology to improve cooking performance, it was felt that a thorough rethinking of the most effective marketing strategy to capture new and developing marketing segments was needed.

Existing Product
Line Competition

Litton's early entry and aggressive marketing program had gained them a leading 33 percent share of the consumer market. In the last three years, in spite of intense competition from General Electric, Sharp, Amana, Panasonic and Magic Chef, Litton's market share had increased while Amana and several Japanese brands had lost market share. The increased product guarantee of some brands to typically include two years on parts and service and five years on the magnetron (the most important oven part), compared with Litton's one year guarantee on parts and labor and two years on the magnetron, was believed to be partly responsible for a current stabliizing of some competitors' sales.

In addition to strong consumer competition, Litton also experienced competition from Sears, Montgomery Ward, and other large retailers selling microwave ovens under private brands. Competition in these markets was characterized by strong price competition.

Technology had recently led to major feature improvements in microwave ovens, with most brands currently offering a variety of options to their basic product. The most common of these options were variable cooking control, a defrost cycle, and a browning unit. With these feature improvements, it was estimated that 80 percent of a family's normal cooking could now be done with a microwave oven.

Litton's early technological advantages had been responsible for the above options. Amana Refrigeration, Inc. had recently begun to fight back with heavy promotion of its "Touchmatic Radarange" which used a digital "mini-computer" to program defrost and cooking time on a touch-sensitive front panel.

However, Litton had pre-empted this competition with the introduction of its new Model 418 with "vari-temp" automatic food temperature control that used a heat probe placed inside the food to automatically stop the cooking cycle when the desired inner food temperature was achieved. Both the Model 418 and the Radarange were perceived as significant advances over previous microwave models.

Along with these feature improvements, prices of microwave ovens had broadened substantially over recent years to include lower and higher priced models. The prices of current models ranged from $250 for a stripped-down version to $500 to $600 for the deluxe models. Most of Litton and Amana sales were near the high end of the price continuum, with the Radarange currently being the most expensive model on the market.

Historical Background of Microwave Ovens

The microwave oven is based on a relatively new technology using radar principles developed during World War II and is still in the early stages of its life cycle. Although microwave cooking was first introduced in 1954, many consumers still do not understand the principles involved or the cooking techniques for most satisfactory results.

Microwaves are a form of radiant energy, and like other common forms (radio waves, visible light, and infrared heat) they have longer nonionizing wave lengths. Microwaves bounce or deflect off metal surfaces and heat by penetrating nonmetallic surfaces where the energy is absorbed by water molecules and converted to heat. The air and nonmetallic cooking utensils transmit this energy without producing heat, and the metal sides of the oven reflect microwaves, so the oven's walls remain cool outside and in during the cooking operation. Microwave cooking takes approximately one-fourth of the time of conventional cooking.

Early models were generally expensive and troublesome appliances. As recently as 1973 the product was not recommended by *Consumer Reports*.[1] At that time there was a substantial amount of discussion and research in process to determine if microwaves could affect the central nervous system, heart, or liver, cause changes in body protein and enzymes, or cause possible genetic damage. Low-level microwave radiation also was believed to interfere with the functioning of cardiac pacemaker implants.

More recently, qualified scientific institutions have issued statements to remove many doubts covering the safety of microwave ovens.[2] The product also has been certified by the Bureau of Radiological Health (BRH) and

Underwriters Laboratories (UL) with certification labels given models that pass the safety tests. However, an updated *Consumer Report* article still cautioned against possible unknown radiation effects.[3]

Benefits of
Microwave Cooking

Because the cooking is fast (for instance, a baked potato can be cooked in 4 to 5 minutes), moisture and flavor are retained and there is less food shrinkage. It also is believed that nutrients are not lost through microwave cooking, and many foods retain their eye appeal.

Since regular serving dishes or paper can be used to prepare food, cleanup time and washing of pots and pans is reduced, and the oven has no "baked on" grease, so it is easy to clean. Soil can be wiped up immediately with a damp cloth or soapy sponge, and grease spatters from browning can be wiped away with a baking soda solution. Both the oven and the kitchen stay cool while cooking is in progress.

Cooked dishes can be reheated in minutes, and leftovers retain their "just-cooked" flavor, since there is little dehydration. Dishes can also be quickly prepared for latecomers or unexpected guests.

Two important disadvantages to microwave cooking include the lack of a browning unit in the portable models and the smaller portable model's oven cavity size (it will not accommodate such items as a large roast). Therefore, the portable microwave oven is suggested as an accessory to a conventional oven and is not recommended for purchase as the sole source of cooking.

Marketing

Market Development

In January 1971, industry estimates showed about 120,000 microwave ovens in use in the U.S. By the end of 1971 that figure had doubled. Market penetration through the end of 1975 in the consumer market is summarized in Table 1.

TABLE 1   *U.S. microwave oven sales (in units)*

Year	Annual	Cumulative
1971	120,000	240,000
1972	290,000	530,000
1973	460,000	990,000
1974	725,000	1,715,000
1975	1,000,000	2,715,000
1976	1,400,000*	4,115,000

*Microwave Industry Forecast

The 1 million microwaves sold in 1975 represent roughly 40 percent of the total number in use at that time, but a market penetration of only 3.8 percent of total U.S. households. The 1976 industry projections represent a growth rate of more than 40 percent.

Microwave ovens were seen as still being in the early growth stage of their life cycle with large numbers of adopter groups just beginning to enter the market.

Market Research

Demographic analysis of present microwave owners, developed from registration questionnaires (see Appendix), produced a profile of the "innovator" segment which is summarized in Table 2.

TABLE 2   *A profile of the "innovator" for microwave ovens (1972-1975)*

Married	*Yes*	*No*		
	90%	10%		
Both spouses working	*Yes*	*No*		
	53%	47%		
Number of children	*0*	*1-3*	*4-6*	*7 or more*
	30%	60%	8%	2%
Residence type	*Homeowner*	*Renter*		
	80%	20%		
	Under 25	*25-55*	*Over 55*	
Husband's age	10%	70%	20%	
Wife's age	30%	60%	10%	
Family income level	*Under $20,000*	*$20,000-$30-000*	*$30,000 and Over*	
	50%	30%	20%	
Education level	*High School*	*College*	*Postgraduate*	*Other*
	40%	40%	15%	5%
Microwave purchase location	*Appliance Store*	*Department Store*	*Furniture Store*	*Other*
	55%	15%	10%	20%

A separately commissioned in-depth study of over 300 California homemakers who owned microwave ovens revealed that the benefits of microwave cooking were perceived as follows by the respondents:

	Major Benefit*	Minor Benefit
Quick meal preparation	80%	10%
Energy savings	60	15
Convenient clean-up	50	15
Moister foods	25	5
Left-over warming convenience	50	10

*Total equals more than 100% due to multiple answers.

The same study also uncovered the following respondent dissatisfactions with microwave cooking.

	Mildly Dissatisfied	Strongly Dissatisfied
Taste of food prepared	30%	15%
Aesthetic appeal of food prepared	30	30
Capacity of microwave oven	30	15
Potential radiation hazard	45	5
High purchase price	35	10

Developing New Market Segments

Litton's prime interest presently is to capitalize on the accelerating acceptance of microwave use among U.S. households. It is felt that new segments of the market are ready to be developed and that the existing marketing strategy of courting "innovators" needs to be modified. Current research supports this contention, predicting that industry market penetration will increase to 15 million microwave units by 1980 and 36 million units by 1985.

Corporate discussions currently are under way to determine whether it is desirable to continue the policy of selective distribution through major appliance outlets, in light of the changing nature of competition and forecasted market. Questions also are being raised concerning the proper role and target of the advertising campaign being prepared for 1977. It is felt that important changes in existing marketing programs may be needed to effectively reach these developing market segments.

Questions

1. What major barriers may have slowed the initial adoption of microwave ovens by consumers? Do any of these barriers remain? If so, how could they be removed?

2. Develop a buyer profile of the next potential market segment, "the early adopters." How would this profile change for the early majority? For the late majority?

3. Suggest a marketing program which could be modified over time to effectively reach these new market segments as the diffusion of microwave ovens accelerates.

Notes

[1] "Microwave Ovens—Not Recommended," *Consumer Reports*, April 1973, p. 221.

[2] "Handbook Buying Issue for 1975," *Consumer Research Magazine*, p. 174.

[3] "Is Microwave Leakage Hazardous?" *Consumer Reports*, June 1976, pp. 319-21.

Appendix: Questionnaire

MICROWAVE REGISTRATION

MODEL NO. MW-_____   SERIAL NO. _____

PLEASE REGISTER YOUR MICROWAVE BY SENDING IN THIS PREPAID POSTCARD.

IT IS NECESSARY FOR YOU TO REGISTER YOUR MICROWAVE OVEN. MANUFACTURERS ARE REQUIRED TO KEEP THESE RECORDS. PLEASE FILL IN THE INFORMATION REQUESTED BELOW, AND MAIL WITHIN TEN DAYS.

YOUR NAME   YOUR DEALER
_____   _____

ADDRESS   CITY-STATE
_____   _____

CITY, STATE AND ZIP   DATE OF PURCHASE
_____
_____

1. Are You Married? _____ Yes _____ No
2. If Married, Do Both Husband and Wife Work Outside the Home?
   _____ Yes _____ No
3. How Many Children Do You Have Living at Home? _____ None
   _____ 1-3 _____ 4-6 _____ 7 or More
4. Where Do You Live? _____ Home _____ Apartment
5. Husband's Age? _____ Under 25 _____ 25-35 _____ Over 45
6. Wife's Age? _____ Under 25 _____ 25-35 _____ Over 45
7. Family Income Level: _____ $10,000 or Under _____ $10,000-$20,000
   _____ $20,000-$30,000 _____ Over $30,000
8. Your Education Status: _____ High School _____ 4-Year College
   _____ Post Graduate _____ Other
9. Where Was Your Oven Purchased? _____ Appliance Store
   _____ Department Store _____ Furniture Store _____ Other
10. What Brand Conventional Range Do You Own? _____

part 5

Consumer
Choice Behavior

Consumer choice behavior is a function of many behavioral processes. In a sense, these cases tend to be comprehensive of all the previous topics of discussion.

The cases following concern store choice and brand choice behavior. Students should consider which factors lead to a choice of a store to shop in or a brand to buy. Furthermore, students should consider the store choice factors which are the more salient for the case under discussion, and why those factors are more important than others in each case situation.

chapter 13

Retail Store
Choice Behavior

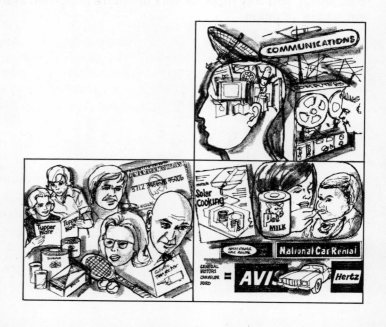

Prime Cut
Steakhouses, Inc.

*This case was prepared by **Dale M. Lewison,** College of Business Administration, University of South Carolina.*

Prime Cut Steakhouses, Inc. is a regional chain of steak house restaurants in what is often described as the "family-priced" steak house field. The Great Plains region of the United States serves as the primary market for the firm's 84 company-operated restaurants and its 120 franchised outlets. By using a marketing mix strategy consisting of standardized product offerings, quick service, uniform quality, convenient locations, and family prices, the firm has attracted a large segment of the Great Plains population.

Management Policies and Marketing Mix

The firm's product mix consists of a standard menu of prepared foods. The menu is restricted to a limited number of steak cuts, specials, and sandwiches. In addition, there is a limited support menu of beverages, salads, side orders, and desserts. Product depth is limited to approximately four items per product line. The limited product mix is part of the firm's operational policy of maintaining strict centralized management control. This policy provides for operational efficiency in the following ways:

1. High volume, low-cost procurement of foods, beverages, and restaurant items.

2. Fewer product procurement costs and requirements because of the limited menu.

3. Consistent product quality throughout the company-owned and franchised restaurants.

4. Fewer preparation problems because of the limited menu.

5. Lower advertising expense per restaurant, since all outlets benefit from the same campaign within the media's market area.

The firm's pricing structure is designed to attract middle-income ($7,000 to $20,000) families. Product-item pricing is based on a single price for a basic meal. The basic meal includes the meat (usually a steak), potato (French fries or baked), and toast. Additional product items are priced separately. The base price plus the individual product-item pricing system is believed to be the most attractive to the widest range of potential consumers. The wide appeal is due to the consumer's desire to select only those items he wants. Essentially, it is the firm's policy to offer a quality product at a reasonable price. This policy has worked for Prime Cut because they have been willing to accept a low unit profit margin, believing that they could generate a high sales volume while keeping overhead to a consumer-accepted minimum.

Management feels that their high sales volume is due to their fast food, self-service policy. The basis of this approach is management's belief that a large segment of its customers must operate within a limited time schedule, which is particularly true of the luncheon trade. Reasonable profits result from greater customer turnover in a limited space during limited trade hours and through lower operating overhead by eliminating table service personnel.

The firm's communication mix consists primarily of newspaper, radio, and television advertisements; however, personal selling and public relations are also employed informally and to a limited extent. The firm invests about 3 percent of its gross sales in promotional activities. General regional promotion costs for Prime Cut Steakhouse are 2 percent of gross sales while individual store promotions account for 1 percent. Part of the firm's promotion costs is invested in special promotional programs. They include: (1) a free ice cream cone with each meal purchased, (2) discount coupons, (3) price specials, (4) newcomer programs such as "Welcome Wagon," and (5) gifts for new babies in the family. Management considers these "special promo" campaigns essential in creating new restaurant patronage, as well as revitalizing former patronage.

The firm's distribution mix consists primarily of a central distribution center which supplies all outlets (company and franchised) with most of the necessary operating inventory. A limited number of perishable items (such as meats, vegetables, and dairy products) are obtained directly from a prescribed list of vendors.

Management believes that an advantage Prime Cut has over conventional restaurants is the standard architecture of its outlets. By using a standardized architectural style, sign, and interior layout, the firm has been able to create wide consumer recognition of its outlets. Each restaurant is of a standard size (90 by 60 feet) with a seating capacity of 180 people. The interior layout is designed to maximize customer turnover during peak demand periods, while providing the consumer with a clean, uncluttered dining atmosphere.

The atmosphere of each of the firm's outlets can be described as a "western" or an "authentic ranch-house style." This style, management feels, is consistent with the people's life style in this region of the country.

The Firm's
Operating Environment

On the national level, Prime Cut has several major chain competitors in the family-priced steak house field which are Bonanza, Pondarosa and Sizzler. While Bonanza and Pondarosa are primarily concentrated in the eastern sections of the country and Sizzler is basically a far-western operation, there are several market areas in which there is direct competition between Prime Cut and the three national chains. In addition, there are numerous smaller regional chains as well as single, independent operations which are in direct competition with Prime Cut. Also, Prime Cut restaurants are located within trading areas which contain a variety of other well-known, nationally franchised restaurants. The competitive impact of Kentucky Fried Chicken, Mc-Donald's, Roy Rogers' Roast Beef, Pizza Hut, Sambo's, and other fast-food chain operations is uncertain since the cumulative attraction versus competitive effects of these restaurants on the sales performances of Prime Cut outlets has not been determined.

Two peak demand periods (the noon and dinner hours) characterize the Prime Cut operation. Prime Cut must maximize sales during peak demand periods to maximize total daily sales. However, daily sales maximization is complicated by the differences in consumers for each of the two peak demand periods. Typically, the noon-hour customers (11 a.m. to 2 p.m.) tend to come from different source areas than dinner-hour customers (5 p.m. to 9 p.m.). Furthermore, there are substantial differences in demographic characteristics and patronage motives for each of the peak-period customers. Prime Cut management believes that these differences must be taken into account in developing the firm's marketing program.

Prime Cut Steakhouses:
An Expansion Program

E.V. Smith, newly appointed vice-president of real estate and development for Prime Cut, is faced with his first major company decision. Smith must recommend to the firm's review board one of four site alternatives for immediate development. The decision is required by the end of the week in order to meet the firm's 1976 expansion schedule of opening two additional outlets per month. Smith's long association with the fast-food industry and the commercial real estate business has given him considerable knowledge and experience in the problems of retail site evaluation and selection.

The four available site alternatives were selected from an original list of twelve alternatives by Mr. Smith's predecessor and the staff of the Real Estate and Development Department. The list was narrowed down by an on-site inspection of the twelve alternatives. Reports indicate that land development and real estate costs were the principal criteria in selecting the four alternatives.

The northeastern area of Killian, Texas (Standard Metropolitan Statistical Area population 1,100,000) is the general trade area location of all four site alternatives. Killian also is the original market area for Prime Cut as well as the firm's corporate headquarters. The northwestern section of Killian has experienced tremendous growth in recent years. With the development of several low-, medium-, and high-income residential areas and a corresponding commercial development, a market has been created that is not being served by one of the firm's eight existing Killian locations.

In an earlier discussion with the firm's president, Mr. Smith got the distinct impression that filling the void in the Killian market was an objective which needed immediate attention. The general location and expansion strategy to which Prime Cut management adheres is market saturation. The policy involves "freezing out" the competition in a local market area by using a distributional pattern of outlets which creates a spatial monopoly. Because the Killian market is the corporate headquarters for Prime Cut, this strategy takes on even greater importance.

Contemplating the importance and the rush nature of the decision, Mr. Smith decides first to clarify in his own mind the nature of the problem. As viewed by Mr. Smith, the major objective is to select the site alternative that offers the greatest sales potential. The current average monthly sales for the firm's existing outlets vary from $30,000 to $60,000. Reasoning that sales potential is primarily a function of locational attributes (all other marketing mix variables are standardized from one store to another), Mr. Smith believes the problem is to determine the site alternative which best serves the type of consumer who patronizes Prime Cut outlets. Realizing that the firm's outlets tend to draw different consumer groups at different peak hours, Mr. Smith decides to start the evaluation by considering a list of locational factors that have served him well in similar past decisions. Locational factors such as accessibility, cumulative attraction, compatibility, interception, store association, competition/saturation, and trade area demographics are, in Mr. Smith's experience, spatial expressions of consumer preference in determining consumer store choice behavior.

Because of the time limitation, Mr. Smith feels that he must base his decision primarily upon the information in the two reports prepared by the staff of his predecessor. (See Tables 1 through 7.) While the reports appear to have been prepared in a reasonably scientific manner, there are certain obvious omissions in the available information such as the lack of demographic data. Mr. Smith feels that he must fill in the demographic and other missing data (at least subjectively) if he is to arrive at the best possible decision within the next week.

Questions

1. What are the relative advantages and disadvantages of each of the four site alternatives?

2. Are there significant differences in the locational requirements and store choice behavior among the four consumer types? If so, what?

3. Which of the four site alternatives should Mr. Smith recommend to the firm's review board? Why?

4. What are the strengths and weaknesses of Prime Cut's retailing mix relative to consumer store choice behavior?

5. In terms of consumer store choice behavior, how appropriate is the firm's locational strategy of market saturation?

TABLE 1   *Customer type based on frequency of patronage*

Customer Type	Patronage Frequency	Average Percentage*	Percentage Range*
Passer-by, drop-in-trade	At least one time	21.6%	15-25
In-vicinity, drop-in-trade	At least once a year	12.1	10-20
Occasional return trade	At least once a month	23.6	15-30
Steady return trade	At least once a week	42.7	35-50
*Percent of all customers for all existing outlets			

TABLE 2   *Customer reasons for patronage (percentages)*

Patronage reason / Customer type	Good Quality Food			Fast Service			Convenient Location			Menu Selection			Reasonable Prices			Store Atmosphere			Other		
	1*	2**	3***	1	2	3	1	2	3	1	2	3	1	2	3	1	2	3	1	2	3
Passer-by, drop-in-trade	9	12	17	16	17	22	40	29	12	21	23	26	12	18	22	1	1	0	1	0	1
In-vicinity, drop-in-trade	16	15	12	16	18	23	30	26	17	20	20	16	15	20	28	2	1	2	1	0	2
Occasional return trade	20	22	20	18	15	20	18	19	20	18	20	15	21	21	25	4	3	0	1	0	0
Steady return trade	25	26	10	15	14	22	15	10	37	23	20	10	20	23	18	2	6	3	0	1	0

* 1 = First choice
** 2 = Second choice
*** 3 = Third choice

TABLE 3   Noon hour origin characteristics *(percentages)*

Origin type / Customer type	Home			Work			Shop[1]			Visit[2]			R and E[3]			Misc.			Total		
	P[4]	S[5]	T[6]	P	S	T	P	S	T	P	S	T	P	S	T	P	S	T	P	S	T
Passer-by, drop-in-trade	0	2	11	1	7	23	0	18	12	1	1	2	1	2	4	0	7	8	3	37	60
In-vicinity, drop-in-trade	0	8	4	14	10	1	30	10	0	6	0	0	8	1	0	8	0	0	66	29	5
Occasional return trade	5	12	1	20	12	0	21	8	1	4	1	0	5	0	0	9	1	0	64	34	2
Steady return trade	11	2	0	40	16	1	14	3	1	2	1	0	3	2	0	4	0	0	74	24	2

(1) Individuals on commercial shopping trips (goods or services).
(2) Individuals on personal visits.
(3) Recreation and entertainment.
(4) P = Primary trading area (0 to .99 miles).
(5) S = Secondary trading area (1 to 2.99 miles).
(6) T = Territory trading area (3 miles or more).

TABLE 4 *Noon hour destination characteristics (percentages)*

Customer type	Home P[4]	Home S[5]	Home T[6]	Work P	Work S	Work T	Shop[1] P	Shop[1] S	Shop[1] T	Visit[2] P	Visit[2] S	Visit[2] T	R and E[3] P	R and E[3] S	R and E[3] T	Misc. P	Misc. S	Misc. T	Total P	Total S	Total T
Passer-by, drop-in-trade	0	1	12	1	10	25	0	8	18	0	2	3	1	3	6	1	3	6	3	27	70
In-vicinity, drop-in-trade	0	2	7	1	3	8	31	17	3	7	2	1	6	0	0	12	0	0	57	24	19
Occasional return trade	3	14	0	16	20	1	22	5	0	4	1	1	5	2	0	6	0	0	56	42	2
Steady return trade	12	2	1	40	13	2	15	3	0	2	0	0	6	0	0	4	0	0	79	18	3

(1) Individuals on commercial shopping trips (goods or services).
(2) Individuals on personal visits.
(3) Recreation and entertainment.
(4) P = Primary trading area (0 to .99 miles).
(5) S = Secondary trading area (1 to 2.99 miles).
(6) T = Territory trading area (3 miles or more).

TABLE 5 *Dinner hour origin characteristics (percentages)*

Origin type / Customer type	Home			Work			Shop[1]			Visit[2]			R and E[3]			Misc.			Total		
	P[4]	S[5]	T[6]	P	S	T	P	S	T	P	S	T	P	S	T	P	S	T	P	S	T
Passer-by, drop-in-trade	0	6	20	1	7	19	1	7	17	0	2	4	1	4	6	1	2	2	4	28	68
In-vicinity, drop-in-trade	0	14	12	1	5	9	15	16	0	3	6	1	4	4	0	5	5	0	28	50	22
Occasional return trade	30	13	1	15	15	0	8	7	1	3	1	0	2	2	0	2	0	0	60	38	2
Steady return trade	34	8	0	27	10	3	10	2	0	2	0	0	1	1	0	2	0	0	76	21	3

(1) Individuals on commercial shopping trips (goods or services).
(2) Individuals on personal visits.
(3) Recreation and entertainment.
(4) P = Primary trading area (0 to .99 miles).
(5) S = Secondary trading area (1 to 2.99 miles).
(6) T = Territory trading area (3 miles or more).

TABLE 6   *Dinner hour destination characteristics (percentages)*

Customer type	Home			Work			Shop[1]			Visit[2]			R and E[3]			Misc.			Total		
	P[4]	S[5]	T[6]	P	S	T	P	S	T	P	S	T	P	S	T	P	S	T	P	S	T
Passer-by, drop-in-trade	0	8	43	0	3	6	1	2	12	1	3	3	0	7	6	0	3	2	2	26	72
In-vicinity, drop-in-trade	2	4	29	5	3	4	10	4	7	1	4	6	1	7	8	1	3	1	20	25	55
Occasional return trade	24	18	4	7	4	1	12	6	0	3	1	0	9	2	0	8	1	0	63	32	5
Steady return trade	48	6	1	8	1	1	12	0	0	6	0	0	10	2	1	4	0	0	88	9	3

(1) Individuals on commercial shopping trips (goods or services).
(2) Individuals on personal visits.
(3) Recreation and entertainment.
(4) P = Primary trading area (0 to .99 miles).
(5) S = Secondary trading area (1 to 2.99 miles).
(6) T = Territory trading area (3 miles or more).

TABLE 7   *Locational survey report, 1976*

Location characteristic[1]	Site alternative 1	2	3	4
A. Residential characteristics				
1. Number of single dwelling units	1,714	2,341	905	3,172
2. Number of multiple dwelling units	670	64	1,248	102
3. Number of transient dwelling units	20	0	50	0
4. Owner-occupied units (%)	42	58	24	67
B. Nonresidential characteristics				
1. Total number of retailing units	94	100	81	57
a. Convenience goods retailers (%)	64	48	61	71
b. Shopping goods retailers (%)	30	42	31	29
c. Specialty goods retailers (%)	6	10	2	0
2. Total number of service units	128	134	311	54
a. Personal service units	24	26	19	35
b. Business service units	6	8	24	0
c. Automotive service units (%)	10	9	4	11
d. Recreation/entertainment units (%)	18	10	15	15
e. Legal, financial, medical service units (%)	16	18	24	7
f. Governmental service units (%)	17	10	10	5
g. Educational service units (%)	5	9	1	10
h. Religious service units (%)	5	8	1	16
i. Miscellaneous service units (%)	3	2	2	1
3. Total number of wholesale units	7	7	21	0
4. Total number of manufacturing units	1	0	2	0
C. Population characteristics				
1. Total population	13,000	15,000	14,000	10,900
2. Mean family income	11,200	12,800	14,100	13,200
3. Low-income population: 7,000 (%)	24	8	10	28

TABLE 7   *Continued*

Location characteristic \ Site alternative	1	2	3	4
4. High-income population: 20,000 (%)	2	12	24	32
5. Nonwhite population (%)	31	8	8	0
6. Elderly population: over 62 (%)	18	6	4	8
7. Teenage population: under 18 (%)	20	35	6	44
D. Site characteristics				
1. Site size: Front footage	80	140	110	100
2. Site size: Total square footage	16,000	19,600	22,000	15,000
3. Site block position	corner	interior	interior	interior
4. Type of location	free standing	free standing	free standing	free standing
5. Number of entrances/ exits	4	2	2	4
6. Footage of entrances/ exits	100	140	100	120
7. Facing street: Number of traffic lanes	4	4	6	4
8. Facing street: Turn on-off lanes	no	yes	yes	no
9. Facing street: Medians	crossable	crossable	uncrossable	crossable
10. Facing street: Speed limit	35	40	45	35
11. Facing street: Average daily traffic volume	19,791	20,213	28,428	14,005
12. Side street: Number of traffic lanes	2	N/A[2]	N/A	4
13. Side street: Turn on-off lane	no	N/A	N/A	no
14. Side street: medians	crossable	N/A	N/A	crossable
15. Side street: Speed limit	35	N/A	N/A	35
16. Side street: Average daily traffic volume	4,952	N/A	N/A	6,200
E. Real estate characteristics				
1. Percent of gross sales	5.25	5.75	5.75	4.75
F. Competitive characteristics				
1. Number of "like" establishments	2	1	2	0
2. Number of specialty sandwich units	6	7	8	2
3. Number of specialty nonsandwich units	7	9	10	2

TABLE 7 *Continued*

Location characteristic	Site alternative 1	2	3	4
4. Number of variety sandwich units	6	6	4	1
5. Number of variety nonsandwich units	9	10	12	2

[1] Location characteristics are for the primary trading area only.
[2] Not applicable

Ready-Market, Inc.

This case was prepared by **Gordon L. Wise,** *College of Business and Administration, Wright State University.*

Ready-Market, Inc., is a small regional chain of grocery supermarkets operating in a midwestern state. The first unit was opened in 1913 in a city of 10,000 population. The success that followed led to the opening of a second store in a neighboring community three years later. At various times during the next fifty years, the firm operated as many as five stores in as many small to moderately sized communities.

Beginning in 1950, Ready-Market began to close its small stores and replace them with larger units. In most of these conversions, the larger stores were opened in the same community where a smaller unit had previously existed. However, by 1973, the firm began to place larger units in a number of cities where the company previously had not had stores.

Plain City:
A New Store

One of the new locations considered was Plain City, a town of 30,000. Plain City is a blue collar, lower-middle socioeconomic class community. Many of its residents are employed in light industries and service industries in the city, while many others work at industrial jobs in several surrounding communities.

Ready-Market's executive staff carefully studied the competitive scene in Plain City before deciding to locate a major unit there. The lack of strong major chain competitors helped influence their choice of Plain City. Other factors included proximity of Plain City to distribution facilities used by Ready-Market and access to a location relatively near two growing middle class residential neighborhoods on the east side of town. This location—with a large drug store and a moderate-size variety store on the same site—featured more than ample space for parking. Because the location site was further from the center of Plain City than any of its competitors, Ready-Market would be able to offer the most spacious and easily accessible parking in town.

Before the Ready-Market store was opened, cost analyses and projections of sales volumes led company officials to believe that the store could break even on a weekly sales volume of $105,000. In an effort to offer as many inducements to customers as possible, Ready-Market's Plain City unit would be lavishly decorated, and carpeting would be used in many areas of the store.

The Competition

As Ready-Market prepared to move into Plain City, a gigantic fire struck the downtown business district. Included among the victims of the fire was Jones Food Center, a major independent grocery supermarket which had long held a fairly strong market position in Plain City. Another strong anticipated competitor also was destroyed by the fire, and its central headquarters announced that the store would not be rebuilt and would cease all operation in Plain City. Jones Food Center later reopened in Plain City, but located in a rather small building with very inadequate parking facilities.

Other major competitors in Plain City include Most-Rite Supermarkets and Konstant Brothers. Both of these are large independent supermarkets which have long held strong positions in Plain City. Each has grown over the years in spite of their mediocre physical facilities. Both are in cramped locations with tight accommodations for display and storage, narrow aisles, and barely adequate parking facilities.

The "Super-Store" Concept

By late 1974, Ready-Market opened its new store in Plain City. This store was patterned after the "super-store" concept with a bakery, delicatessen, a full-service restaurant in the store, a flower shop, and a spacious seafood section.

Aisles were unusually wide. Only the most modern and beautiful fixtures were installed, and lighting was emphasized throughout the store. Each of the special departments (delicatessen, bakery, restaurant, produce, etc.) were given spacious prime locations in the store and many of the floor areas were carpeted. It was announced that the store would operate twenty-four hours a day and seven days a week.

The store was opened with the customary promotion and fanfare. Door prizes, free gifts, and numerous specials were featured. Response from Plain City residents was instant and gratifying. Average weekly sales immediately passed $130,000 and climbed steadily to nearly $145,000. At that point sales appeared to peak and then began to fluctuate between $120,000 and $140,000.

Accounting statements soon showed that the estimated break-even weekly sales figure was too low. Over the period of the first six months of operation, the profit from the Plain City unit was barely existent.

To counter the situation, Ready-Market began to offer more price specials. After some considerable internal debate, the company decided to cease its heavy use of newspaper advertising and concentrate more on promotional pieces mailed directly to the homes of residents of the Plain City area.

A Study of the Market

In an effort to determine whether further steps could be taken to expand market penetration in the Plain City area, Ready-Market conducted a market research study designed to identify and measure such factors as: What features and services are most desired by Plain City consumers from the grocery supermarkets which would serve them? What image does Ready-Market have for the major patronage-inducing factors (price, location, promotion, etc.)? What image do its major competitors have? Where are the competitive strengths and weaknesses possessed by Ready-Market?

A personal interview was conducted in more than 300 homes in the Plain City area. The selected sample was patterned in such a way that an approximately equal number of respondents were drawn from the geographical areas in the "natural" market of each of the four major Plain City supermarkets. Respondents were given approximately twenty-five possible features/services available through a supermarket and asked to indicate for each whether they believed the dimensions were "very important," "somewhat important" or "not at all important" to them in choosing a grocery supermarket. Responses to these features/services are shown in Table 1. The responses are shown in three categories: all respondents in the samples, respondents who do at least some shopping at Ready-Market, and respondents who do most of their shopping at Ready-Market.

Respondents then were asked to choose from among all of the features/ services those which they considered the single most important and the second most important in selecting a supermarket. Responses to these questions are shown in Table 2.

A series of direct questions was asked of all respondents. These questions dealt with such matters as: Which store in Plain City does the most advertising? Has the lowest prices? etc. Responses to these questions are shown in Tables 3 through 8.

Respondents then were asked to use several patronage factors to evaluate each of the Plain City supermarkets in which they shopped. Table 9 provides a summary of responses to these questions

After all of the data was gathered and the results were presented, the management of Ready-Market turned its attention to analysis of the results in light of a less than acceptable profit performance.

Some members of the management staff wondered whether they were expecting too much from the Plain City unit. After all, the store had captured approximately 24 percent of the Plain City grocery dollar. Konstant Brothers had a 23 percent market share and the Jones Food Center had 12 percent. Only Most-Rite with 41 percent enjoyed a larger market share than Ready-Market. However, Ready-Market management was generally unhappy with the profit figures and all agreed that some action must be taken.

TABLE 1   Responses to supermarket features and services

Feature	Total Response Sample (%)			Shop "Some" at Ready-Market (%)			Shop "Most" at Ready-Market (%)		
	Very Important	Somewhat Important	Not Important	Very Important	Somewhat Important	Not Important	Very Important	Somewhat Important	Not Important
Store is located close to my home	59.3	26.8	13.9	58.8	27.2	14.0	61.2	26.5	12.2*
Very wide aisles	54.1	32.5	13.4	50.9	34.2	14.9	63.3	26.5	10
Lots of parking	84.7	12.4	2.9	82.5	15.8	1.8	89.8	8.2	2.0
Employees easy to find if I need help	69.9	21.5	8.6	67.5	21.1	11.4	65.3	22.4	12.2
Low prices	90.4	7.2	2.4	91.2	7.0	1.8	91.8	4.1	4.1*
High quality food products	90.0	8.6	1.4	89.5	9.6	.9	85.7	12.2	2.0
Friendly, courteous employees	82.3	15.3	2.4	83.3	14.0	2.6	83.7	14.3	2.0
Offers many well-known national brands	64.1	25.4	10.5	59.6	29.8	10.5	59.2	32.7	8.2
Locally-owned; not part of a big chain	17.7	25.4	56.9	11.4	28.9	59.6	2.0	30.6	67.3*
Stays open 24 hours	20.6	18.7	60.8	25.4	24.6	50.0	36.7	26.5	36.7*
Has a delicatessan	14.4	21.5	64.1	14.9	21.9	63.2	26.5	20.4	53.1
Wide selection of food products	85.2	12.0	2.9	83.3	23.3	4.4	89.8	6.1	4.1
Has a bakery	19.6	29.2	51.2	21.9	29.8	48.2	26.5	28.6	44.9
Offers a wide variety of produce	85.6	12.1	2.1	87.1	11.8	1.1	88.9	8.3	2.8
Small store, with everything close together	5.3	10.1	84.6	4.4	8.8	86.7	4.2	8.3	87.5

TABLE 1   *Continued*

Feature	Total Response Sample (%)			Shop "Some" at Ready-Market (%)			Shop "Most" at Ready-Market (%)		
	Very Important	Somewhat Important	Not Important	Very Important	Somewhat Important	Not Important	Very Important	Somewhat Important	Not Important
New store with modern equipment and fixtures	25.0	31.3	43.7	23.9	27.4	48.7	29.2	16.7	54.2
Puts coupons good for reduced prices in mailers or in the newspaper	55.0	22.0	23.0	56.1	21.1	22.8	51.0	16.2	32.7
Offers many nonfood items	28.2	25.8	45.9	30.7	27.2	42.1	36.7	12.1	51.0
Has an express check-out lane	72.3	16.5	11.2	79.6	12.9	7.5	72.2	16.7	11.1
Offers weekly specials	71.8	19.6	8.6	67.5	21.9	10.5	63.3	24.5	12.2
Offers cash to nonprofit organizations for collecting cash register tapes	17.8	28.8	53.4	19.5	26.5	54.0	14.6	29.2	56.2
Has a restaurant	8.6	8.6	82.8	12.2	10.5	77.2	20.4	6.1	73.5*
Offers free carry-out service	57.4	22.5	20.1	58.8	21.1	20.2	71.4	14.2	14.3
Neat and clean	97.1	2.4	.5	96.5	2.6	.9	95.9	2.0	2.0
Offers a wide variety of meat and fish	84.1	11.1	4.8	83.3	8.8	7.9	89.8	6.1	4.1

* Significant at .05

TABLE 2 *"Forced choice" responses to supermarket features and services*

Feature or Service	Most Important	Second Most Important	Total First and Second
Low prices	41.1%	20.6%	61.7%
Neat and clean	8.6	14.4	23.0
High quality food products	10.0	12.4	22.4
Wide selection of food products	9.1	8.1	17.2
Friendly, courteous service	7.2	7.2	14.4
Store is located close to my home	6.2	7.2	13.4
Offers a wide variety of meat and fish	5.3	3.8	9.1
Offers a wide variety of produce	1.4	5.7	7.1
Offers many well-known national brands	2.4	4.3	6.7
Lots of parking	1.0	2.9	3.9
Offers free carry-out service	1.4	2.4	3.8
Very wide aisles	—	3.3	3.3
Has an express check-out lane	1.9	1.4	3.3
Employees easy to find if I need help	1.4	1.4	2.8
Puts coupons good for reduced prices in mailers or in newspaper	.5	1.4	1.9
Locally-owned; not part of a big chain	.5	.5	1.0
Stays open 24 hours	1.0	—	1.0
Has a delicatessan	—	.5	.5
Offers weekly specials	.5	—	.5
Has a restaurant	—	—	—
Offers cash to nonprofit organizations for collecting cash register tapes	—	—	—
Has a bakery	—	—	—
Offers many nonfood items	—	—	—
New store with modern equipment	—	—	—
Small store; everything close together	—	—	—

TABLE 3   *"Which Plain City grocery store does the most advertising?"*
            (controlling for the store shopped most frequently)

Response	Overall Sample	Ready- Market	Most- Rite	Konstant Brothers	Jones
Ready-Market	10.5%	26.5%	4.8%	6.7%	—
Most-Rite	41.1	24.5	59.0	17.8	59.1%
Konstant Brothers	21.1	10.2	14.5	53.3	4.5
Jones	1.4	—	1.2	—	9.1
Don't know	25.8	38.8	20.5	22.2	27.3

Note: Differences observed in the data presented in this table were found to be
      statistically significant at the .05 level.

TABLE 4   *"Which Plain City grocery store do you think has the lowest*
            prices?" (controlling for the store shopped most frequently)

Response	Overall Sample	Ready- Market	Most- Rite	Konstant Brothers	Jones
Ready-Market	9.1%	24.5%	4.8%	2.2%	4.5%
Most-Rite	56.5	36.7	86.7	26.7	50.0
Konstant Brothers	8.1	2.0	1.2	31.1	—
Jones	3.3	4.1	—	2.2	18.2
Don't know	23.0	32.7	7.2	37.8	27.3

Note: Differences observed in the data presented in this table were found to be
      statistically significant at the .05 level.

TABLE 5   *"Which Plain City grocery store do you think has the highest*
            prices?" (controlling for the store shopped most frequently)

Response	Overall Sample	Ready- Market	Most- Rite	Konstant Brothers	Jones
Ready-Market	42.1%	10.2%	63.9%	42.2%	40.9%
Most-Rite	2.9	2.0	—	6.7	4.5
Konstant Brothers	19.1	22.4	21.7	13.3	9.1
Jones	11.5	20.4	9.6	8.9	—
Don't know	24.4	44.9	4.8	28.9	45.5

Note: Differences observed in the data presented in this table were found to be
      statistically significant at the .05 level.

TABLE 6 "Which Plain City grocery store would you most likely recommend to a friend who had just moved into town?" (controlling for the store shopped most frequently)

Response	Overall Sample	Ready-Market	Most-Rite	Konstant Brothers	Jones
Ready-Market	18.7%	65.3%	1.2%	8.9%	—
Most-Rite	44.5	16.3	92.8	6.7	4.5%
Konstant Brothers	19.1	6.1	2.4	73.1	9.1
Jones	7.7	2.0	1.2	—	63.6
Don't know	10.1	10.2	2.4	11.3	22.7

Note: Differences observed in the data presented in this table were found to be statistically significant at the .05 level.

TABLE 7 "Which of the following Plain City stores has (in your opinion) the best produce department?" (controlling for the store shopped most frequently)

Response	Overall Sample	Ready-Market	Most-Rite	Konstant Brothers	Jones
Ready-Market	43.5%	72.2%	34.6%	42.5%	38.1%
Most-Rite	19.6	8.3	38.5	—	4.8
Konstant Brothers	21.2	2.8	19.2	52.5	4.8
Jones	6.5	5.6	1.3	2.5	33.3
Don't know	9.2	11.1	6.4	2.5	19.0

Note: Differences observed in the data presented in this table were found to be statistically significant at the .05 level.

TABLE 8 "Which of the following Plain City stores has (in your opinion) the best meat department?" (controlling for the store shopped most frequently)

Response	Overall Sample	Ready-Market	Most-Rite	Konstant Brothers	Jones
Ready-Market	34.2%	63.9%	29.5%	27.5%	23.8%
Most-Rite	23.9	5.6	43.6	10.0	9.5
Konstant Brothers	16.3	—	12.8	47.5	—
Jones	9.8	8.3	3.8	5.0	42.9
Don't know	15.8	22.2	10.3	10.0	23.8

Note: Differences observed in the data presented in this table were found to be statistically significant at the .05 level.

TABLE 9   *Consumers' competitive image of Plain City supremarkets (1-5 scale)*

(1)	Ready-Market	Most-Rite	Konstant Brothers	Jones Food Center	(5)
Very low prices	3.11	2.30	3.12	3.02	Very high prices
Friendly, courteous employees	1.96	1.78	1.67	1.71	Unfriendly, discourteous employees
Very clean	1.47	1.74	1.80	1.89	Very dirty
Highest quality products	1.71	1.87	1.93	2.18	Low quality products
Very good advertising	2.33	1.65	2.00	2.05	Very poor advertising
Has good specials	2.50	1.69	2.22	2.29	Does not have good specials
Has a good selection of food products	1.51	1.73	1.73	2.18	Has a poor selection of food products
Plenty of parking	1.35	1.84	1.79	2.44	Not enough parking
I like this store very much.	1.96	1.69	2.07	2.00	I don't like this store.

Questions

1. From the data presented in the case, how would you characterize the criteria used by Plain City grocery shoppers in choosing a store at which to shop? Are there other important choice criteria overlooked in the study? If so, what?

2. How well do the store characteristics of Ready-Market match the choice criteria used by Plain City grocery shoppers?

3. Ready-Market has 24 percent of the Plain City market. Based on the consumers' choice criteria and the store's perceived characteristics, should Ready-Market expect a larger market share, about what they have, or a smaller market share? Explain.

4. Develop what you feel Ready-Market's strategy should be in the Plain City market. Based on the data, describe the promotional approach you would use, i.e. advertising, sales promotion, etc.

5. What model(s) of store choice behavior might be helpful to Ready-Market management in considering marketing strategies for future store locations? Explain.

chapter 14
Brand
Choice Behavior

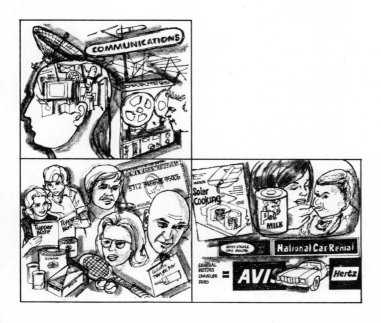

Sweetbriar Pharmaceutical

This case was prepared by **John F. Willenborg** and **Robert E. Pitts,** College of Business Administration, University of South Carolina.

The Sweetbriar Pharmaceutical Company's research staff has been working on a variety of deodorants and antiperspirants in the company laboratories for over a year. Historically, the firm has produced a relatively small line of soaps and other cleaning products for both industrial and consumer markets. It has been particularly successful selling heavy-duty cleaners to manufacturing firms in the southeastern United States but, recently, has enjoyed some success with antiperspirant soap sold to distributors, primarily retailers, who sold the soaps as distributor-branded items. That success has prompted management to initiate laboratory research on formulations of underarm products.

The market for deodorant-type products was in something of a state of flux in mid-1976. As a result, the Sweetbriar management team was even more optimistic about the opportunity for a new brand to make inroads into the market than they had been when the laboratory work had been initiated. For example, the rapid rise in market share of aerosol sprays had leveled off, due primarily to the possible links between fluorocarbons given off by such sprays and both pollution and disease. Also, increasing publicity regarding the relatively high cost of such sprays vis a vis "roll-ons" and "sticks," had prompted some firms to begin producing their products in the latter forms.

Laboratory tests of the potential Sweetbriar products were extremely favorable. The best formulation seemed to be one which could be packaged as either a spray or roll-on. In terms of effectiveness, it was judged to be better than most deodorants, but not quite as effective as the most popular antiperspirants. As such, the problems of excessive wetness and short-term effectiveness which were often associated with deodorants were minimized. Similarly, skin irritation of which some consumers complained when antiperspirants were used was largely avoided by the new formulation.

Hopeful that the laboratory-tested product could be introduced at the earliest possible date to take advantage of changing market conditions, the top management team asked the marketing manager, D. A. Disbrow, to initiate some market research which would serve as the basis for some important decision making. The key question as perceived at this time was how the new product was to be positioned in the market, that is, how would it relate to competing products and toward which part of the total market would the product be directed?

Although Disbrow had been with Sweetbriar for almost ten years, he had limited experience with carrying out marketing research efforts. The firm's product line had been fairly stable over the years, and there had been little perceived need for the research. In some cases, the retailers and other distributors had conducted limited research and reported the results to Sweetbriar. The industrial market customers saw an even lesser need to do research. However, Disbrow was a fairly astute marketer and felt that he could effectively find answers to the relevant questions.

In order to optimize the product positioning strategy, Disbrow felt that he should learn more about what consumers look for when buying deodorants. A clear understanding of the factors underlying purchase decision was necessary, according to Disbrow, for development of both a promotional campaign theme and overall approach, whether the product were to be marketed to distributors or directly to consumers.

Because the firm did not have a research staff, Disbrow contacted a medium-sized research firm in the heart of Sweetbriar's primary market area (Southeast United States). The firm presented two alternatives: (1) a full-fledged survey of randomly selected consumers conducted on a face-to-face basis, with stratification of the sample according to a wide range of demographic characteristics; and (2) a personal interview exploratory study with a small number of consumers, leading to a mail survey of randomly selected consumers who are members of a consumer panel maintained by the research firm. The panel study would not deal with a representative sample of all consuming groups, but with approximately 500 adult household members in the medium and upper income categories in the market area. Costs of each study were estimated to be $25,000 and $5,000 respectively.

Disbrow speculated that there were not likely to be major differences in the brand choice factors among different socioeconomic groups. Therefore, it would not be necessary to carry out the expensive study. He also felt that a well-conceived research plan that would generate responses from several hundred persons should provide enough insight into the basic positioning problem. While the firm was not overly cost conscious, Disbrow felt that the cost differential also was a strong factor influencing the choice of research alternatives at this point in time.

The research firm first surveyed 100 panel members, asking simply, "When you buy deodorant for your personal use, what factor(s) influence your choice of brand?" Of those factors listed, each was also ranked in order of its importance to the buyer. The survey generated a list of twenty-eight factors influencing purchase. Based on comments supplied by the respondents, a list of the ten most important factors was developed for use in the second stage of the research effort. (See Figure 1.)

The consumer panel then was mailed the questionnaire which asked each person to rank the ten factors in terms of their relative importance in

FIGURE 1   *Factors in purchase decisions used in consumer panel*
              survey

Another person has recommended it.
Is a good value for the money.
Prevents wetness.
Prevents odor.
Is on sale.
Doesn't irritate.
Is available in stores where I usually shop.
Is easy to use.
Does its job from morning until night.
The brand is well known.

purchasing deodorant. In addition, panel members were asked to indicate the brand of deodorant they most recently purchased. Although many different brand purchases were specified, Disbrow was particularly interested in the best-selling brands. Table 1 shows the average (median) ranks given to each of the ten factors both on an overall basis and classified according to the brand in use by each panel member.

When presented the data, Disbrow quickly noted that the factor of most importance to the consumer was that the product "prevents odor." No significant differences were apparent based on brand last purchased. Overall, the attribute "lasting from morning until night" was second in importance. Interestingly, purchasers of Brand B, the second most popular brand, felt that the attributes "prevents wetness" and "doesn't irritate" were even more important.

The two price-related attributes ("is a good value for the money" and "is on sale") were of some importance overall, particularly to purchasers of Brand C, who rated the two factors significantly higher than the panel as a whole. Disbrow was anxious to discuss the results with one of the firm's recently hired summer trainees, who had some experience in data analysis in her college program.

The trainee, Jennifer Gregg, suggested that the results be analyzed in terms of differing socioeconomic characteristics such as income, race, and education. Also, she felt that males and females probably differed in their purchases of specific brands and that some further insight into the market might be obtained by looking at such data. In Table 2 are data indicating reported purchases of the five leading brands by sex of the purchaser. Also presented are the estimated market shares held by each brand on a national scale as reported by the industry.

When the rankings of the ten product attributes were analyzed in terms of socioeconomic characteristics, no statistically significant differences were found. That is, income and other similar factors did not seem to account for differences in the rankings given to product attributes.

Ms. Gregg then suggested another approach. Rather than looking at one product attribute at a time, she felt that Disbrow should investigate the possibility that there were patterns of evaluation of the entire set of attributes which could be discovered and which would help to differentiate among

TABLE 1   *Relative importance of specific factors in purchasing deodorant by brand last purchased*

Purchase Factor	Median Ranks Assigned by Panel Members*					
		Brand Last Purchased				
	Overall	Brand A	Brand B	Brand C	Brand D	Brand E
Personal recommendation	7.5 (10)	6.5 (9)	5.5 (7)	5.8 (10)	8.5 (10)	8.3 (9)
Good value for the money	4.1 (5)	4.3 (6)	4.4 (5)	2.9 (4)	3.8 (5)	5.1 (5)
Prevents wetness	2.3 (4)	1.5 (3)	1.6 (2)	3.0 (5)	2.9 (4)	3.1 (4)
Prevents odor	1.2 (1)	1.3 (1)	1.2 (1)	1.2 (1)	1.2 (1)	1.4 (1)
Is on sale	5.8 (8)	6.5 (9)	6.0 (9)	3.4 (6)	6.5 (8)	6.0 (6)
Doesn't irritate	2.2 (3)	2.0 (4)	2.7 (3)	2.1 (2)	2.0 (3)	1.7 (2)
Available in stores where I usually shop	5.3 (7)	5.2 (8)	5.5 (7)	3.7 (8)	5.8 (7)	6.0 (6)
Is easy to use	4.8 (6)	4.2 (5)	5.2 (6)	3.5 (7)	5.0 (6)	6.4 (8)
Works from morning until night	2.1 (2)	1.4 (2)	3.0 (4)	2.2 (3)	1.8 (2)	3.0 (3)
Brand is well known	6.7 (9)	4.5 (7)	8.3 (10)	4.5 (9)	7.3 (9)	8.8 (10)
	n = 456	n = 136	n = 96	n = 96	n = 72	n = 56

*Median based on 1-10 ranking, with 1 as "most important." Numbers in parentheses are rank within each brand category.

TABLE 2   *Male-female purchases of deodorant brands*

Brand	Percent of Panel		Percent of Total	Market Share**
	Male	*Female**		
A (n=136)	17.6%	82.4%	29.8%	20%
B (n=96)	37.5	62.5	21.1	15
C (n=96)	54.2	45.8	21.1	16
D (n=72)	22.2	77.8	15.8	10
E (n=56)	42.9	57.1	12.3	8

*Female household members were 67 percent of the 456 respondents to the survey.

**As reported by industry sources. All other brands account for 31 percent of the U. S. market.

different types of potential customers. She proposed that the data be subjected to a "cluster analysis" to see if respondents could be assigned to different classes (clusters) on the basis of their purchase factor ratings. The results of the cluster analysis, which was carried out by a statistician in a local data processing company, are shown in Table 3.

Six clusters of panel members were found to exist. It was immediately apparent to Disbrow that these groupings were different from those based on brand of deodorant purchased. For example, persons in clusters 3 and 6 did not assign nearly as much importance to "prevents odor" as persons in other clusters. Cluster 4 persons were notably unimpressed by brand name. They purchased on the basis of sale prices and availability at the stores where they usually shopped. Other differences also appeared to exist, but Disbrow was not certain how to proceed with his analysis of the data in Table 3 or in Tables 4 and 5 which were also given to him by the local data processors. He was anxious to sit down with Ms. Gregg and together work on the analysis. He hoped that he could report to top management on his findings relative to deodorant purchasing within a few days.

TABLE 3   *Relative importance of specific factors by cluster**

| | Median Ranks Assigned by Panel Members** | | | | | |
| | | | Clusters | | | |
Purchase Factor	1	2	3	4	5	6
Personal recommendation	6.0	9.1	4.0	3.0	7.5	1.1
	(9)	(10)	(5)	(10)	(8)	(1)
Good value for the money	5.0	4.7	4.0	1.4	6.0	2.1
	(7)	(6)	(5)	(3)	(6)	(2)
Prevents wetness	1.2	3.1	2.5	1.6	3.8	9.3
	(2)	(3)	(2)	(6)	(4)	(9)
Prevents odor	1.1	1.5	3.5	1.0	1.4	8.7
	(1)	(1)	(4)	(1)	(1)	(8)
Is on sale	6.5	6.5	5.0	1.5	8.4	3.2
	(10)	(7)	(8)	(4)	(9)	(3)
Doesn't irritate	1.5	2.2	2.5	1.6	2.7	6.1
	(4)	(2)	(2)	(6)	(3)	(6)
Available in stores where I usually shop	5.2	6.7	6.8	1.2	6.4	4.8
	(8)	(8)	(10)	(2)	(7)	(4)
Is easy to use	4.5	4.2	6.5	1.5	5.7	5.8
	(6)	(4)	(9)	(4)	(5)	(5)
Works from morning until night	1.2	4.6	4.5	1.8	2.0	7.6
	(2)	(5)	(7)	(8)	(2)	(7)
Brand is well known	4.3	8.2	2.0	2.0	9.0	10.0
	(5)	(9)	(1)	(9)	(10)	(10)
Percentage of sample	20%	34%	10%	16%	18%	2%

*Each cluster includes respondents with similar rankings of purchase decision factors.
**Median based on 1–10 ranking, with 1 as "most important." Numbers in parentheses are rank within each cluster.

TABLE 4   *Male-female purchasers by cluster*

| | Percentage of Males vs. Females by Cluster | | | | | |
Purchaser	1	2	3	4	5	6
Male	10%	43%	17%	36%	18%	10%
Female	90	57	83	64	82	90

TABLE 5   *Brand recently purchased by cluster*

Brand	Percentage of Brands by Cluster*					
	1	2	3	4	5	6
A	58%	24%	50%	36%	18%	0%
B	17	29	17	18	27	20
C	17	10	0	27	0	60
D	8	24	17	18	27	20
E	0	14	17	0	27	0

*Each cluster includes respondents with similar rankings of purchase decision factors.

Questions

1. What do Tables 1 and 2 describe regarding the factors influencing the purchase decision of deodorant? How is brand choice related to the importance ascribed to deodorant attributes?

2. Based on the information presented, how should Sweetbriar's deodorant product be positioned in the market? Explain.

3. What do the data in Tables 4 and 5 indicate about the relative importance of purchase factors for each of the clusters described in Table 3?

4. Would you recommend that additional consumer research be undertaken before introducing the product? If so, what? Explain.

5. If additional research were to be conducted, what data should Disbrow collect?

6. If it can be assumed that each cluster in Table 3 describes a group of persons according to the product benefits they desire, what characteristics or factors would you emphasize in developing a different product for each group? What should be the key elements of Sweetbriar's promotional campaign? Explain.

part 6

Marketing
Communications

Having studied the basic concepts of attention, perception, learning, attitude change, etc., the student now is asked to apply these fundamental concepts to specific marketing activities, namely advertising and salesmanship.

In this part you will read about the Brick Association, which is a trade association interested in stimulating greater awareness of the variety of uses for brick as well as to combat the rising use of other construction materials. The Davenport Music Store case is concerned with the interpretation and use of research results pertaining to the dyadic interactive effects between salespersons and clients when variations in "expertise" are used. Part B of the C&S Bank case focuses on the bank's sales personnel and their effect on the bank's image and customer relationships.

chapter 15

Advertising

The Brick Association of
North Carolina

*This case was prepared by **James M. Clapper** of the Babcock Graduate School of Management, Wake Forest University. The author wishes to thank Corbin E. Garton, general manager of the Brick Association of North Carolina, for his extensive co-operation in this endeavor. This case is intended to serve as the basis for classroom discussion rather than to illustrate either effective or ineffective handling of an administrative situation.*

For the brick industry in North Carolina, 1975 was one of the worst years in the industry's history. North Carolina brick sales declined for the third consecutive year. Total sales were 800 million units,[1] the lowest total for the state since 1965. Clearly, a large portion of the problem could be attributed to the severe recessions experienced in the housing industry during the period of late 1973 to 1975. However, there also was evidence that brick was facing an erosion in its market to competitive building materials.

As Figure 1 shows, growth in the dollar value of brick shipments nationally has not been keeping pace with growth in the construction industry in general. Recent sales history in North Carolina seems to reflect this trend and has become cause for great concern among the state's brick manufacturers.

Responding to this concern, Corbin E. Garton, General Manager of the Brick Association of North Carolina (BANC), together with the BANC Marketing Promotion Committee began to explore actions the association as the major representative of the industry in the state could take to revitalize brick sales in North Carolina.

Background on the
Brick Industry

Structure

Brick manufacturing is a $360 million a year industry nationwide. Manufacturers are located throughout the country but are most heavily concentrated in the states of the Southeast. Historically, firms in this capital-intensive industry have been small, family-owned and managed operations. This still is

FIGURE 1   *National brick shipments and total construction (1960–1974)*
Source: U.S. Department of Commerce statistics

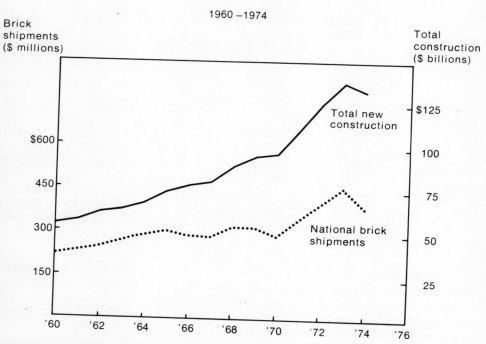

largely true today with approximately 65 percent of the firms having annual sales of less than $3 million. A strong production orientation has been the tradition in the industry with the result that today the industry enjoys perhaps the highest level of production efficiency that can be found among any of the building material industries.

Because of the comparatively high costs of shipping finished brick, manufacturers have found it largely uneconomical to compete for business in markets that are better served by firms located closer to the market in question. As a result, the brick industry is characterized by high levels of intraregional competition but significantly lower levels of interregional competition.

Brick Markets

Brick is widely recognized within the construction industry as a high quality building material. Available in a wide variety of colors, sizes, and forms, and with a variety of performance characteristics, brick has many diverse uses.

In a study conducted for the Structural Clay Products Institute, the national association of the brick industry, Arthur D. Little, Inc. identified seven different segments of the brick market. These segments include:

1. Commodity commercial. Includes warehouses, industrial plants, a high percentage of motels, low-rise offices, and most stores. Consumption in this segment amounts to approximately 12 percent of national brick sales.

2. Prestige commercial. Includes high-rise office buildings, some motels, stores, and monumental structures. This segment accounts for approximately 1 percent of national sales.

3. Institutional. Includes schools, hospitals, and religious buildings and accounts for approximately 11 percent of national sales.

4. Single-family, two- and three-family homes. Consumption in this segment is approximately 34 percent of sales.

5. Multifamily housing. Includes structures with four or more units and represents 27 percent of sales.

6. Other miscellaneous building types (principally entertainment). Represents 2 percent of sales.

7. Nonbuilding uses. Includes such uses as fireplaces, chimneys, patios, culverts, paving, walls, etc., and represents 13 percent of sales.[2]

Marketing Practices

Despite the recognized quality and versatility of brick products, total demand for brick has not grown at the same pace as has the demand for competitive products. Many people both within and outside the industry believe that the cause of this poor competitive performance is the fact that marketing practices in the industry have remained rather primitive compared to those of other industries. According to the Arthur D. Little report:

> "Few efforts have been made to discover the real needs of the consumer or specifier, and even today the industry is fairly remote from the decision-making process that affects its sales. Although companies have increased their sales force in the recent past and a few use advertising and other promotional methods, the production orientation still predominates. Informal conversations between two or more brick manufacturers are invariably centered upon machine design, plant labor problems, production costs, and other manufacturing considerations. The industry has long operated, and continues to operate, in a marketing vacuum and has abdicated its promotional responsibilities to the dealer and distributor and to the regional and national association."[3]

Reliance on dealers and distributors for marketing and promoting brick has not been a particularly effective strategy. Building material dealers and distributors commonly carry a wide variety of competing lines, serving as outlets not only for brick but also for such commodities as concrete block and wood products as well. Thus, dealers do not perceive their own interests as being directly aligned with those of the brick industry. Further, dealers in the building material field typically play very passive, order-taker roles, dispensing technical and price information but making little effort to influence customer choices.

Brick manufacturer associations, however, have not faced the most advantageous circumstances in trying to market brick. These associations are voluntary organizations supported by assessments agreed upon by the member manufacturers themselves. As a result, these organizations have tended to reflect the priorities of the individual member firms. The associations are largely staffed with engineers and other technically oriented people and thus are able to do an excellent job in such areas as research and development and manpower training. However, few of the associations have the strength, interests, or capabilities to carry on an effective marketing effort on behalf of their members.

The promotional efforts that have been carried on in the industry have been directed at contractors and design professionals. These efforts have taken two basic forms, promotion of the various uses of brick and promotion of the quality of brick construction. Nonbuilding uses of brick especially have been singled out for promotion by the industry. The primary quality themes which have been used include brick's low maintenance, permanence, and aesthetic appeal.

Pricing among firms in the industry has been very competitive. When "in-place" costs are compared, brick also is priced competitively with most other building materials. The only market segments in which brick has any price disadvantage are the housing segments. In these segments, brick must compete with wood siding. Costs vary widely from area to area and fluctuate rapidly over time, but the "in-place" cost for wood per square foot of wall area is roughly half that of brick. However, at the prices prevailing in late 1975, for a home with 2,000 square feet of floor space, the initial cost differential would be less than $1,800. In addition, this cost would be more than recovered in maintenance savings over the life of the house.

The Industry in North Carolina

North Carolina is known as the "Brick Capital of the Nation" because of the state's pre-eminence in the industry. The twenty-two manufacturers located in the state produce approximately one billion bricks annually or roughly 15 percent of the entire nation's output. North Carolina has been the nation's leading brick producer for over twenty years.

While the industry situation in North Carolina largely parallels that of the industry at large, the firms in the state do have two advantages. First, North Carolina manufacturers have not relied as heavily on dealers and distributors to sell their product. The twenty-two firms in the state employ over 100 salespeople and secure approximately 90 percent of their sales as direct sales, a figure that compares very favorably with the national average of approximately 30 percent. As a result of this high percentage of direct sales, North Carolina firms are closer to their markets. The firms gain valuable feedback through their salespeople as to market conditions, trends, and competitive activity. The second relative advantage is that North Carolina has one of the strongest regional manufacturers' associations in the nation.

Brick Association of North Carolina

In 1943, a group of progressive-minded manufacturers within the state founded the Brick and Tile Service, Inc. partly because they felt it more economical to support engineering and research and development, and generally to promote the common interests of the industry within the state. Known today as the Brick Association of North Carolina, this organization has grown continually to the point where twenty-one of the twenty-two manufacturers in the state are members, and BANC is the largest regional association in the industry.

BANC currently employs a professional staff of four people and operates on an annual budget of $200,000. As the major representative of the industry within the state, BANC performs a number of varied tasks. For example, BANC is responsible for the highly regarded high school brick layer training program in the state. The organization also provides educational programs for member-firm employees such as seminars for salespeople on the energy conservation advantages of brick. Other important activities include the rendering of design assistance to architects and contractors, the accumulation of marketing and economic statistics, and the representation of the industry's interests before governmental agencies such as the Department of Labor, the Environmental Protection Agency, and the State Utilities Commission.

BANC's direct promotional activities on behalf of the industry have been limited in the past to the production of promotional and technical literature aimed at various members of the construction and design professions. The quality of BANC's work in this area is attested to by the heavy demand for its publications by other brick associations and their members who wish to use them in their own marketing areas.

In 1973, BANC launched its first statewide effort to reach the ultimate consumer. A brief radio campaign was run, emphasizing the availability and maintenance advantages of brick. Sales continued to decline in 1974 and 1975, however, and the BANC membership decided not to commit scarce funds to consumer advertising during this period. Toward the end of 1975, the Marketing Promotion Committee of BANC again reviewed the industry situation to assess what action BANC should take during the upcoming year.

The Present Situation

Mr. Garton offered the following assessment of the situation faced by the North Carolina brick industry at the beginning of 1976.

"In recent years, the brick industry has not continued to get its fair share of the market. The whole industry has been geared to production. The attitude of a lot of people has been that sales are just a necessary evil, and this has been the case up until not too many years ago. We have been going along for years and years doing very little in the way of marketing and marketing research. About the time of the Arthur D. Little report (1972) we began to realize this. At that same time, however, the industry experienced one of the biggest years it has ever had. Ironically, the boom in sales at that time contributed in part to our present problems. During this period of great demand, the industry just was not able to take care of all the orders coming in. In the housing market in particular, contractors began building with other than brick and the first thing we knew, they found out people would buy them. During this time, there was also a *tremendous* campaign by the lumber industry. It started on the West Coast with what we call the 'California contemporary design' and began to move across the country, finally arriving here in the Southeast. The result has been that now people think of contemporary as wood. In a modern contemporary home everything is wood. If you look at any of the shelter magazines, you will see that they feature wood houses. We realize now that it is necessary for us to take action.

"In the past, we have done almost no advertising to the consumer. All our promotion has been aimed at the contractors and the design industry. Yet these people are moving more and more into wood houses and as long as they can sell them, they're going to continue to build them.

"The nature of the building industry in this part of the country has changed. Where the bulk of the business used to be done by a man building three, five or ten houses a year, now the large project builder represents a greater percentage of the business. Our salespeople find it much harder to sell to these people. They are most heavily influenced by economy of initial cost. They're not concerned about maintenance, energy savings, or life cycle cost.

"A similar situation seems to exist in the multi-family market. We've been losing ground there, too, so we've done some surveys to try and find out why. About the only conclusive result we've got is that builders and apparently renters are more interested in amenities such as swimming pools and tennis courts than they are in quality construction.

"As I say, all this led us to feel we have to get involved in a consumer promotion program because we have to make the consumer want brick. Until recently there has been a decided consumer preference for brick. But now it appears to be a new ball game. Older home buyers still display a preference for brick. They seem to like its sturdiness, permanence and security. Most younger people, on the other hand, don't seem to view these things with the same importance. We've got to make this younger segment understand the many advantages of brick. This is the reason we are considering launching a multimedia, statewide advertising campaign."

The Proposed Advertising Campaign

After analyzing the situation, the BANC's Marketing Promotion Committee decided that the need for a consumer advertising and promotion program could not be denied. Accordingly, BANC contacted the advertising firm of Cleland, Ward, Smith and Associates, Inc. and solicited ideas for such a program. The committee established the budget for such a program at $75,000 to be paid through a special assessment of the member firms. The Appendix contains material from the proposal which grew out of these discussions. Mr. Garton and the Marketing Promotion Committee are about to present this proposal to the full membership of BANC for approval.

Appendix

Proposed Advertising and Promotion Program, Spring 1976 (February—April)

  I.   Reason for campaign.
      Necessity to create consumer demand for brick residential construction.

  II. Campaign objectives and goals.
      To make the ultimate consumer, particularly those in the 20 to 50 age bracket, demand brick for residential construction. This would be done by using all media to make consumers aware of the many advantages of brick in residential construction—energy savings, low maintenance, permanence, and lasting beauty. Brick is available in all sizes, textures, and colors. Brick is a natural material—crafted with earth and fire! Brick doesn't fade, peel, rot, or dent. Show that small extra cost for a brick home is more than paid back every year of the mortgage life. Feature brick as the *now* material for contemporary homes and carefree living. The final goal will be to increase brick sales in residential construction throughout the state.

  III. Campaign theme: Brick doesn't cost—it pays.

  IV. Budget as recommended by Marketing Promotion Committee: $75,000. (See below)

  V.   Select media: magazines, radio, T V and billboards, Also include P.R. program.

  VI. Create multimedia campaign based on theme. Copy attached.

  VII. Place ads in media and coordinate with member promotion.

  VIII. Analyze and evaluate campaign. Develop marketing evaluation program. (See below)

Budget Detail (IV.)

Media Cost

Magazines
  Better Homes & Gardens
    N. C. circulation: 178,000
    March and April
    Full page, 4-color at $2,126.50 $ 4,253.00

Radio
  N. C. news network
    58 stations
    February 1—March 20

6—30 sec. spots/week/7 weeks	= $ 4,920.00	
March 21—April 30		
12—30 sec. spots/week/6 weeks	= $ 7,712.00	
Total radio	= $12,632.00	
Less 2% Discount	= $ 253.00	
	$12,379.00	$12,379.00

Television
  10 stations to blanket state
  All networks 30 sec. spots
  February—April $36,000.00
Billboards
  86 boards $ 8,110.00
    Total media cost $60,742.00

Production Costs

Magazines
  Color separations, plates $1,000.00
Radio
  Commercial production
  3—30 sec. spot including
  30 sec. tape dubs for members $ 500.00
Television
  T.V. commercial production $4,500.00
  2—30 sec. spots 1—10 sec. dubs $ 250.00
Billboards
  90 posters at $10.00 $ 900.00
P.R. Program $2,250.00
    Total $9,400.00

Total Production Cost

Media $60,742.00
Production and P.R. $ 9,400.00
    Total $70,142.00
    Contingency allowance $ 4,858.00
    Total $75,000.00

EXHIBIT 1   *Campaign ideas*

RADIO SCRIPT

Cleland,Ward,Smith
& Associates,Inc.
ADVERTISING AND PUBLIC RELATIONS

3238 REYNOLDA ROAD
WINSTON-SALEM, N. C. 27106
TELEPHONE 919-723-5551

Client ___BANC___

Product ___Brick___

Commercial Number ___#1___

Length ___:30___

> Picture your dream home ... built with old-fashioned
> elegance ... or traditional comfort ... or, with striking
> contemporary boldness! Then, picture your dream home
> built of brick ... natural, beautiful brick. Brick
> blends, naturally, with its surroundings ... lending
> itself, beautifully, to every home style. When your
> dream home comes true, insist on brick ... modern,
> beautiful, natural North Carolina brick ... made by
> members of the Brick Association of North Carolina.
> Brick ... naturally beautiful ... beautifully natural.

RADIO SCRIPT

Cleland,Ward,Smith
& Associates,Inc.
ADVERTISING AND PUBLIC RELATIONS

3238 REYNOLDA ROAD
WINSTON-SALEM, N. C. 27106
TELEPHONE 919-723-5551

Client ___BANC___

Product ___Brick___

Commercial Number ___#2___

Length ___:30___

> Naturally, when you're planning your dream home, you'll
> consider costs -- and not just the initial costs. Figure
> continuing costs, too -- energy and maintenance costs.
> Then, figure on brick! Maintenance-free brick saves
> energy and energy dollars so that, really, brick doesn't
> cost ... it pays, in so many ways! When your dream home
> comes true, insist on brick ... energy-saving, money-saving
> brick made by members of the Brick Association of North
> Carolina. Brick ... naturally beautiful ... beautifully
> natural.

Cleland,Ward,Smith
& Associates, Inc.

ADVERTISING AND PUBLIC RELATIONS

201 N. BROAD STREET SUITE 301
WINSTON-SALEM, N. C. 27101
TELEPHONE 919-723-5551

NEWS RELEASE

For Further Information Contact:

Ellen Tripp, CWS

FOR: IMMEDIATE RELEASE

February 16, 1976

Nature of Service or Business

Brick Ass'n of N. C., P. O. Box 6305, Greensboro, N. C. 27405

RESEARCH LAB GIVES NOD
TO BRICK OVER GLASS FOR
BUILDING, ENERGY SAVINGS

A comprehensive study by a Texas research laboratory reinforces
the masonry industry's contention that brick buildings are excep-
tionally economical in several ways. The Texas State Building
Materials and Systems Testing Laboratory (TSBMSTL), an official state
gacility governed by representatives from the nine participating
state universities, compared ten different exterior wall types
for a typical hypothetical 15-story office building.

They found that "increased window area with either of the
two types of glass considered has the effects of increased development cost, increased construction cost, increased equity requirements, increased operating cost and reduced return on investment."

Summarizing the laboratory's comparison between a glass and a
brick building, the report notes that the brick building saved 9%
in initial construction costs and nearly 34% in required cash equity.
The brick version also reduces heating and air conditioning bills
by 9.8% and annual operating costs by nearly 4%. Maximum rate of
return on investment is estimated to be 28% higher with the brick.

Looking at heating and air conditioning alone, it was found
that insulating reflective glass walls cost about 30% more than
tinted glass walls and nearly 85% more than conventional brick
masonry walls. Although they are more efficient in conserving

energy than the tinted glass, they still use about 2-1/2 times
more energy than brick.

Although foundation and structural framing costs are considerably higher for brick construction the overall building expenditure
is much lower with a savings of $848,735 in initial costs and
$1,040,549 in total development and building costs.

The optimum glass building used all glazing in an anodized
aluminum frame with sealant. The glass was one-inch thick insulating glass with one pane of 1/4" clear plate and one pane of 1/4"
tinted reflective (metallic) plate. The spandrel glass was 1/4"
standard color plate with insulation behind the spandrel.

The comparative brick structure featured conventional brick
masonry with 10-inch double walls consisting of 4 inches of brick,
2 inches of insulation and 4 inches of lightweight concrete block
with the interior walls plastered, finished and covered with two
coats of paint. The building's 20% window area was tinted glass
1/4" thick. Costs were based on average prices in Dallas during
the spring of 1975 and included contractors' profits and overhead.

Additional information on the study is available from BANC,
the Brick Association of North Carolin (P. O. Box 6305, Greensboro,
N. C. 27405.)

Proposed Campaign Evaluation (VIII.)

1. Total all home building permits by month for N. C., for a 9–12 month period
in 1975.

2. Request statistics from brick companies (confidential) of brick sold each
month in residential market.

3. From above data, figure average number of brick per house. This would
give our base data.

4. Continue during three month campaign and in nine-month period following
for comparison to use in evaluation of the campaign.

5. Requirements: Each member would give estimate of bricks used in residential construction each month as a percent of in-state sales.

Figures would be needed for each month, beginning in March 1975
through December 1976.

Would like to have figures for 1975 by January 1976 and then update each
month.

EXHIBIT 2   *Media presentation*

Cleland, Ward, Smith
& Associates, Inc.
ADVERTISING AND PUBLIC RELATIONS

3238 REYNOLDA ROAD
WINSTON-SALEM, N. C. 27106
TELEPHONE 919–723-5551

TELEVISION SCRIPT

Client___BANC_____

Product___Brick_____

Commercial Number___1_____

Length ___:30_____

VIDEO	AUDIO
ART: VICTORIAN HOUSE WIPE ON BRICK	Old-fashioned elegance ...
CUT: BUNGALOW WIPE ON BRICK	traditional comfort ...
CUT: CONTEMPORARY HOUSE WIPE ON BRICK	or contemporary boldness.
DISSOLVE TO YOUNG COUPLE WITH PLANS BOOKLET	Let your imagination soar! Picture your dream home ...
DISSOLVE TO SHOT CONTEMPORARY HOUSE	built of natural, beautiful brick.
DISSOLVE TO LS HOUSE WITH TREES	Brick blends naturally with its surrondings
DISSOLVE TO TCU HOUSE AGAIN	... Brick saves energy ... and energy dollars naturally ...
CUT TO CU HAND AT THERMOSTAT	Heating energy ...
CUT TO CU COOLING SYMBOL	Cooling energy ...
CUT TO CU PAINT CAN	Maintenance energy.
REPEAT YOUNG COUPLE WITH BOOKLET	Really, brick doesn't cost ... It pays: in so many ways.
SPLIT SCREEN: COUPLE & HOME	When the dream home you're imagining comes true,
DISSOLVE HOUSE	insist on brick ...
HOUSE WITH TREES: SUPER	naturally beautiful, beautifully natural.
Brick Association of North Carolina	

Questions

1. Evaluate the proposed advertising plan. What consumer need(s) is the campaign appealing to?

2. What would be the best way, in your opinion, to segment the ultimate consumer brick market? For example, would it be better to appeal to a particular

life style, social class, or psychological need such as aesthetics or security? What advertising theme would you use to appeal to the segment you have chosen?

3. How does the market segment you have suggested alter the media mix for the promotional effort?

4. How would the advertising campaign change over time with respect to scheduling? That is, would you distribute your advertising evenly over time or concentrate on a larger effort at some point in the campaign?

5. How would your promotional *approach* toward the commercial and institutional markets differ from the one you have suggested for the ultimate consumer?

Notes

[1] Some of the figures in this case have been disguised at the request of the Brick Association of North Carolina. Nevertheless, the general relationships among the figures in the case have been preserved.

[2] "The Brick Industry: An Industry at the Crossroads," Arthur D. Little, Inc., Report C–73958 (Cambridge, Mass., March 1972), pp. 18–22.

[3] Ibid., p. 64.

chapter 16

Salesperson - Client
Interaction

Retail Selling and Customer Purchasing Behavior: The Davenport Music Store

*This case was prepared by **Arch G. Woodside,** College of Business Administration, University of South Carolina. Copyright © 1976.*

Bill Davenport, owner and manager of the Davenport Music Company, Augusta, Georgia, recently purchased two cases (48 units) of HCC–2001, Head and Capstan Cleaner Kit for resale in his store. The kit included two felt pads, the head cleaning solution, and cartridge to be used to clean 8-track tape players. The product was manufacturered by Becht Electronics, Burbank, California.

Bill Davenport made the following statement to his two salespersons in his store concerning the HCC–2001:

"All music tapes lose the oxide coating when being played, making the player dirty and harmful to tapes, so the item has real and universal utility to the owner of any 8-track player. A very small percentage (probably less than 5 percent) of tape player owners have a tape player cleaning cartridge, and these are the old abrasive type, which can scar the head and do so little for the capstan. Also, such devices do not have the selling appeal of a current hit recording, so most retail tape outlets do not offer such a device. Most outlet operators are not even aware of the need for periodic cleaning.

"It is normal for the user to play his unit until it becomes unusable and/ or it begins to destroy expensive tapes one after another. Then, the unit is taken for repair to a shop, where it is repaired by a thorough scrubbing with a solvent.

Competition

None of the six competitors of the Davenport Music Store in Augusta, carried the HCC–2001 or a similar product. The six competitors were visited by a "shopper" hired by Bill to buy "some type of cleaning stuff or kit" for his tape player. Two competitors had knowledge of such devices but stated that demand was not great enough to carry them.

Product

The HCC–2001 was somewhat technically complex and its safe use was assumed to be important to a user since the product had to be connected to the tape player. The kit was mounted on cardboard, enclosed in a plastic container, and had a suggested retail price of $1.98. Operating instructions were printed on one side of the cardboard.

Pricing Study

Bill Davenport expressed concern about the suggested retail price of $1.98 for the cleaning kit. The retail markup on the product was 50 percent; his revenue was $.99 per unit sold.

Bill believed the kit was unlikely to sell in substantial numbers without active salesperson support. Bill wanted his two salespersons to attempt to induce customers who had just purchased one or more tapes to make an additional purchase of the cleaning kit. However, the low price of the item did not appear to justify the time and effort of the salesperson to present a sales pitch to potential customers. Consequently, Bill decided to sales test different prices of the product in his store.

Bill noticed that the cleaning kit was similar in size and shape to 8-track music tapes priced between $3.00 and $5.00 in his store. He believed customers might perceive the two products are similar.

Therefore, Bill decided to vary the price and also vary the salesperson's behavior in selling the cleaning kit. He knew from the marketing research course he had in college that he should randomly assign customers, each to one particular "price treatment." He decided to test two different selling pitches on the customers which he labeled "expert" and "nonexpert" conditions.

Four prices were selected for testing: $1.98, $2.98, $3.98, and $5.98. Bill used this wide range of prices to ensure some significant price effects in the experiment. The complete research design is shown as Table 1. He planned to use a total of 270 customers as participants in the study.

Procedure of
Research Study

The salesperson attempted to induce customers who had just purchased one or more tapes to make an additional purchase of the cleaning kit. Selected customers were randomly assigned to one of the eight treatment conditions or to the control group. Descriptions of treatments were typed and copies placed below the cash register in the store after the copies were randomly mixed. Space was available on the copies to record purchase information. Blank copies represented the control group assignment.

Customers examining 8-track tapes were selected unobtrusively as subjects in the experiment. While a selected subject was examining the tapes, the salesperson looked at the top treatment copy under the register

TABLE 1   *Research design for cleaning kit study*[1]

(n = Sample Size)			
	Expertise		
Price	*Expert*	*Nonexpert*	n
$1.98	n = 30	n = 30	60
$2.98	n = 30	n = 30	60
$3.98	n = 30	n = 30	60
$5.98	n = 30	n = 30	60
Total	n = 120	n = 120	240

[1]Control group of n = 30 customers also used. Members of the control group were not given a sales pitch, and the product was priced at $1.98.

and administered that particular treatment. A display box containing twenty of the cleaning kits was placed near the cash register throughout the experiment. A 6 × 6 inch card appeared on the display box. The words "8-Track Tape Cleaner Kit" and the price were placed on the card. Different cards were used for the different price treatments. Prices were not listed on the cleaning kits. Purchase response was recorded immediately after the customer left the store. The copy of the treatment administered remained in its top position until the next subject was selected. The salesperson removed the previous customer's treatment copy at this time, noted the role for the new subject, changed the display card if necessary, and administered the treatment when the subject approached the cash register.

The treatments consisted of the eight combinations of the four price levels and the two expert-nonexpert levels. A total of thirty customers was assigned to each combination and to the control group.

The salesperson asserted his or her own prior purchase of the musical tapes being bought by the customer in all treatment conditions except the control group. Levels of perceived expertise were defined as the salesperson's oral instructions on how to operate the tape cleaner versus expressed inability to operate the cleaner. Specifically, the following appeals were used:

Expert. "I hope you enjoy the tapes. They are of very good quality. I have these same ones in my collection and play them often. Here is a device we have on special that will clean the dirt and tape oxide from the guides, the head, and especially the drive wheels of your tape player. You just put a few drops of this cleaner on these two pads, stick it in just like a tape, and let it run for about ten seconds while you wiggle this (pointing to head of cleaning bar). It will keep the music clear and keep the tapes from tearing up by winding up inside the player. It's only (price stated on card). Would you like one?"

Nonexpert. "I hope you enjoy the tapes. They are of very good quality. I have these same ones in my collection and play them often. Here is a thing we have on special that they tell me will keep your tape player clean. I don't really know how it works, but you can read the directions right here on the package as to how to use it and what it does. I never have used one, and really don't know anything about playing tapes except how to listen to them, but this thing is supposed to help the tape player a lot. It's only (price stated on card). Would you like one?''

Customers in the control group did not receive any sales presentation but could purchase the product from the display box on the counter near the cash register. Any questions asked about the product by these customers were answered by the salesperson. No customer was rejected for requesting information. The salesperson responded to questions in the treatment role as required. The amount of additional information requested by the customer was recorded. Few customers requested further information.

Store policy was to accept cash, check, or charge card, and no discrimination was made for method of payment.

Results

The results of the sales tests for the eight price and expertise combinations are shown in Table 2. Results for the control group also are shown in Table 2.

A total of twenty-four (80 percent) of customers receiving the expert and $1.98 price treatment purchased the product, while only 3.3 percent of those

TABLE 2   Results of purchasing behavior

Price	Expertise	Purchase	No Purchase	Number of Customers
$1.98	Expert	80.0%	20.0%	30
1.98	Nonexpert	30.0	70.0	30
2.98	Expert	70.0	30.0	30
2.98	Nonexpert	36.7	63.3	30
3.98	Expert	66.7	33.3	30
3.98	Nonexpert	40.0	60.0	30
5.98	Expert	13.3	86.6	30
5.98	Nonexpert	3.3	96.7	30
1.98	Control	13.3	86.7	30

receiving the nonexpert and $5.98 treatment purchased the product. A total of four (13.3 percent) of the customers in the control group purchased the product.

The price and demand relationships for the two expertise conditions Bill *expected* to find are shown in Figure 1. He expected a shift to the right in the demand curve from the low expertise to the high expertise conditions. He also expected price to affect demand less in the high expertise versus low expertise conditions (a more vertical demand curve or a demand curve which is less elastic to price changes).

Bill wanted to know if the price changes produced much of an effect on demand. He also wanted to know if the expert sales pitch substantially in-

FIGURE 1   *Expected price and expertise effects on demand*

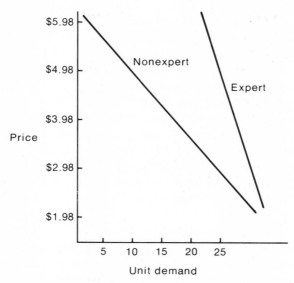

creased sales compared with the nonexpert sales pitch. Looking at the data in Table 2, Bill thought he might set the retail price at $2.98 and offer his two salespeople 50¢ extra for each kit sold.

However, he first wanted to develop separate additional tables to study the effect of price alone and expertise alone on customer purchase behavior. He also wanted to graph the purchase behavior shown in Table 2 and compare his graph to Figure 1.

Questions

1. Construct a table showing purchase and nonpurchase percents for the four prices. Do not include the control group results.

2. Construct a table showing purchase and nonpurchase percents for the two expertise conditions (combine the price results for each expertise condition).

3. Graph the demand curves for the two expertise conditions and compare the observed results with the expected results shown in Figure 1.

4. What actions would you recommend to Bill Davenport? Should he price the kit at $2.98? Should the salesperson make a pitch to customers to buy the kit? If yes, what type of sales pitch?

5. What other factors should Bill Davenport consider in his evaluation of marketing the cleaning kit?

6. What general managerial implications are suggested from Bill's study?

The Citizens and Southern National Bank of South Carolina: Introducing Customer Service Banking (Part B)

*This case was prepared by **Billy Silver,** vice-president of marketing communications, The Citizens and Southern National Bank, Columbia, South Carolina.*

One of the cornerstones of successful banking is the rapport that bank employees develop with their customers in a face-to-face and day-to-day situation. Whether they be tellers, secretaries, or financial loan officers, bank employees who come into contact with present and potential customers influence the perception which customers have of their bank.

Selling Financial Services

Today, banks offer more financial services than ever. However, studies indicate that employees have become highly specialized in operations and processing and obtain a very low level of overall banking knowledge. These factors tend to facilitate a lack of desire and ability on the part of the employee to take advantage of opportunities to sell services and thereby contribute to profitable growth.

When employees do attempt to sell, it often is done in a haphazard fashion, principally because there is a lack of knowledge on how to sell and a lack of product knowledge of what to sell. Even when employees are adequately prepared to sell, studies indicate that they are not properly motivated to do so, nor is the bank organizationally and formally set up to encourage this selling atmosphere.

In addition, banks expect good customer relations to be learned through practice on the job. Each new employee must become as skillful as the most experienced one in order to stay even. Banks are not judged by management policies, advertising, or bank buildings, but by the treatment which customers receive when they come in contact with a bank employee. In essence, how well a bank employee services and treats the customer and communicates what the bank is actually offering determines the customer's attitude toward the bank. Therefore, the need exists to maintain uniform, consistent, high-quality customer service and customer relations at all times to maintain the proper image and reputation of a bank.

The Customer's
Viewpoint

C&S is concerned about the way customers perceive their bank, especially through personal contact. C&S customers have three ways of contact with the bank:

1. *Face-to-face contact* at the banking office where the customer either has a regular contact or just deals with anyone who is available to assist.

2. *Telephone contact* made directly to the banking office or to another area in the bank. A phone call may be made directly to someone who is a regular contact or to anyone who can aid in solving problems or answering questions.

3. *Bank-by-mail* where the customer sends a transaction directly to a particular banking office or just to the bank in general.

Customers have four ways they deal with the bank:

1. Process transactions. Most transactions are processed in the banking office face-to-face, while the mail is used to process the second highest number of transactions. Of the three ways a customer contacts the bank, telephone ranks lowest when the customer processes a transaction.

2. Open new account or apply for a loan. Both of these transactions occur most often in a face-to-face situation in a banking office. Opening new accounts or making loan applications are very infrequently initiated by mail or phone.

3. Seek information. Most often when a C&S customer or potential customer is seeking information, he does so in the banking office. The second most often used method is by telephone, and the least often is mail.

4. Make a complaint. When a customer makes a complaint, he does so face-to-face in a banking office and equally as often by telephone. Occasionally he uses the mail for voicing a complaint.

Customer Needs

Customers have two types of needs, financial and psychological. A bank must satisfy both needs to keep customer business, to make them receptive to suggestions, and to generate recommendations in acquiring new customers.

For the bank to achieve its objectives, it must provide customers and the community with satisfaction of their basic financial needs. However, most banks do not really understand what customers want nor expect from a bank in fulfilling their psychological needs.

C&S management believes that psychological needs for bank services can be categorized into the three following areas:

1. Competency. The customer wants and expects the bank and its staff to be competent and to know the job that needs to be done. If the staff does not know how to do a job, the customer will want to know why that individual is there. This, of course, will cause concern about the type of bank with

which he or she deals. The customer expects the staff member to exhibit the following characteristics: (a) a complete knowledge and proficiency in operational procedures; (b) an ability to explain C&S policy and procedures that he may not see the need for or understand; (c) a knowledge of C&S and its services; and (d) a fast, accurate, efficient, and confidential service.

2. Courtesy. The customer also wants and expects courtesy. The degree to which a bank—through its staff—makes a customer feel welcome, important, appreciated, and at ease when he goes into the bank to discuss a problem, makes a deposit, cashes a check, or opens an account, has an effect on keeping the customers loyal and encouraging noncustomers to become customers. But this courtesy is more than just mechanically going through the motions of calling people by name, smiling at appropriate points during the conversation and transactions, and using courtesy words. The customer expects the staff to be pleasant and friendly whenever he is face-to-face with a service representative. He expects them to exhibit an attitude of genuine courtesy, not just mechanical courtesy.

3. Concern. Do the bank employees exhibit a real concern that they are properly serving the customer in every way possible? Are the bank employees continually looking for new ways to help customers? Are they looking for problems the customers may be having, or needs they may not be aware of and suggesting solutions to their problems or needs? This concern of being personally interested in helping customers solve problems is what separates C&S Bank from other banks, and the C&S staff, tellers, and Customer Service Representatives, from any other bank's staff.

Customer
Service Program

The following statement was recently issued to all bank employees:

"We at C&S are launching a new customer service program to expand our relationships with present C&S customers and to develop new relationships with other members of the consumer banking community. The success of this program depends upon you, the employee, who comes in contact with our customers on a day-to-day basis. I have outlined the following points of the program."

The outline follows.

Program Objectives and Purpose

In every contact with a customer or prospective customer, whether face-to-face, by telephone, by mail, or by a member of the customer contact staff, the *purpose* of this program is to make that contact the most effective possible in satisfying the customer's financial and psychological needs while at the same time satisfying the bank's need for improved growth.

The objectives of the program are the following:

1. Creating the most favorable impression of C&S Bank in the minds of customers who come into contact with C&S employees.

2. Satisfying customer psychological needs—needs for recognition, for appreciation, for courtesy, etc.

3. Satisfying customer financial needs by offering or suggesting new or additional C&S services which will help provide solutions to their problems and needs, or assist them in reaching their goals.

The basic thrust of the Customer Service Program should be developing lifetime customers for C&S National Bank.

Program Concept

The concept of C&S's Customer Service Program is that the customer contact staff member has an obligation as a representative of the bank to do four things in all of his or her contacts with bank customers or prospective customers:

1. Portray the desired image of C&S Bank.

2. Provide the highest level of quality banking service.

3. Satisfy customer psychological needs by exhibiting outstanding customer relations in all of his or her dealings with customers and prospective customers, and develop close rapport with regular customers.

4. Satisfy customer financial needs by offering or suggesting C&S services which will help provide solutions to customer problems, satisfy customer needs, or assist them in achieving their financial goals.

Philosophy of Program

Good customer relations and sales awareness are an important part of everyone's job, and consistent good customer relations and high sales performance are expected of all customer staff members.

The program operates on a continuous, low-pressure basis with emphasis on "offering maximum assistance to customers so that they will receive the full benefit of their C&S relationship" rather than "just trying to sell something." By following this philosophy, it is virtually impossible to offend customers and prospects. In addition, this philosophy also reduces the amount of unprofitable business generated since customers and prospects are sold only those services they need and want.

The philosophy of the C&S Customer Service Program is based on providing this total customer development effort to all C&S customers and prospective customers. The emphasis is on determining customer needs and suggesting additional customer services and solutions.

Desired Image

A new image is desired to help portray the type of bank C&S wants to become. The desired image incorporates what people in C&S trade areas should perceive C&S Bank to be and includes the following:

Substantial

Leading

Friendly and dignified

Bank for the public

Up to date

Active and progressive

Wants your business

The Staff's Role

Studies have shown that 80 to 90 percent, and even up to 95 percent of all contacts with customers and prospective customers are with bank customer contact staff level employees. This includes tellers, safe deposit custodians, contact secretaries, and others who meet the customers face-to-face every day. The customer contact staff includes the people the customer thinks about when thinking about our bank. They are the interpreters of the bank, its services, its policies, its procedures, its advertising, and its image. This job has three dimensions:

1. Internal operations and procedures.

2. Customer service and customer relations.

3. Business development (suggesting services).

Through these three job dimensions, we can provide the highest level of quality banking service and customer satisfaction by being competent, courteous, and concerned. Details concerning these job dimensions are described briefly below.

Internal operations and procedures   This is the dimension of the staff member's job that has to do with handling the internal aspects of processing banking transactions. All customer contact staff members need to be familiar with the proper operational skills and procedures and need to be familiar with the right method of handling each banking transaction.

They need to have a good working knowledge of each of the operational transactions they are expected to know and be able to perform every duty involved in carrying out these transactions and procedures. They need to be able to settle accurately and usually at the first of each day.

Customer service and customer relations   Customers want and expect competency, courtesy, and concern and to be treated as individuals. They do not wish to be treated merely like an account number or part of a herd. The C&S staff should make every attempt to provide the most courteous, pleasant, and friendly service to each customer that they meet each day. They need to:

1. Be quick, accurate, and efficient in their transactions, and adjust their speed to differences in customer traffic flow.

2. Be familiar with the policies of the bank so that they can answer questions pertinent to policies and procedures, as well as explain misunderstood policies and procedures.

3. Make an appealing impression upon C&S customers by being courteous, pleasant, friendly and helpful, and to help them feel welcome, important, appreciated, and at ease.

4. Attempt to establish rapport with each regular customer.

5. Present a pleasing outlook by smiling and greeting customers.

6. Have patience with customers to help satisfy their complaints.

7. Take an interest in customers by finding out more about them and looking for ways that they might help them.

8. Make an effort to learn and use the names of regular customers and show an interest in their families and jobs.

Business Development (suggesting services)

Many of our present C&S customers and prospective customers do not know about the many services the bank offers or how they may benefit from using them. Many customers are now using other financial institutions for services that C&S can provide.

With the opportunity to meet customers and to learn about their needs, the bank staff should take an active role in trying to spot customer needs and problems so that services might be suggested to satisfy their needs or problems. As an example, the typical teller serves anywhere from 25 to 150 customers per day. If each customer needs between two and eight additional services they either do not have or are obtaining from another financial institution, the C&S staff has enormous opportunities to uncover these needs, explain the services that will satisfy these needs and how C&S can provide the service better.

Benefits of the Concept, Philosophy, and Objectives

Benefits to the customer   Benefits to the customer include:

1. Assurance of receiving the best in quality banking service.

2. Assurance of receiving outstanding customer service which means that transactions will be handled properly, efficiently, and quickly; that questions will be answered knowledgeably; and that bank policies and procedures will be explained intelligently.

3. Assurance of receiving the best in customer relations—receiving courteous, pleasant, and friendly service and knowing that C&S staff members are taking a personal interest in him and his banking business.

4. Assurance of having his financial needs satisfied by concerned staff members who are constantly on the lookout for needs and problems so that they may suggest solutions.

Benefits to the bank   C&S will achieve a higher level of growth and profitability for the following reasons:

1. Retention of present customers. Fewer customers will be moving their business from C&S to another bank because they were not receiving

the high level of service and proper customer relations that they wanted and expected.

2. Expansion of relationships with present customers. Because the staff will be looking for new ways to help existing customers by analyzing their needs and problems and suggesting solutions through the use of new and additional banking services, present customers will become more profitable to C&S.

3. Addition of new customers. Although promotion of C&S will play a role in attracting new customers, the major impetus in obtaining new customers will be favorable word-of-mouth advertising by satisfied C&S customers.

The staff at C&S was asked to make any comments or ask questions concerning the memorandum, the new customer service concept, or its implementation.

Questions

1. Do you feel that the psychological needs of bank customers identified in the case are the most relevant to banking services or even basic consumer needs for banking services? Explain.

2. Evaluate the C&S Customer Service Program. What are its strengths? Its weaknesses? How would you improve it?

3. What behavioral selling concepts is C&S using in its Customer Service Program? What other behavioral selling concepts might C&S consider in selling its bank services? How would you translate these concepts into practice?

part 7

Cross-Cultural
Buying Behavior

This part is divided into two sections—marketing in foreign countries and marketing from abroad to consumers in the United States. The first case deals with an American firm marketing abroad, and the second case examines a United Kingdom company marketing in its home country as well as considering a market effort in other European countries. Finally, the third case discusses the efforts of a German company to market in the United States.

Students should consider the differences in consumption behavior, attitudes, product perceptions, product and brand choice criteria, etc. between the American consuming market and those of other countries.

chapter 17

Marketing Abroad

Home
Products, Inc.

*This case was prepared by **Brian Toyne,** College of Business Administration, University of South Carolina.*

In September 1976, James Bradley, vice-president of marketing for the Wet Soups Division of Home Products, Inc., was wondering what strategy he should follow to enter the United Kingdom's wet soup market with a line of condensed soup products. His assistant, Tom Bennett, a recent MBA graduate with a major in international marketing, had collected some preliminary data on the U.K. soup consumer and on the experience which their major competitor, Campbell Soup, Inc., had had in the United Kingdom. Mr. Bradley must have a proposal outlining his strategy for entering the British soup market on the president's desk in one week.

Company Background

Home Baking, Inc., was founded in 1948. This firm, which supplied pies, bread, and other flour-based baked products to the food retailing and catering industries in the Southeast, merged in 1955 with a small, but nationally known producer of wet soups, sauces, and salad dressings. The new company then operated under the name Home Products, Inc., (HPI) and was organized into two divisions, the Baking Division and the Wet Soups Division. By 1976, the company's markets extended across the U.S. and into Canada.

From its origin, the brand name Home Made became increasingly strong and was eventually given to all of the company's branded products. As a result of the company's decision to include Canada as a market for its products, the name was registered in 1962 for use internationally.

Within HPI, the Wet Soups Division (WSD) proceeded with its original activities after the merger, namely the development of additional soups, sauces, and salad dressings. The following list indicates the range of consumer products which the division markets: salad dressings (several varieties), tomato ketchup, mayonnaise, condensed wet soups (over twenty varieties), gourmet soups (two types of clam chowder, vichysoisse, green turtle, etc.) and several kinds of sauces (shrimp, tartar, horseradish, spaghetti, etc.).

By 1975, WSD's products had become an important factor in the wet soup and sauce markets, accounting for about 5 percent of these markets' aggregated annual sales. By this time, WSD had become a troublesome competitor for Campbell Soup, Inc., and H. J. Heinz Company, which were its major competitors in the United States and Canada.

The total sales of Home Products in 1975 were more than $143 million. Profits before taxes were more than $13.3 million. WSD accounted for about 35 percent of total sales and contributed $6.1 million in before-tax profits.

The International Competitive Environment

Direct investment in foreign facilities generally is an alternative to exporting from the company's home base. The most frequent reason for making a direct investment abroad is that the company's exports are confronted with foreign trade barriers. This is particularly true in the case of the larger free-trade regions, such as the European Economic Community (EEC) and the European Free Trade Association (EFTA). The EEC was formed in 1957 and resulted in the eventual elimination of all restrictions to the free flow of goods, capital, and persons among member nations, and the creation of a common external tariff. The original members of this agreement were Belgium, France, Italy, Luxembourg, the Netherlands, and West Germany. Members of EFTA, on the other hand, rejected the idea of total integration implied by the EEC agreement. While the member nations favored a free flow of industrial goods among member nations, they sought the freedom necessary to establish their own external tariffs. The original members of EFTA, formed in 1960, included Austria, Denmark, Norway, Portugal, Sweden, and the United Kingdom. In January 1973, Britain, Denmark, and Ireland left the EFTA and joined the EEC.

Partially in response to the formation of the EEC and partially because of its domination of a saturated U.S. market, Campbell decided to move overseas in 1958. H. J. Heinz, a practiced foreign marketer, was already well established in Europe at this time and, along with the Swiss dry soup mix firm of Knorr, dominated most of the European markets. Nestlé, another Swiss firm, also was a formidable European competitor.

By 1973, Campbell had plants in Australia, Austria, Belgium, Britain, Canada, France, Italy, and Mexico. Its net income from these subsidiaries in 1973 was $10.6 million.

H. J. Heinz had started exporting its products in 1886 and had established its first overseas plant in Britain in 1905. It had additional plants operating in Argentina, Australia, Canada, Denmark, Ireland, Italy, Japan, the Netherlands, Portugal, Mexico, and Venezuela. Net income from these foreign subsidiaries in 1973 was $20.2 million. Campbell and H. J. Heinz each enjoyed total sales in 1973 amounting to about $1.2 billion.

The British
   Market

The Campbell Soup Experience

Oscar Wilde once noted that the U.S. and England were two great nations separated by the same language for, in spite of many similarities, there are vast differences in nuance and emphasis. David Dutton, a one-time managing director of one of Britain's largest advertising agencies, once explained the impact that these differences have on American businesspeople: "It is perhaps understandable that Americans tend to enter the United Kingdom with a bit too much self-assurance. They feel at home here and are bound to make mistakes."

James Bradley was well aware of this potential problem. He had recently re-read a March 1967, article in *Sales Management* about the problems Campbell had encountered during its first ten years overseas. Notwithstanding its vast resources and marketing expertise, Campbell made the typical American mistake when it entered the British market in 1959. As a result, it had only secured about 15 percent of the British market between 1959 and 1966. H. J. Heinz, which can only boast of about 5 percent of the U.S. market, is the dominant force in the British soup market with about a 60 percent market share. In fact, Heinz has been in Britain so long and has established itself so well that many Britons think of it as a domestic company.

Bradley learned that Campbell's first mistake was a failure to explain to the average consumer just how to prepare its condensed soups. The British consumer, accustomed to the ready-to-eat Heinz soups, was unaware of Campbell's condensed soup concept. Since no one had explained about adding a can of water to the soup, Campbell's soups were at some disadvantage on the retail shelf because of their smaller size. In spite of an avalanche of advice, it took Campbell two years to embark on the necessary educational advertising and promotion programs to sell the British on the idea of condensed soups.

Bradley also learned that Campbell had further compounded the problem by initially refusing to tailor its flavors in soups to foreign tastes. For example, the British were unaccustomed to the taste of Campbell's original tomato soup. It was too sweet. The taste of well-established and branded local varieties, such as those offered by Heinz, were so different from Campbell's flavor that it was not until Campbell had made significant changes in its soups' flavors that sales perked up.

Bradley felt that Campbell also erred in its advertising. The British consumer, not so greatly influenced by a "youth culture" as the American consumer, found many of the firm's initial advertising efforts too youthful and fanciful. The British are accustomed to a degree of realism in their advertising that borders on the trite. Although the company's advertising has been modified to some extent, it is still too transatlantic in concept. The movie theater commercial, practically nonexistent in the U.S., is a prime medium in England as well as in a number of other European countries. Several countries, Britain included, do not allow commercials on their government controlled television networks. Campbell's movie commercials, still strongly characteristic of so much U.S. advertising, especially on television, is viewed as being too slick, vapidly unreal, and determinedly youthful.

The United Kingdom Report

In anticipation of a move into the British market, Mr. Bradley had Tom Bennett arrange for some preliminary market research. Tom had contracted with the British market research firm of Benson and Brooke to determine the significant factors affecting the soup service decision. What was being served and why was of particular interest to Tom.[1]

Although Tom was aware that tastes and cultures were not constant across national boundaries, he had chosen not to have any taste or product concept tests made in the British market at this time. These tests had been delayed because there was some question over the type of tests to be employed; monadic, blind, and brand comparisons were some of the alternatives that had been considered.

During March, a probability sample of 500 British homes were interviewed on all seven days of each week. The ten-page questionnaire used by Benson and Brooke dealt with such issues as the frequency and importance of soup-serving decisions. Specific questions dealt with who ate the soup, how much they enjoyed it, and at which meal soup was served. Most questions referred only to the soup served at the previous day's meals. Additional information also had been requested which was to assist Bradley in determining the seasonal effect on demand. This information was important since Campbell had found that its soups were subject to a seasonal effect which left its British plant unproductive for about one-third of the year.

Household eating patterns from the survey showed that 94 percent of the families ate yesterday's dinner at home, 56 percent ate lunch at home, and 28 percent served snacks. The latter group tended to consist of families with children between the ages of 3 and 14, high incomes, and a high educational level. The group who ate lunch at home tended to consist of families whose wage earners were blue collar workers. Table 1 indicates the kinds of soups that were served on these three occasions.

TABLE 1   *What kind of soup was served yesterday?*

Type of Soup	Type of Meal		
	Snacks (%)	Lunch (%)	Dinner (%)
Condensed	50	21	16
Ready-to-eat	32	48	33
Dry soup mix	18	15	0
Homemade	0	16	51

The general frequency of serving soup as an appetizer and as a meal are presented in Tables 2 and 3. About 73 percent of the households served soup as an appetizer 84 percent of the time. Twenty-seven percent of the households never served soup as an appetizer. The question as to which type of soup was served as an appetizer and as a meal was not asked.

When these results and their accompanying remarks were compared to WSD's research on the U.S. consumer, some interesting differences were noted. These differences are presented in Table 4.

Most American consumers considered soup "quick and easy" to prepare and therefore ideal for late morning or early afternoon snacks. They also thought that when combined with sandwiches, soup is good as a "light

TABLE 2   Frequency of serving soup as an appetizer

| Frequency | Type of Meal | | |
	Snacks (%)	Lunch (%)	Dinner (%)
Daily	0	0	8
Several times a week	0	15	12
Once a week	0	21	39
Less often	100	64	41

TABLE 3   Frequency of serving soup as a meal

| Frequency | Type of Meal | | |
	Snacks (%)	Lunch (%)	Dinner (%)
Daily	5	9	0
Several times a week	51	37	17
Once a week	26	34	38
Less often	18	10	45

TABLE 4   Comparison of United States and British soup consumers

| | Type of Meal | | | | | |
| | Snacks | | Lunch | | Dinner | |
	U.S.	British	U.S.	British	U.S.	British
Percent of consumers eating three types of meals at home	69	28	22	56	82	94
Percent of consumers serving soup at these meals	83	32	58	52	21	49

lunch." On the other hand, "because we must eat plenty of greens to stay healthy," salads were the most frequently served appetizer at dinner.

Since most British consumers consider sandwiches a more "substantial meal for growing children," only a small number of them served soup as a snack. British families who serve lunch at home consider it very important that their "working menfolk" eat a full, hot meal, so soup is used to "round out the meal." When soup is served at dinner, the reason most frequently given is that it helps "reduce the cost of the meal."

As Table 5 shows, the British soup market has extreme seasonal demand which coincides with climatic changes. Sixty-nine percent of the year's total volume of soup sales occur in the six months beginning in October. During the remaining six months, the drop in soup sales is offset by a corresponding increase in the sale of salad greens and hors d'oeuvres.

FIGURE 1   *Seasonal analysis of soup market (percentage of annual total market sales, bimonthly)*

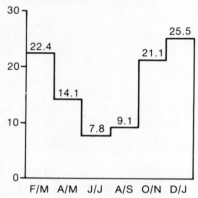

International Extension Alternatives

The following is the report Tom Bennett prepared for Mr. Bradley:

"I have prepared five alternative strategies for extending WSD's operations into Europe. Since I do not feel that our transatlantic move should be restricted to the United Kingdom, I have outlined basic strategy alternatives for entering any new national market.

"I feel that our company can grow by using one or a combination of the following three approaches. Basically we can undertake further penetration of existing national markets to increase market share, extend our product line into new product markets in a single national market, or we can expand by extending our existing operations into new countries and areas of the world. The latter method is geographical expansion and, I feel, is pertinent for entry into the United Kingdom and eventually into Europe. The following five strategic alternatives are available for extending our operations geographically:

1. Product Communication Extension.
2. Product Extension—Communication Adaptation.

3. Product Adaptation—Communication Extension.

4. Product Adaptation—Communication Adaptation.

5. Product Invention.[2]

These alternatives, along with the factors that should influence our selection, are presented in Exhibit 1. At this point, I will explain each of these strategy alternatives.

EXHIBIT 1   *Strategic alternatives for geographical extension*

SOURCE: Warren J. Keegan, *Multinational Marketing Management* (Englewood Cliffs, N. J.: Prentice-Hall, Inc., 1974), p. 234.

Strategy	Product Function or Need Satisfied	Conditions of Product Use	Ability to Buy Product	Recommended Product Strategy	Recommended Communications Strategy
1	same	same	yes	extension	extension
2	different	same	yes	extension	adaptation
3	same	different	yes	adaptation	extension
4	different	different	yes	adaptation	adaptation
5	same	—	no	invention	develop new communications

Product Communication Extension

"When adopting this approach, a company sells exactly the same product with the same advertising and promotional themes and appeals it uses in the United States. The method has great appeal to most multinational corporations because of the cost savings that are associated with this approach. Two major sources of savings are manufacturing economies of scale and the elimination of product research and development costs. Also associated with this method are the substantial economies associated with standardization of marketing communications. Pepsico has been extremely successful with this method. However, when Philip Morris attempted to take advantage of U.S. television advertising campaigns that have a sizable Canadian audience in border areas, they found that the significant taste differences between the Canadian straight tobacco and the U.S. blended tobacco was too great, and they had to withdraw their U.S. brands from the Canadian market.

Product Extension-Communication Adaptation

"When a product fills a different need or serves a different function under use conditions that are the same or similar to those in the domestic market, the only adjustment required is in marketing communications. The appeal of the product extension—communication adaptation strategy is its relatively low cost of implementation. Since the product remains unchanged, research and development, tooling manufacturing setup, and inventory costs associated with the addition of a new product are avoided. The only cost is in identifying different product functions and the reformulation of the marketing communication program. An example of this approach is the sale of outboard motors in many foreign countries. Instead of being used for recreational purposes as is the case in the U.S., they are used mainly for fishing and transportation. Therefore, the marketing communications program must be changed to fit a different product use.

Product Adaptation—Communication Extension

"A third approach is to extend, without change, the basic marketing communication strategy developed for the domestic market, but adapt the domestic product to local use conditions. This approach assumes that the product will serve the same function in foreign markets under different use conditions. Gasoline, agricultural chemicals, household appliances, and clothing are examples of products that need to be changed for climatic, soil, environmental, and fashion differences but which still serve basically the same use.

Product Adaptation—Communication Adaptation

"When there are differences in environmental conditions of use and in the function that a product serves, a strategy of product adaptation and communication adaptation is indicated. This is, in effect, a combination of strategies two and three.

Product Invention

"This strategy alternative is most frequently used in less developed countries where the potential customers do not have the ability or the purchasing power necessary to buy the product. Under these circumstances, the strategy involves the invention or the development of an entirely new product designed to satisfy the identified need or function at a price that is within reach of the potential customer. This approach can be rewarding if product development costs are not prohibitive.

"I have developed these five strategy alternatives based on my research of how other firms have expanded operations geographically. Our problem now is to determine which broad strategy should be used and, specifically, how WSD can implement the chosen strategy."

Mr. Bradley feels that Bennett's report offers sound alternatives and is now faced with selecting the best strategy for WSD, given the available information.

Questions

1. In what ways does the British soup consumer differ from the American soup consumer? Which of these differences are most important in deciding upon a marketing strategy for WSD?

2. What lesson should Mr. Bradley have learned from the Campbell Soup experience in the British market? How will this affect Mr. Bradley's decision?

3. For each of the five strategies developed by Mr. Bennett, how might WSD adapt its product and communications programs to the British soup consumer?

4. What other information would you want about the British soup consumer in order to select the best strategy alternative? How would this information be used?

5. How should WSD handle the disrupting seasonal demand for soup in the British market?

6. Locate information on the French, German, and Italian soup consumer. Would you use a different strategy in each of these markets? Why?

Notes

[1] Benson and Brooke and the data presented are fictitious and are for illustrative purposes only.

[2] These strategy alternatives are presented in Warren J. Keegan, *Multinational Marketing Management* (Englewood Cliffs, N.J.: Prentice-Hall, Inc., 1974), pp. 227–234.

Hardy's and Company, Ltd.

This case was prepared by **Peter Doyle,** *University of Bradford Management Centre, West Yorkshire, England, 1CH–575–620. Copyright* © *1975. Adapted for use in this casebook.*

Paul Wilcox, a management consultant specializing in marketing, was asked by Hardy's managing director to give a second opinion on the company's proposed advertising expenditure. Hardy's was a well-established, publicly-quoted company with over 200 High Street shops (downtown) spread throughout the U.K. selling furniture and carpets. Turnover in 1973 amounted to almost £ 30 million.

In the previous three years, Hardy's had withdrawn from media advertising, reflecting skepticism on the part of Harold Fisk, the managing director, about the value of such expenditure. Nevertheless, because of changes and increasing competition in the furniture industry, he was reconsidering his earlier position. A leading London advertising agency had been briefed and had subsequently proposed an advertising appropriation in 1974 at an annual rate of £650,000.

The U.K.
Furniture Industry

In 1973, retail sales of furniture and carpets amounted to over £800 million. Annual growth since 1960 averaged 2.5 percent in real terms, but it was extremely sporadic, largely due to the industry's vulnerability to government economic action. Commentators, both inside and outside the industry, were optimistic about long term industry growth. The most frequent justification for this view was comparison of U.K. expenditure per capita on furniture with other countries.

The general quality of U.K. furniture is regarded as low by European standards. The industry is characterized by many small manufacturers— around 1,500 operating in 1972. Retailing, too, is highly fragmented. Multiples (more than ten outlets) have a relatively low share of turnover (27 percent) compared to many other sectors of retailing (e.g. clothing and footwear, 57 percent; grocery, 43 percent), and independents are relatively powerful.

TABLE 1   *Furniture expenditure in various countries*

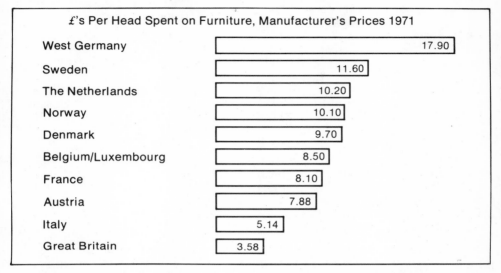

£'s Per Head Spent on Furniture, Manufacturer's Prices 1971	
West Germany	17.90
Sweden	11.60
The Netherlands	10.20
Norway	10.10
Denmark	9.70
Belgium/Luxembourg	8.50
France	8.10
Austria	7.88
Italy	5.14
Great Britain	3.58

In recent years, significant changes have taken place in the furniture trade. Larger manufacturing units were emerging in certain sectors of the trade. In retailing, independents were slowly losing out to multiples. In the multiples section, department stores (the biggest groups being United Drapers Stores, House of Frazer, and Debenhams) accounted for about 15 percent of furniture sales. The most rapidly growing retail sectors, however, were discount stores and mail order.

Discounting generally has grown tremendously since the late 1960s. Although their impact on furniture sales has been slight so far, it is recognized that they present a formidable threat to traditional retailers. A typical example is Status Discount, Ltd. which has recently opened its first discount furniture store offering brand leaders at discounts of 15 to 20 percent in a 40,000 square foot out-of-town site. Similar stores are planned elsewhere in the near future. Mail order furniture advertising is also growing rapidly, notably through the Sunday color supplements. This has attracted specialist retailers but also some of the discounters and more recently Times Furnishing, the largest of the multiples which competes directly with Hardy's in the High Street. In 1972, however, discounting and mail order still probably amounted to under 10 percent of furniture sales.

A significant growth of new specialist retailers has also occurred. Over the past three years, Habitat, started by designer Terence Conran, has become a significant force with its fourteen shops in major cities and a mail order business. It uses an "up-market" appeal supported by a strong image and modernly designed, quality furniture at reasonable prices. Other innovators are Schreiber and G-Plan which manufacture conventional furniture but market it with considerable flair through tightly controlled retail agents, supported by relatively heavy brand advertising. In 1973, Schreiber's turnover was £30 million, almost double that of the previous year. (See Table 2.)

TABLE 2 *Structure of the retail furnishing trade*

SOURCE: 1971 Census, "Trade and Industry"

	All Outlets	Multiples	Cooperatives	Independents
Turnover (£thousands)	676,600	182,900	15,500	478,200
Outlets	23,125	2,013	254	20,858
Persons engaged	92,646	17,530	1,675	73,441
% share				
Turnover	100.0	27.0	2.3	70.7
Outlets	100.0	8.7	1.1	90.2
Persons	100.0	18.9	1.8	79.3
Turnover/outlet (£thousands)	29.3	90.9	61.0	22.9
Turnover/person (£thousands)	7.3	10.4	9.3	6.5

Competition

The largest retailers are the general furniture multiples such as Times Furnishing, Hardy's, Courts, Williams, Henderson-Kenton, and Allied Carpets. With profit margins at about 12 percent, Hardy's is also one of the most profitable of the groups. In 1973, profits before taxes were around £3 million. (See Table 3.)

The managing director told Wilcox that Hardy's growth has come from a policy of opening new stores in central locations. The older stores were smaller with frontages of under fifty feet, and the company has tried to obtain newer sites with a larger frontage (100 feet is thought about right). Hardy's success, he said, is not due to particularly unique factors. The stores offer furniture of adequate quality at competitive prices, backed by effective hire-

TABLE 3 *Turnover and branches for various multiple furniture retailers (1971–72)*

SOURCE: Annual reports

	1971-1972 t/o (£millions)	Branches	T/o (£thousands) per Branch
Times Furnishing	60.0	500	120
Hardy's	25.0	205	122
Court's	16.9	75	225
MFI Discount	10.5	9	500
New Day	10.2	108	94
Williams	8.7	80	109
Henderson-Kenton	6.1	52	117
Allied Carpets	6.1	20	203

purchase facilities aimed at the largest segment of the population. Hardy's has avoided the tendency to move "up-market," believing that its real strength and popularity is at the lower-middle to working-class end of the market. He also feels that the store has a relatively greater appeal to older households. (See Table 4.)

TABLE 4   *Social grade definitions and average weekly food expenditure, 1973*

SOURCE: *Market Research Society Yearbook* (London: Market Research Society, 1974).

	Social Grade	Occupation of Household Head	% of Adults	Expenditure (£)
A :	Upper-middle class	Higher managerial, administrative, or professional	2.4	6.8
B :	Middle class	Intermediate managerial, administrative, or professional	11.0	
C1:	Lower-middle class	Supervisory or clerical and junior managerial, administrative, or professional	22.8	6.5
C2:	Skilled working class	Skilled manual workers	32.5	7.2
D :	Working class	Semiskilled and unskilled manual workers	23.0	6.1
E :	Lowest levels of subsistence	State pensioners or widows (no other earner), casual or lowest-grade workers	8.3	

The Advertising Agency Proposals

Fisk told Wilcox that he recognized that Hardy's has not been a marketing-oriented company. Fisk is an accountant by training, and the company is still family controlled with most of the management having been with the company for many years and without real management training or extensive experience in other companies. Consequently, while Hardy's is still doing well, he recognizes that the future will demand changes in its existing policies.

After spending intermittently on advertising during the 1960s, Fisk has abandoned all expenditure except for direct mailings in specific areas to announce new store openings. He believes that these savings have increased profits since there has been no obvious fall-off in sales. He also points to a recent report of the trade association which suggests that advertising has only a minor influence on furniture purchases and choice of stores. Never-

theless, the recent increase in furniture advertising has increased his uncertainty about advertising, and he feels that it could be dangerous for
Hardy's if it stands aside in the increasingly competitive environment. For
this reason, he has asked an agency for its views about whether advertising
would be effective and, if so, what type of program would be necessary.

TABLE 5   *Reasons for selecting retailer*
SOURCE: Furniture Trade Research Association

Reasons	% of Respondents (546)**
Dealt with before	56.2
Good reputation	46.7
Stocks item wanted	42.6
Convenient location	39.3
Good display and wide range of products	39.3
Terms offered*	31.8
Local advertising feature	4.5
Decor consulting services	3.5

  *Covers both discount and HP terms
**Percentages show more than 100 percent, since respondents gave more than
  one reason. Each figure is a percentage of 546.

TABLE 6   *Influences behind purchases*
SOURCE: Furniture Trade Research Association

Influences	% of Purchases
In-shop display	21.6
Visiting different shops	17.3
Discount	15.5
Brand/make importance	13.9
Salespeople's advice	7.7
Manufacturer's catalog	5.9
Window display	5.7
Favorable credit terms	4.6
Family/friends' recommendations	4.2
Magazine articles and/or advertising	3.6
	100.0%

Base: 1543 postal respondents

The agency expressed no doubt that advertising has a major role. On
the size of the appropriation, the agency's report states:

"The company turnover is currently £30 million per annum, and we have
aimed at a modest sales increase of 10 percent, i.e., £3 million. To achieve
this goal, we estimate that we would need to spend an absolute minimum of

10 percent of the expected increase, i.e., £300,000. This figure is in fact under 1 percent of an expected turnover of £33 million. Advertising to sales ratios can vary from as little as 0.5 percent to 10 percent of turnover depending upon various market factors. However, we believe a realistic budget on a turnover of £33 million is 2 percent of turnover, i.e. £650,000."

The agency recommended that media should be chosen after a two-month test in the Tyne-Tees TV region (where there are twenty-seven stores) and the Midlands TV area (fifteen stores). To give an idea of the media which could be tested, Table 7 shows estimates of the costs of an effective two-month campaign in Tyne-Tees using alternative media.

TABLE 7   *Estimated costs of effective two-month test campaign in Tyne Tees using alternative media*
SOURCE: Advertising agency

Medium	Dimensions of Advertisement	Campaign Cost	Est. Adult Coverage	Est. Average Frequency of Exposure	Est. Cost per 1000 Adult Exposure
National press	Page × 7	£5,579	70%	8.0	50p
Local press	Page × 8	22,674	60	8.0	£2.36
Television	30 sec × 13[1]	6,825	80	8.0	53p
Posters	16 sheet × 350	4,200	85	160	15p
Transport	bus-side × 150	1,800	75	160	7½p
Radio	30 sec × 15	2,000	30	8.0	42p
Leaflets	750,000 × 1[2]	4,500	85	1.0	£2.74

[1] Test rates

[2] Excluding print costs

In making its creative proposals, the agency said its objectives were two:

1. to make people aware of Hardy's.

2. to create an increase in store traffic and sell more merchandise.

This would be achieved by:

a. Creating a memorable phrase which is linked to the Hardy's logo and is relevant to the basic proposition—"Big Hearted Hardy's."

b. Linking this phrase with a clear, understandable, and attractive proposition which *appears* to offer more than the competition—"£250 of furniture right now without paying a penny deposit and with up to three years to pay."

Fisk feels that neither he nor anyone else in the company has the marketing expertise to judge objectively these proposals. Before making the £650,000 commitment, he believes a second opinion from Wilcox would be worthwhile. (For additional data, see Tables 8–12.)

TABLE 8   *Manufacturers' advertising expenditure, 1970–1972 (£thousands)*
SOURCE: MEAL (London: Legion Press, 1973).

	1970	1971	1972
Carpets	£1,648	£1,412	£1,057
Bedding	686	457	607
Furniture	1,627	1,861	2,754

TABLE 9   *Advertising expenditure of various multiples, 1970–1972*
SOURCE: Retail Business, Economist Intelligence Unit, 1973

| | *£thousands* | | | | | | | | |
| | 1970 | | | 1971 | | | 1972 | | |
	Press	TV	Total	Press	TV	Total	Press	TV	Total
Cavenham-Woodhouse	160	—	160	260	10	270	355	20	375
Court's	6	—	7	—	—	—	75	—	75
Grange	17	20	37	16	23	38	28	33	61
Times	27	120	147	95	50	145	200	10	210
Waring and Gillow	10	—	10	38	—	38	95	—	95
Williams	115	—	115	118	—	118	215	—	215

TABLE 10   *Changes in consumer durables expenditure 1964 to 1973*
SOURCE: "Monthly Digest of Statistics," Her Majesty's Stationery Office, January 1974.

Year	All Consumer Durables (£millions)	Furniture (£millions)	Electricals (£millions)	Car Registrations (thousands)
1964	£1,109	£443	£409	99
1965	1,157	467	431	94
1966	1,229	501	349	89
1967	1,253	501	377	93
1968	1,352	531	412	93
1969	1,401	521	419	82
1970	1,536	546	485	92
1971	1,801	661	600	109
1972	2,125	747	720	139
1973	2,449	826	846	137

TABLE 11   *Balance sheet*

	1972 (£thousands)	1973 (£thousands)
Capital	5,811	5,811
Capital reserves	779	828
Unappropriated profit	4,433	4,778
Debts and mortgages	2,027	2,019
Minimum interest	307	307
Deferred tax	1,023	1,987
Current liabilities		
Creditors	3,299	3,374
Tax	1,953	1,383
Overdrafts	2,384	4,002
Dividends	711	650
	8,347	9,409
Total	14,380	15,730

	1972 (£thousands)	1973 (£thousands)
Current assets		
Stocks	2,996	3,047
Debtors	11,961	13,550
Investments	100	93
Cash	8	13
	15,065	16,703
Current liabilities	8,347	9,409
Net current assets	6,718	7,294
Fixed assets		
Freehold properties	4,196	4,832
Leasehold properties	2,529	2,648
Fixtures and fittings, etc.	937	956
Total	14,380	15,730

TABLE 12   *Hardy's and Company, Ltd.*

Year	Turnover (£thousands)	Pretax Profit (£thousands)	Share Price (P)	Employees	Stores
1964	7,682	1,064	87	N/A	115
1965	10,711	1,459	105	N/A	131
1966	12,407	1,716	96	N/A	204
1967	15,407	1,747	109	N/A	198
1968	20,370	2,130	101	2,259	207
1969	22,229	2,408	104	2,355	209
1970	22,745	2,309	90	2,176	211
1971	24,050	2,504	132	2,307	215
1972	24,568	2,889	125	2,459	218
1973	27,754	3,262	135	2,401	221

Questions

1. How do you feel about the advertising agency's method of determining a "realistic" advertising budget? Would you use a different budget method? If so, what?

2. Evaluate the advertising agency's creative proposal. What is the appeal being suggested? Is it appropriate for the U.K. lower-middle and working classes?

3. Should Hardy's place a major effort into advertising, or should it consider other marketing and promotional mix variables as more important? If so, which variables and why?

4. Identify the fundamental changes in the U.K. furniture market, and describe how they will affect Hardy's overall marketing program.

5. How do the furniture decision-making process and consumer needs of U.K. consumers differ from those in West Germany? Italy? France? United States? Describe how marketing and advertising strategies would differ across these cultures. (Note: The student should consult available literature to answer this question.)

chapter 18

Marketing in the U.S.A.

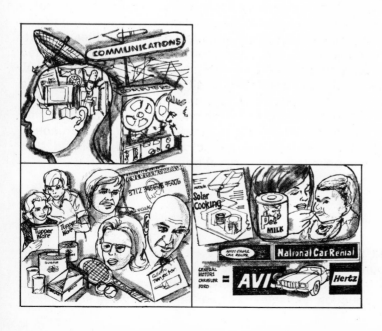

Bauer-Schmidt, GmbH:
Selling in the United States

*This case was prepared by **Brian Toyne**, College of Business Administration, University of South Carolina.*

In 1964, Bauer-Schmidt, a large German company, introduced a line of dry soup mix products to the U.S. market. By 1968, export sales in the U.S. had grown to $3.1 million. Because of this success, the company decided to establish a U.S. subsidiary and build a plant in the United States. The plant, located in Newark, N.J., was opened in 1973 for a cost of about $3 million.

To support this overseas operation, Bauer-Schmidt, Inc., the U.S. subsidiary, undertook an intensive marketing campaign during 1973-1975, costing $1.5 million. The campaign was designed to promote the use of dry soup mixes by the U.S. soup consumer and to develop new distribution channels to reach these consumers through all reputable convenience food stores. Sales for 1974 and 1975 were set at $4.9 million and $7.2 million, respectively. Actual sales, however, fell considerably short of these estimates as sales for 1974 totaled $4.1 million and for 1975, $4.6 million.

Since the opening of the plant had encountered no difficulties in start-up, acquisition of supplies, or financing, the short-fall in sales was attributed to an improperly developed marketing campaign. However, a quick review of the campaign by an internal marketing audit committee found that the company's place and pricing policies were competitive with the wet soup products marketed by competing U.S. firms, and that the promotion had been adequate for the introduction of the product line. (The promotion campaign had been supported by 12 percent of anticipated 1974 and 1975 sales, considerably above the U.S. industry's 9 percent average.)

History of the Company

Bauer-Schmidt had been formed in 1921 by Herman Bauer and Gunther Schmidt, two accountants who had met while working for Knorr, a Swiss-based multinational firm. Originally, Bauer-Schmidt was engaged almost exclusively in the production and sale of two varieties of dry pea soup mixes.

Over the years, due to its success, the company began high volume production of these soup mixes. During this period, it also broadened its soup mix line through the development and marketing of additional varieties of soups. By 1965, the company's share of the German market reached 80 percent.

With the formation of the European Economic Community (EEC) in 1957, the company expanded its operations to include the other five member nations. By 1968, it had plants operating in France, Italy, and Belgium. The company also entered the United Kingdom in 1961 after this country joined the European Free Trade Association (EFTA) formed in 1960. Although sales in the United Kingdom had not reached expectations, exports to the other EFTA countries kept the British plant relatively well utilized. In aggregate, Bauer-Schmidt had about a 20 percent share of the European market.

The United States Market

The company entered the U.S. market in 1965 with a limited line of dry soup mixes. Initially, this was a small operation with the soup mixes being supplied by the German plants. By 1967, sales had reached $2.9 million and the German plant was being over-utilized. To correct this high-cost situation, the French and British plants were used to help supply the U.S. market.

Specialty stores, such as delicatessens and the gourmet sections of stores such as Neiman-Marcus, were the major outlets for Bauer-Schmidt's soup mixes. Very little promotion had been needed. Wholesalers and large retailers had requested the company's products. Most advertising was done locally by the retailers without company incentive.

The product was packaged in a $4'' \times 4'' \times 3/8''$ rectangular container with a sealed wax envelope. The envelope contained a four-serving soup mix. Since it was felt that the consumers who shopped the specialty stores were seeking something unusual, the labelling and directions on one of the $4'' \times 4''$ surfaces was in German. English was used on the other surface with the word "imported" boldly written in the upper right-hand corner. The soup was identified also in English along two of the four $3/8''$ edges of the container.

The product, priced at 85¢ per envelope, sold for nearly three times that of Lipton's dry soup mixes. The wholesalers and retailers had assured Bauer-Schmidt that the high price, along with the fact that the soups had not been modified for the U.S. palate, were justified because "The U.S. customer was looking for the European taste." These assurances had proven correct.

The 1973–1975 Marketing Strategy

As a result of the decision to build a plant in the United States, Bauer-Schmidt decided to evaluate its U.S. marketing strategy. To support the new plant, it was necessary for the company to more than double its 1968 sales from $3.1 million to $7.9 million. To achieve this objective, the company realized that it had to attract a broader spectrum of customers and to shift from a selective to an intensive distribution system. The evaluation resulted in several significant changes in the company's U.S. marketing strategy. These changes, along with explanations, are summarized below.

Product   As a result of several extensive consumer taste and product concept tests conducted in 1970 and 1971, the company decided to modify the taste of all of its U.S. products. To further "Americanize" the product, all labelling and directions were in English. The word "imported" also was dropped. Since the U.S. consumer was found to react favorably to the original colors and script used on the imported containers, these were retained. In addition, the contents of the wax envelope was increased from four to six servings. A review of the major competitor's products and the market tests indicated that a six-serving package would be more favorably received. The package was enlarged to 4" × 4" × ½".

The directions on the package were expanded to include instructions for making sauces and dips. The product concept tests had indicated that approximately 20 percent of the U.S. consumers used dry soup mixes for these purposes.

Price   An evaluation of the pricing situation for dry soup mixes resulted in a price reduction from 85¢ to 49¢ per package. The company felt justified in making this price reduction because of the anticipated greater demand and the elimination of transatlantic transportation costs and U.S. tariffs. The price also would be more in line with the company's new distribution system and the target market. While the price was still above that of its competitors, the price would be supported by an image of superior quality and taste.

Place   During 1973, the U.S. subsidiary hired fifty experienced sales representatives. It was their task to gain acceptance for the company's product among general service wholesalers and large convenience food retailers. Since these intermediaries generally considered the product "untested," they were given above-tradition discounts to carry the product. These additional costs were budgeted as promotion expenses by Bauer-Schmidt. While the intermediaries indicated a willingness to carry the soup mixes because of the company's previous successes in the U.S., they generally were of the opinion that the U.S. customer would not accept the concept of dry soup mixes. One wholesaler, who subsequently declined to carry the soups, informed Bauer-Schmidt that an intensive educational program would be required. Bauer-Schmidt had unsuccessfully offered to provide him with an advertising allowance to carry on such a campaign for his region.

By the end of 1973, the company was very satisfied with the progress it had made in developing an intensive distribution system. The company was represented in all fifty states and had agreements with a majority of the major supermarket chains to carry its products. In addition, the supermarket chains had indicated a willingness to position Bauer-Schmidt's soups at eye-level to catch the attention of the shopper. This network of distributors and retailers was further expanded in 1974.

Promotion   The promotion campaign was divided into two parts. Approximately $300,000 was expended in developing the new distribution system. The money, distributed on a per capita basis by state, was used for trade advertising, the sales force, and trade discounts. An additional $1.2 million was used to introduce the company's "new" line of soup mixes. The marketing department wanted to convey three principal points: (1) that the dry soup mixes were completely new, (2) that they were convenient, both for preparation and storage, and (3) that the mixes were ideal as light lunches and as appetizers for dinner.

The $1.2 million was distributed among the various media and promotion methods in the following way: television ($600,000), newspapers ($100,000), magazines ($175,000), sampling ($200,000), coupons ($20,000), and advertising allowances ($100,000). These promotional efforts, while covering all fifty states, were confined to 263 Standard Metropolitan Statistical Areas.

Television was used because of its ability to show the product in actual use, for instance, a consumer preparing and serving a soup. Newspapers were used because of their announcement effect and their influence on local trade. Magazines, however, were used because of their color advantage and their selective audiences. Sampling, although expensive, was considered important because of its ability to introduce the new product directly to the consumer. Sampling was restricted to the major SMSAs. Coupons, good for 10¢ off the purchase of the company's pea, chicken, and tomato dry soup mixes, were used to induce trials and thereby change consumer habits.

Post Strategy Review

The marketing department of Bauer-Schmidt was equally divided over what should be done to stimulate sales. One faction strongly believed that the solution was to undertake an aggressive and intensive educational program. They argued that the U.S. consumer, not accustomed to the concept of dry soup mixes, needed to be educated to this concept and shown that this type of soup was easy to prepare and better tasting than the wet soups she was purchasing. They further argued that the campaign was launched on the premise that because of the company's delicatessen and gourmet successes, it had a ready market for its products. This did not prove to be the case. The market now being sought was not so willing to change, and not actively seeking an unusual taste experience.

The other faction believed just as strongly that U.S. consumers would not be educated to the concept of dry soups, and cited Lipton's small market share as compared to Campbell's share as evidence of the reluctance to change. They further argued that a new market had to be found and suggested that the new dry soup mixes be relabeled and sold as sauce and dip mixes and that the delicatessen and gourmet markets be recaptured, with the re-introduction of European products with the word "imported" omitted from the German-English label.

Questions

1. To what do you attribute the lack of success which Bauer-Schmidt experienced in the U.S. soup market?

2. Which plan proposed by the marketing department in its post strategy review would you accept? Or, would you suggest an alternative proposal? If so, what? Why?

part 8

Complete Analysis of Consumer Behavior

This part has many interesting and unusual cases. "The New Car Dilemma" is a case written from the consumer's point of view and traces over time the family decision-making process, changes in attitudes, perceptions, learning, etc. as told by the consumer.

"Managerial Use of Behavioral Concepts: Its Interface with Consumer Protection" is a collection of four case vignettes concerning customer complaints to the Office of Consumer Affairs. Although somewhat humorous, the vignettes deal with important behavioral issues.

The Healy case, "Marketing the Marketing Club," is short in length, but in using the case in class, Professor Healy found that it generated tremendous enthusiasm; so much, in fact, that the students used their new insights to resurrect their faltering Marketing Club to a solid body of over 100 members.

These cases are intended to provide students with situations in which they can integrate the body of behavioral concepts they have studied throughout the course. Students must determine the more relevant concepts to apply in each case.

chapter 19

Comprehensive Cases

Pathcom, Inc. and the CB Market:
Even the Smokey's a Good Buddy
in the Bodacious World of CB

*This case was prepared by **Denis F. Healy,** College of Business and Economics, University of Delaware. The material in this case has been obtained from a variety of published sources. The case has been prepared for teaching purposes only and is not intended to be evaluative of industry or company structure, conduct, or performance.*

The CB radio has struck the market by storm. Rapid, if not explosive, acceptance of the innovation has catapulted a major new industry into existence—and with little, if any, participation from the traditional consumer electronics producers. As the product concept moves through various market phases, companies are challenged to learn more about the consumer decision process and to adapt marketing strategies to changing market requirements and opportunities. Pathcom, the leading producer of CB radios in the United States, like its competitors, is faced with the need to adapt and to know about market characteristics. This case presents a comprehensive view of the industry and future trends. In addition, information is provided about Pathcom and its marketing practices. Analysis and discussion is sought about such issues as the consumer decision process, its marketing implications, the product life cycle, and competitive reactions at each stage. In addition, the analyst is asked to comment on information needs and marketing management issues.

Introduction

In 1971, the CB radio was still virtually unknown to the U.S. consumer, nearly a quarter century after its introduction to the market. Between 1947 and 1973, only 850,000 CB licenses were issued and over 70 percent of these were issued to electronics hobbiests. In 1973, speed limits were reduced to 55 mph ("double nickel"). To protect themselves from the lurking police cruisers ("smokey bears"), truckers ("18-wheelers") purchased CB units in large numbers. Those without CBs are termed "bear bait" by CBers. The growth of CBs among truckers and the growing awareness of its safety and entertainment value spread to consumers. In January 1973, CB license applications numbered 26,682. In January 1975, 79,375 were issued. And, by January 1976, 544,742 applications were awaiting processing at the FCC's center in Gettysburg.[1]

The country experienced a CB explosion with industry sales growing from 800,000 units in 1973 to 1.9 million in 1974 and to 4.3 million in 1975. Estimates for 1976 sales vary, but most authorities figure that they will be in the range of 8 to 10 million units. Demand still exceeds supply, but the gap is closing rapidly as firms expand capacity or enter the market for the first time. Demand for 1976 is estimated to be about 12 million units, and sales are estimated to be in the range of $1.9 billion to $2.5 billion, making the CB market the second largest consumer electronics market in the country and a strong contender for the top position held by color television.[2]

In addition to direct product sales, several other huge markets have opened, such as recordings (C. W. McCall's "Convoy" sold 5 million copies); a TV series ("Movin' On"); movies (such as "White Line Fever"); and publications (a $2.95 paperback dictionary of CB terms, *CB Land,* sold over a quarter of a million copies).

As one can imagine, the growth of companies in the industry has been astonishing. Hy-Gain, one of the leaders, reported first quarter 1976 sales of five times that for the same period in 1975. Pathcom, the dominant supplier in the U.S., has experienced sales growth from $2 million in 1972 to $52 million in 1975. For the first six months of 1976, Pathcom reported sales of $63.7 million compared with $15.7 million for the same period of 1975, a four-fold increase.[3] In addition, net income growth between 1975 and 1976 kept pace with sales.

The Personal Communications Market

Never before had it been possible for the mass market to enjoy two-way communication with unnamed people over a distance of five to fifteen miles. The advent of CB, two-way radio service (Class D) has made it possible for truckers, shut-ins, traveling salespeople, and the First Lady ("First Mama") to have something in common and to be able to share experiences without direct personal contact.

According to *Time* magazine, CB radio has had the largest impact on communications since the advent of the telephone. CB allows the user to be creative and actively involved in a two-way medium in contrast to television where he is passive and nonparticipating. The cultural impact is yet to be assessed but seems to involve a change in American slang and the development of "an egalitarian, anti-authoritarian philosophy."[4]

CB is making an indelible mark on society. New modes of expression have opened for many and a whole new world has become available. In fact, one CB purchaser told me he had just purchased a CB and that he had driven the highways near his home for several hours, totally oblivious to the time and completely absorbed by the conversations he heard or participated in.

Amitai Etzioni, a world renowned sociologist, feels that CB permits its user to take on a false personality, becoming whatever one wishes to become —tall, rich, beautiful, etc. Etzioni believes that the CB allows people to relate to others without getting too involved or completely investing themselves in the relationship.[5]

The Side Effects of CB Fever

In addition to providing a release from the tension and tedium of driving, the CB has become useful in the public safety area. Many CBers have started to use the radio as a means of helping drivers in distress, reporting stolen or dangerously driven vehicles ('Harvey Wallbangers"), and in helping each other avoid traffic tie-ups. In fact, many police vehicles are equipped with CBs, as well as their land mobile radio sets. An organization of CBers, REACT (Radio Emergency Citizens Teams) has a membership of over 70,000 in all fifty states. Since its founding in 1962, it claims to have responded to 35 million emergency calls of which 12 million were highway accidents.[6]

Of course, the medium has its problems, too. Prostitution rings ("Pavement Princesses") have begun to use CB radios to entice prospects. People have come to abuse the rights of others to use the twenty-three channels ("ratchet jaws") to the point that some say that all one can hear in metropolitan areas is "one loud buzz." The gap between supply and demand for the sets has stimulated widespread theft of units from autos and shops. On the other side, CB radios have become another tool in the thief's bag. The CB frequently is used by criminals to relay information about police activity in the vicinity of a crime. Finally, the abuse of CB power output regulations has resulted in the development of linear amplifier units which, while extending the range of units, cause television and radio interference, the source of which is all but impossible to identify or stop.[7]

To date, it has been difficult to deal with most of these problems with the exception of the channel overload situation. The Federal Communications Commission (FCC) augmented the number of channels for CB usage from twenty-three to forty, effective January 1, 1977. In addition, the FCC has tightened the type acceptance specifications for CBs, a move the major producers hope will upgrade the industry image and force out marginal suppliers. The ultimate channel expansion is still at issue with the FCC. An interim measure, which some believe is essential for continued growth of the industry, is an expansion to 115 channels. Many consider this a mere "Band-aid" with total expansion of the spectrum available for CB usage considered the longer run solution. If the potential market is to be tapped, it is apparent that the number of channels and the available frequency range will have to be expanded.

Characteristics of the Market

Contrary to popular belief, today's CB purchaser is not only a truck driver or blue collar worker, but rather he or she comes from a much broader spectrum of society. For instance, the CB has become almost as important as a briefcase to field salespeople. As one source reports:

> "It is believed that the average buyer is a 35-year old who earns $15,000 per year. He is a high school graduate with some college, married, and lives in a three- to four-bedroom home.

The man has a 50/50 chance of being a blue or white collar worker, he is outdoor-oriented and has a 75 percent probability of watching football on television. A recent Gallup poll found the user to be male, 18–34 years of age, $7,000–$15,000 income. It also found that 7 percent of households had CBs." [8]

In addition to purchaser characteristics and trends, there are significant shifts in where CBs are used and where they are purchased. As shown in Table 1, the major growth area in usage between 1974 and 1975 was in passenger vehicles where a shift from 62 percent to 75 per cent was experienced.

TABLE 1   *Mobile equipment usage*
SOURCE: Jon D. Gruber, "Institutional Research Report—Pathcom, Inc.," Robertson, Coleman, Siebel, and Weisel, Member, New York Stock Exchange, Inc., San Francisco, May 25, 1976. Reprinted from *Popular Electronics* 1975 and 1974 surveys.

	1975		1974
Passenger car	70.1%	} 75.1	62.0%
Personal van	5.0		
Personal truck	27.2	} 36.4	45.2
Commercial truck	9.2		
Recreational vehicle	12.4		8.6
Boat	4.9		6.2
Farm vehicle	2.2		2.8

Purchasing patterns are changing as well. Table 2 presents survey results from *Popular Electronics* for the period 1973 through 1975. As might be expected, there has been a move away from the specialist type outlet to the department and discount stores as the market for CBs has widened.

TABLE 2   *CB radios place of purchase*
SOURCE: Jon D. Gruber, "Institutional Research Report—Pathcom, Inc.," Robertson, Coleman, Siebel, and Weisel, Member, New York Stock Exchange, Inc., San Francisco, May 25, 1976. Reprinted from *Popular Electronics* 1975 survey.

	1975		1974		1975	
CB/communication dealer	36.5%	} 72.2	53.0%	} 80.0	38.2%	} 81.5
Electronics store	35.7		27.0		43.3	
Department store	11.1	} 23.3				
Discount store	6.9		16.1		16.7	
Automotive supply	5.3					

The Potential Market for CBs

The market potential for CBs is large compared to current levels of penetration. One estimate, prepared by securities dealer, Robertson, Coleman, Siebel, and Weisel, as part of an underwriting progress report on Pathcom is shown in Table 3.

TABLE 3   *Demand model*
SOURCE: Jon D. Gruber, "Institutional Research Report—Pathcom, Inc.," Robertson, Coleman, Siebel, and Weisel, Member, New York Stock Exchange, Inc., San Francisco, May 25, 1976. Reprinted from *Popular Electronics* 1975 survey.

End Market	No. of Vehicles (Millions)	CB Sets in Use (millions) Current	Possible	Percentage of Penetration Current	Possible
Passenger cars	100.0	5.0	30.0	5%	30%
Small trucks	22.0	1.0	10.0	5	50
Long-haul trucks	3.0	1.5	3.0	50	100
Boats	2.5	0.5	2.0	5	50
Campers/recreation vehicles	5.0	1.0	5.0	20	100
Home/office	60.0	2.0	15.0	3	20
Portable use	N/A	1.0	10.0		
Total		12.0*	75.0–80.0		

*March 1, 1976.

Assuming the 75–80 million unit estimate is accurate, there are still a number of factors affecting the rate of market growth. Should only minor channel expansion plans be adopted, for instance to forty channels, then the market could reach saturation by 1980 with annual sales to that point of about 15 million units. If, on the other hand, major channel expansion plans are implemented, as are expected by many, then a sizable replacement market might be created in addition to the first set market. Should this be the case, the growth of the market might be extended or the annual sales level after the channel expansion could be larger than in the minor expansion scenario.

The Future of the Industry

As the demand for CB radios has skyrocketed, it becomes apparent that the rate of growth in the future will be shaped in large part by the extent and type of regulations the FCC imposes on the industry. The FCC has adopted an expansion of the Class D channels from twenty-three to forty, effective January 1977, and is discussing the creation of a new Class E Citizens Band FM Service. If adopted, these changes would result in a large number of new channels and would require design changes which would significantly increase production costs.

Other considerations about the market also are important to such companies as Pathcom. The following statement appeared in its prospectus for a 600,000 share common stock offering:

"At present the CB radio industry is experiencing remarkable growth, and demand for CB radios currently exceeds supply . . . At this time the number of such buyers, the number of persons who will purchase two or more units, and the size of the replacement market cannot be estimated. Therefore, no assurance can be given that the current unprecedented rate of growth in CB radio sales will continue. A reduction in demand for CB radios would have material adverse effects on company operations, which presently are heavily concentrated in the CB radio business."[6]

In addition to these uncertainties, the industry is faced with several other major concerns dealing with pricing and the impact of competition not yet visible in the industry. The pricing concern is related to the pricing strategies that may be adopted as the gap between demand and supply is closed.

The second area of major uncertainty is related to the potential impact outsiders, such as the major consumer electronic producers, might have on the established CB suppliers over the next few years as the industry shakes out and as demand growth slows.

CB Radio Suppliers

As with many new products, there are a large number of suppliers in the market today. In the 1976 Personal Communications Show over fifty suppliers displayed products. There are perhaps as many as eighty assemblers in the field today. Again, as is typical of such markets, there are a few dominant producers: Pathcom, E. F. Johnson (Sears supplier), Tandy (Radio Shack), Midland, and Hy-Gain. The total output capability of the industry for 1977 is expected to be about 15 million units. In a few years many authorities suggest that the field will have been narrowed to ten companies or less and the composition may not include the current top ten.

The entry rate of the more traditional and large consumer electronic companies such as Motorola, G. E., Panasonic, Sharp, Superscope, RCA, and others is expected to pick up speed rapidly in 1977-1978. This is an obvious threat to the established producers, but most of the aforementioned companies do not appear to have strong distribution ties in the channels employed by the present CB companies.

Another group of possible entrants to the market are the semiconductor producers such as National Semiconductor. However, because of the comparatively low semiconductor content of the CB compared to the hand calculator or the videogame, for instance, it is not likely that a semiconductor company would be attracted to a major committment in the CB field. If the FCC decides to allow CB operation at higher frequencies, there is the possibility that semiconductor technology or some of its offspring could make a mark and displace current producers who could not, nor care to, adapt.

The Pathcom Story [10]

Like many of its counterparts in the CB market, Pathcom was virtually unknown to the mass market until a few years ago when it entered the CB field. The company was founded in early 1971, and by 1973, net sales were over $2.9 million.

Pathcom, located in Harbor City, California, occupies facilities covering 360,000 square feet. In 1976, employment was approximately 1,000 people with over 850 in production, 35 in product development and engineering, and 115 in sales, advertising, and administration. The company is organized along functional lines and includes operations, engineering, marketing, finance, order service, and administration.

A summary of sales and income since commencement of operations in February 1971 is shown in Table 4. In each year of its operation the company has derived over 90 percent of its net sales and net income from the sale of CBs and related equipment. It also is a producer of nonCB items such as business/industrial radios, marine radios, scan monitor receivers, and communications accessories. The company has achieved and maintained a leadership position in the market and claims to enjoy the largest market share of CB units sold.

TABLE 4   *A summary of sales and income for Pathcom, Inc. (1971–1975)*
Source: Pathcom, Inc., *1975 Annual Report*, p. 18.

	Year Ended December 31				2/1/71 to
	1975	1974	1973	1972	12/31/71
Net sales	$52,193,640	$14,438,626	$5,089,470	$2,093,835	$645,718
Net income	5,315,131	962,337	355,621	109,626	27,044

Pathcom is in a unique position in the industry because it is the only major supplier with significant domestic production and multiple offshore suppliers. In addition, it has a strong product line and access to important channels of distribution.

Robertson, Coleman, Siebel, and Weisel view Pathcom's strengths as (1) U. S. based production with ability to react quickly to changing market conditions, (2) strong brand identification (PACE) associated with quality and performance, (3) strong distribution, service availability nationwide, and effective advertising, (4) financial strength, (5) highly capable top management, and (6) strong market position due to its being the largest in the industry.[11]

Products and Product Development

In 1976, Pathcom had over thirty models of CB radios marketed under the PACE name. Between 75 percent and 80 percent of sales are for mobile units with 15 to 20 percent of sales in base stations and the remainder in portable units.

The company was one of the first to use semiconductor technology and may still be the only one to use a one chip, one crystal, digitally-synthesized CB radio. This technology allows for easy and inexpensive expansion of the channels available to the expanded format adopted by the FCC. Since all but the low end of the line has such large scale integration technology, inventory obsolescence is avoided and retrofitting of existing equipment is feasible.

Distribution and Support [12]

Pathcom markets mainly through a two-step distribution channel. It is represented by seventeen independent commissioned sales organizations containing a total of over 100 salespersons. Most of the distributors and retailers also sell competing lines. No single outlet accounts for more than 5 percent of sales. No direct-to-customer sales are made by Pathcom.

The CB units are sold to over 1,000 independent distributors who in turn sell to a wide variety of retail outlets. Original equipment manufacturer sales are not entertained by the company. Pathcom believes that the auto aftermarket is a major market that will survive the turbulence of the life cycle currently being experienced in the industry. As a result, much of the attention of the company is being directed to the auto dealer who would be the major seller/installer of the CB radio in the future. Pathcom's distributors are directing their attention to the major chain department stores such as Sears, Penney's, May's, and Bullocks. In addition, Pathcom is installing regional service centers to supplement its several hundred independent service stations and the central facility in Los Angeles.

Beyond these tangible evidences of support, Pathcom in 1976 expanded advertising to $6 million nationally in a variety of media. Television is the latest vehicle and will become nationwide by 1977. In 1976, the company advertised in a number of national magazines such as *Time* and *Newsweek,* as well as in such vehicles as United Airlines' *Mainliner Magazine.* The company also advertises in trade publications and other periodicals and furnishes in-store display material and literature to support distributors' activities.

Diversification into Other Markets [13]

In 1976, about 3 percent ($3.5 million) of the company's sales were in nonCB areas, such as business/industrial and marine two-way radios. The market potentials are quite large, however. For example, business/industrial is a $600 million market, and Pathcom already has access to it through its existing channels of distribution. The marine radio field is a little more complex and is currently in a turmoil as a result of recent FCC regulations requiring all AM marine radios to be replaced by VHF–FM equipment by January 1977. Pathcom sales into marine products in 1976 was slightly over $1 million. The company is committed to expansion in this market.

Management Concerns

In coming to grips with areas of major threat and potential, Pathcom management has identified the following:

> "Additional competition could result in an increased supply of lower quality and/or lower-priced CB radios, and these and other factors could result in an oversupply of CB radios and a reduction of present profit margins. Moreover, the entry into the market of large, well-known electronics companies with large engineering and advertising budgets could result in substantial additional competition based on technology, brand name recognition, and distribution strength. Changes in FCC regulations also could initiate technological competition." [14]

Questions

1. Place yourself in the position of a marketing executive for Pathcom and comment on the following:

   a. What are the implications on marketing effort at this stage of the industry and company life cycle?

   b. What kinds of information about consumer shopping and purchasing behavior are needed to properly mount a marketing communications campaign?

   c. What, if anything, can be done to encourage repurchasing and/or increase the number of CB units owned by present users?

   d. What can be done to stimulate new demand for CBs?

   e. Some would argue that CB is a fad, much as the hula hoop. What evidence exists to support or refute this contention? What are the implications for firms if you conclude it is a fad?

2. Now take the position of a major consumer electronics organization's marketing executive and assume that you are contemplating entry into the CB market. Formulate responses to each issue in question 1 above.

3. Discuss the implications for marketing decision making of the consumer learning process associated with the adoption of CB by the mass market.

4. Outline the likely steps in the consumer decision process associated with the purchase of a CB unit. Also, outline and discuss the kinds of market information you would seek to better define the process and to formulate marketing strategies.

5. In the context of product positioning notions, what are some possible areas for strengthening Pathcom's current position? For repositioning the CB concept?

6. For each stage of the consumer decision process associated with the purchase of CB equipment, outline and briefly discuss the marketing management implications in terms of market segmentation possibilities and programming of the marketing mix.

7. For each stage of the product life cycle, what are the likely distributions of consumers at each stage of the decision process, and what pieces of marketing information would you seek to assist you in formulating marketing strategies to cope with the emerging stages of the life cycle?

8. What recommendations would you make to Pathcom for evaluating the effectiveness of its advertising and general promotional programs?

Notes

[1] "The Bodacious New World of CB," *Time,* May 10, 1976, p. 78.

[2] Pathcom, Inc., *1975 Annual Report,* p. 7; See also Lem Buckwalter, *The Wonderful, Wacky World of CB Radio* (New York: Grosset and Dunlap, Inc., October 1976) for a complete guide to CB radio.

[3] Pathcom, Inc., "Second Quarter Report to Shareholders for the Period Ended June 30, 1976."

[4] *Time,* May 10, 1976.

[5] Ibid., p. 79.

[6] Ibid., pp. 78–79.

[7] Ibid.

[8] Jon D. Gruber, "Institutional Research Report—Pathcom, Inc.," Robertson, Coleman, Siebel, and Weisel, Member, New York Stock Exchange, Inc., San Francisco, May 25, 1976.

[9] Pathcom, Inc., "Common Stock Prospectus," January 21, 1976, p. 14.

[10] Compiled from Pathcom, Inc., *1975 Annual Report* and "Second Quarter Report to Shareholders for the Period Ended June 30, 1976."

[11] Gruber, "Institutional Research Report," pp. 13–14.

[12]Ibid., pp. 16–17.

[13]Ibid., p. 17.

[14]Pathcom, Inc., "Common Stock Prospectus," p. 17.

The New Car
Dilemma

This case was prepared by **John F. Willenborg,** *College of Business Administration, University of South Carolina.*

In 1972, our children, Stephen and Laura, were 5 and 3 years old, respectively. While my wife and I were in reasonably good control of the problems attendant with growing children, a crisis situation showed signs of developing. The 5-year old was due to start school in September on a 5-day per week basis.

There were few public kindergartens in the state and none nearby our home. Privately-operated kindergartens, of course, provided no means of transportation. The alternatives seemed clear: (1) skip kindergarten, or (2) sign Stephen up in a private kindergarten and provide transportation.

Our automobile inventory had been one—a 4-year Pontiac Catalina— since my wife Martha's Volkswagen had been stolen several years earlier. The Pontiac replaced the only other car I had ever owned, a 1958 Chevrolet Biscayne, bought as a used car in 1964.

As early as the summer of 1971, Martha had reminded me of the need to buy a second car when transportation to school became necessary. On many occasions after the Volkswagen was stolen, she complained about the inconvenience of being a one-car family. Needs had to be anticipated. If a shopping trip was in order, it had to be done in the evening, or on the weekend when stores were crowded, or when she could drive me to work and pick me up in the evening.

Unanticipated needs presented the worst problems. "What if one of the children had an accident and I was without a car?" Martha had asked. "What would I do?"

When the Pontiac required service, everyone was inconvenienced. It was particularly unpleasant for me because I usually drove the car to the university and back home in the late afternoon. Thus, I felt the problem to an even greater degree.

A fairly strong case for a second car was being constructed. I had always agreed with the existence of a need, but felt that we had learned to live with the inconveniences very well. There seemed to be a clear-cut economic advantage to having only the Pontiac. Therefore, I put off serious consideration of the issue as long as possible. After all, the thought of having to draw upon hard-earned savings was not a pleasant one. Nor was the prospect of car payments for one to three years very bright. And when would the Pontiac need to be replaced? It was already nearly four years old.

In January 1972, Christmas-related bills came due, and we dipped into our savings account. The inconvenience of the fall semester with me coming home early to let Martha use the car, or Martha taking me to work and picking me up, was temporarily pushed out of my mind. I reminded her several times that it would be difficult to afford a car in the upcoming months, particularly since my salary at the university ended in June (I was on a nine-month contract).

In April, I was forced to cancel two tennis matches because the logistics of the car could not be worked out to accommodate family needs. In May, the Pontiac's water pump had to be replaced for the second time in less than six months.

Just before final exams in late May, Martha remarked one evening that she had stopped in at a Datsun dealership that day and had checked the prices. The salesperson on duty had indicated that Datsun was involved in a national campaign for the environment. Whenever a person took a test drive in a Datsun, the company would plant a tree some place in the United States. Martha said she didn't have time to drive the car then. "Why don't we stop in and drive one on Saturday?" she asked me.

"Martha, that's just a gimmick some ad agency dreamed up. Big deal. They probably won't plant the tree anyway."

On Saturday, we drove several Datsuns. The kids had a ball in the back seat. (The salesperson didn't think he and the kids would fit in the back seat, so we went out by ourselves.) Both of us shared the opinion that the cars were a bit smallish, but fairly comfortable. My father (who is 6'3") had always said that he wouldn't buy a car unless he could wear a hat while sitting behind the wheel (it was cold in Iowa and he had sinus trouble). I'm also 6'3" and had to bend slightly to see out of the front window and to avoid messing my hair. When I mentioned that to Martha, she reminded me that she would usually be driving the little car.

I commented further that the car seemed "tinny" and that all the colors were "garish." She agreed, but countered with, "It sure moves out faster than the Pontiac. Would be great in heavy traffic."

"That's true," I said.

After we had signed our request that Datsun plant a tree somewhere, we climbed back in the Pontiac and headed home.

By the time we had finished our test drive, it was after 5:30 p.m., and we were in the middle of rush-hour traffic. The drive home lasted nearly a half-hour. We were both acutely aware of the time and distance involved. "How would you like this trip every time the Datsun needed service?" I asked Martha.

For several weeks, the subject of the new car was not mentioned. One evening in early July, we were both "turned on" by a T.V. commercial for a car which had been selling well since its introduction into the market, the

Mercury Capri. Martha and I agreed to get a baby-sitter for the children the next afternoon and look at the Capri and some other small cars.

When we arrived at the Mercury dealership, we looked around the lot (I didn't want to attract the attention of a salesperson, whose presence looking over my shoulder always made me nervous). We saw several cars that seemed to fall into the small-car category, but none of them were very exciting. Finally, we saw a bright red Capri, conspicuously parked directly in front of the showroom. The door was unlocked, so I started to get in, finding that the seat was pushed too far forward to allow me to get past the steering wheel. After several minutes, I was able to push the seat back far enough to get in. I found myself looking through the upper third of the windshield. My head was flush against the roof, and, if I hunched forward, I could see some distance in front of the car. "Maybe it has a reclining seat back," I speculated.

"Martha, close the door so I can get a feel for the size of this thing." The first time she pushed the door, it didn't close. When I moved my elbow, the door closed on her second try.

When I got out, I said, "No way. Japanese must make this car for Japanese. (I didn't realize the car was not manufactured in Japan.) I don't care how fast it'll get to 60 miles per hour. I couldn't ride in this thing for ten minutes before I'd have to get out and stretch!"

"But it's a beautiful little car. I'd love to drive one," Martha said.

I looked up and saw a salesperson approaching. "Let's go up the street and look at the Dodges and Plymouths. I think their cars have more room. They're generally made 'boxier' and more conservatively."

The Dodge-Plymouth dealer's lot was packed with new cars, in contrast to most other lots we'd passed. There were many cars in the Falcon and Dart categories. The colors were not attractive, but there were many from which to choose. We talked to the salesperson who was confident he could find the color combination we wanted.

"What do you think, Martha?" I said on the way home. We had spent nearly an hour talking to the salesperson, looking at his card file of cars in stock, and trying to get a feel for how much of a reduction he would give us from the sticker price. We drove a Dart Swinger within a several block radius of the showroom. "Lots of room in those cars—not bad-looking either. And I think we can really get a great price. Did you ever see more cars in the lot? They really are overstocked."

"Looks pretty good. I agree," Martha said. "But I felt like we were driving in a box. And it had rather poor acceleration, don't you think?"

"Well, it is going to be a second car, you know."

She seemed disappointed. "I'll go by the Chevy place tomorrow. A lot of people are buying Vegas, I hear. Or is it Novas? I'll take a look at them on the way home."

The next day, at the site of the largest Chevrolet dealer within 100 miles (according to their advertisement), I found exactly one Nova (the big seller), and it was a sort of sherbet orange color that didn't appeal to me at all. There were many Vegas, all seemingly the same dark green color. I drove one and asked the salesperson about a piece in the paper recently about factory call-backs of Vegas. He agreed that there had been some problems, but didn't think they were serious. "Only one chance in a thousand that the defect will show up," he noted.

Despite my feeling that a Chevy was a sound car (my 1958 was a gem), I couldn't get "turned on" by the Vega, and the Nova was not readily available. And I liked the Dodge Dart Swinger better, anyway.

When Martha and I discussed the matter that evening, we wondered about the next step. "What about Fords?" she querried.

"Wouldn't have one if it was given to me," I replied. "The most economical model they make is the Pinto, and I've heard nothing good about them. In fact, two of my marketing colleagues, Bill and Taylor, have been driving one for free. Ford is involved in some promotional program with universities across the country, and they've given the cars to marketing professors who are to get their students involved in projects with the car, research, and test driving, and whatever else they can think of."

"Why don't you get good deals like that?" she asked, sounding frustrated over the whole thing. "Let's go look at a Maverick."

"Okay, but I think we're at a disadvantage with American cars. The manufacturers are already tooling up for the 1973 models. We'll have to take what's left and the best ones are already sold. But, we can look."

It was ten days or so before I could get motivated to go looking again. We agreed that the Pinto was too small and, apparently, put together with bailing wire. The Maverick was a plain little car, not exciting at all. I liked its looks except that it had this crazy little shelf across the front (just below the dashboard) and no glove compartment. If the shelf were used, I speculated, a sudden stop would mean flying objects in the front seat. We weren't impressed overall, but I did drive a Maverick briefly. It handled nicely in traffic and had pretty good acceleration. But I just couldn't get "turned on" by that crazy idea for a dashboard.

It was now mid-August and the start of school was less than three weeks away. "What's next?" I wondered.

"How about a Toyota?" Martha asked one night.

"I had thought about that possibility, but the dealership is way over near the Datsun dealer. The prospect of having to take the car over there for service is not pleasant. And I understand they are a bit more expensive than the comparable Datsuns."

Martha then reminded me of a new dealership which she had driven by, much more accessible than the original one. It sold only Toyotas (in contrast to the other, which also sold Volvo and Mercedes) and was advertising heavily on the radio. I recalled seeing recently a Toyota Mark II (one of Toyota's more expensive models) and being impressed with it. "Well, what do we have to lose? We can go tomorrow afternoon."

The showroom of the new Toyota dealer (Toyota Town) displayed four cars: a Mark II, two Corollas (one a station wagon), and a Celica (a new sporty-type Toyota). We walked around and looked at price stickers for about ten minutes before a salesperson came over and introduced himself as Fred. We asked all the relevant questions about mileage, trunk space, and service. The Corolla got slightly better mileage than the Mark II, but the Mark II had slightly more horsepower. The rear seat in the Corolla folded down, greatly increasing the storage capacity. The Mark II had a lot of extras for more comfort and had somewhat more interior room. There were more Corollas from which to choose. Obviously, the Mark II cost more (about 15 percent more on sticker price than the Corollas).

Fred explained that Toyota's model year began in January or February or whenever the cars were ready. So, there would be no problem in obtaining cars during August or September. However, he wasn't sure about the Mark II, because it was to be upgraded to a much larger car with six cylinders in 1973. When I asked Fred why, he said he didn't know.

While we were test driving the Mark II, I asked Fred, "What do we really have to pay for a Mark II like the one in the showroom? How much below the sticker price?"

"The sticker price on foreign cars is what you pay. There is a very small margin on them. They're not like American-made cars. I might be able to get you fifty bucks off, but that's about it. And demand is very high for Toyotas. We haven't been able to get all the cars we want."

"Come off it, Fred," I said. "You have a new dealership and your competitor (Thom's) has been in business for years. You mean to say you'll let them beat you out of a sale on a price basis?"

"Well, I don't know. You're right to some extent. We are trying to establish ourselves in this market. Just tell me which car you want and I'll see what I can do."

I liked the Mark II I had driven and I think Martha did, too. It seemed to be made better than the Datsuns, roomier than the Capris and Pintos, and there were quite a few on the lot from which to choose. The price was the big hangup, and I didn't like the Corolla well enough to buy it at the lower price.

Back at the showroom, while Fred went to get some brochures for us, we looked at the cars on the floor again. Martha sat in the Celica. "Sure wish we could buy a sports car like this one," she said.

"But it's not practical for us. Look at the back seat. There's not enough room for one person. The trunk is very small. And we'd be paying for the fancy instrumentation. And this has off-white upholstery. Wouldn't the kids have a time with that!"

On the way home, Martha again remarked that she had liked the Mark II, but that she still thought the sports car was a good idea. She liked Fred. She thought the new dealership probably would treat its customers with great care. But, most of all, she wanted to buy a car and have it over with. I argued that Fred ought to be willing to take less for the Mark II. So I said I would go over to Thom's in the morning and see what they would do price-wise.

The salesperson's name at Thom's was Harold. When I told him we were looking at cars at Toyota Town, he said he could beat any price they offered by $100. He had several Mark IIs and one Celica. "How about letting me drive the Celica around the block?" I asked. When I got into the car, I slid the seat back all the way and was surprised that I was very comfortable. And since the seat also reclined, I had plenty of head room when the seat back was lowered a notch. On the highway, the engine did not falter noticeably when I turned on the air conditioning (which had happened on most of the other small cars I'd driven). The car handled well and I began to appreciate the sports car features.

When I got back, Harold was ready to sell me either the Celica or any Mark II on the lot. I put him off because the ride in the Celica had changed some of my decision criteria. The need for trunk space didn't seem so pressing (we wouldn't travel long distances in it anyway); the back seat was certainly large enough for two small children; and a sports car would have good resale value. "Let me talk it over with my wife," I said.

When I got to the office, I called Fred and told him what Harold had said about the price. Fred was quiet for a minute, then said he didn't know how Harold could do it. But, he said he would do what he could for me. I said that we might come back over in the evening.

I told Martha about the price dealings, but not about my impression of the Celica. That evening, we went to Toyota Town again. While we waited for Fred to return from dinner, we looked at the Mark IIs in the lot again and then ended up in the showroom in the Celica with the white upholstery. "Do you think we could get by with a car like this?" I asked.

When she answered enthusiastically in the affirmative, I asked, "What about the lack of trunk space? What about the light upholstery? What about the higher price?" Her answers corresponded almost exactly with those I had arrived at that afternoon. She agreed that the white upholstery was not practical, but the other points were minor. She looked dumbfounded when I said, "If we can get a different color with different upholstery and can get Fred to come down further on the price, should we buy the Celica?"

Before she could answer, Fred returned and I asked him about other models. He said he could call around to other dealers and ask, but the Celicas were big sellers and he wasn't optimistic. "We'll have more cars shipped into Jacksonville about September 1, but we never know what we'll get," he said.

I shook my head. "I don't know, Fred. We like the Celica, but not the white upholstery. I'd like to deal with you, but Thom's is willing to beat your price on either a Mark II or a Celica. Any suggestions?"

He took out a pad and began to figure. "On the Celica, I can give you this price (about $50 higher than Thom's). But I can't even do that if I have to call around and get a car from another dealer."

"Fred," I said, "sell me this Celica at the same price that I could get the one at Thom's and I'll take it with the light upholstery." Fred didn't look happy, but said he would ask his boss (the same strategy followed by every salesperson I'd ever dealt with).

While he was gone, Martha said I was being ridiculous to quibble over $50. She also pointed out that if we waited for a new shipment at Jacksonville, school would have started, and there would be no guarantee that we'd get the right color anyway. I had already thought of that, but didn't want to give in. When Fred returned, he said, "I got him to take off another $25, but that's rock bottom." Now I did have a dilemma. I looked at Martha and her look was unmistakeable. I told Fred that we'd take it.

In the weeks that followed, several things of interest happened. I noticed that the car had received a safety inspection in April. Thus, it had been in the showroom for at least that long before we bought it. I calculated that we had spent $400 more than we had intended, had less trunk space, and got poorer mileage than we had been looking for. I saw several gold Celicas with black interiors (the color I had liked) on the road.

On a more positive side, I noted that a foreign student of mine, who was very soft spoken and clearly conservative, had purchased a new Dodge Dart Swinger. I was relieved that I hadn't pursued that idea further. In January, I read that the Celica had won an award as Import Car of the Year for 1973. Even more significant was the favorable reaction of some of my colleagues who vowed to me that they were going to talk their wives into letting them buy a sports car next time, too. I didn't describe to them the way in which I had made the decision to buy the sports car.

Questions

1. Was the decision process typical or atypical? Explain.

2. Comprehensive decision process models dealing with buyer behavior have been developed in recent years. Explain how the decision process in this case conforms to or departs from such models.

3. Prepare a flow chart describing how the "new car dilemma" was resolved.

4. Does the process described in this case seem to represent one decision with many stages or many different decisions? Describe the major and minor influences on each stage or on each decision.

5. Explain which of the following concepts have applicability to the decision making in this case and describe how they apply: reference group influence; family influences; attitudes; brand loyalty; learning processes; family life cycle; personality; prepurchase and postpurchase dissonance.

Managerial Use of Behavioral Concepts:
Its Interface with Consumer Protection

This case was prepared by **Creighton Frampton,** *School of Business Administration, University of Richmond.*

The Office of Consumer Affairs (OCA) of the Department of Agriculture and Commerce of the State of Virginia receives complaints from consumers concerning deceptive advertising and other consumer problems. Staff limitations prevent the agency from investigating every complaint, but all complaints are accepted and reviewed. Only complaints of deceptive acts, not covered by the authority of another agency, are investigated in depth. The following are incidents which have been reported to OCA.

Incident 1: Personal Selling—
The Principle of Empathy

Three weeks ago, Mr. and Mrs. Smith bought a new automobile. And now the Smiths feel they were cheated and want their money back. The Smiths' story goes like this:

"My wife and I had been thinking about buying a new car for over a year. I usually do business with the A. B. Car Company. I bought my last three cars from them and have been satisfied with each one, but I saw a lot of TV commercials for a new dealer named Economy Car Company that promised the best deal in town. Well, like my wife says, as tight as money is today, I thought we ought to at least look into what they had to offer.

"We went by Economy one Wednesday afternoon and started looking around the showroom. They had some fine looking cars, but the prices didn't look low to me. After a few minutes, a salesperson came over and introduced himself and began asking a lot of questions concerning the price range and type of car we needed. He seemed interested in our problems, but the wife felt he got 'too personal'. We finally narrowed down our choice between two models. The salesperson arranged for us to take a test drive so we could compare how both cars performed on the road. I noticed he kept asking my wife questions and pointing out the various features of the car to her, but she didn't say much. She never does talk much outside of the home.

269

"When we got back from the last test drive, the salesperson suggested my wife and I go into his office and talk the purchase over between us. He said he had something to check on and would leave us alone for about ten minutes. Well, I welcomed the opportunity to talk things over with the missus without his interference. When we were alone, I told my wife I liked the more expensive car but was not sure it was worth the extra dollars. She said she felt the cheaper car was the better buy, but we should stop by the old A. B. Car Company and see what they had to offer since the prices here seemed rather high. We agreed to tell the salesperson we would think over the proposition and come back a week later. We still had a few minutes to wait for the salesperson, so we just shot the breeze about my wife's upcoming election for president of the garden club.

When the salesperson returned, he began to chat about some of his other customers and their wives. I remember his mentioning that Mrs. Jones, the president of the PTA, had just bought a car like the expensive one we were considering. We had a cup of coffee with him and talked for about fifteen more minutes. The next thing I knew the salesman was slapping me on the back and telling me I had made a wise purchase.

"Well, everything was O.K. for several weeks. I liked the car even though I felt I had spent more than I should have. Then my wife comes home one day and tells me she had learned from the wife of a salesperson at A. B. Car Company that the Economy Car Company had placed listening devices in all its offices. She explained the salesperson had eavesdropped on what was supposed to be our private conversation. Well, she has been in a bad mood anyway since losing the garden club election, and this invasion of our privacy has her burned up. I think we were tricked into buying this car and I want my money back."

A brief check of the company's sales offices by OCA revealed that they do contain listening devices. When the manager of the company was questioned concerning the listening devices, he made the following statement.

"The most important characteristic for a salesperson to develop is empathy. He must be able to determine what is on a customer's mind so he can see the problem through the customer's eyes. Unfortunately, this is often difficult. Customers seldom reveal their true needs and fears to a salesperson. By using the listening device, my sales staff is able to determine where the real blocks to closing a sale lie. This allows them to meet the customer's needs more efficiently. Both the customer and the salesperson benefit from this progressive selling technique."

Questions

1. One well-founded behavioral principle of personal selling is that successful sales representatives are ones who have empathy toward clients. What are your opinions about the method the Economy Car Company used to obtain consumer information? Does it differ from other behavioral research techniques? Where is the boundary between methods which are ethical and those which are not?

2. Are there any federal or state laws which pertain to this situation? If so, what are they? If not, would you propose one? What?

3. What action as an OCA board member would you take in this situation? Explain.

Incident 2: "MUD"—
Satisfying Consumer Wants

A group of vacationers returning from Chapel Hill, North Carolina, has raised a complaint against a small grocery store operator. The store has been selling a type of clay found in the area as a food supplement. The clay usually is mixed with food to add bulk. To obtain more information on the case, a telephone call was made to the grocer. The following notes were made during this conversation.

The grocer was questioned to determine if he were misrepresenting a product or making any false product claims.

Grocer: "I don't deceive nobody. It's mud, and I have it marked 'MUD.' I don't have to tell what it's good for and how to use it. My customers already know all about it."

OCA: "Why do your customers buy this mud?"

Grocer: "It's cheap and they like the taste. Heck, with the way prices is going up, mud is almost all my customers has got money to buy."

OCA: "Is it really safe to eat this mud?"

Grocer: "Folks 'round here been eating mud for years, and nobody ever complained about getting sick from it."

OCA: "Don't you feel that you are taking advantage of the poor and uneducated?"

Grocer: "Why, heck, some of my best customers is them knee-jerk liberals over yonder at the university. They eats it up like chitlins and they ain't dumb. They is educated."

OCA: "How can you justify selling a product that has no food value?"

Grocer: "I'm providing a service by making the mud easy to get. Before, folks had to go out and dig it up themselves. I also do the processin' and baggin'."

OCA: "Then you intend to continue selling mud?"

Grocer: "Sure do. As long as folks want to buy it, I'll sell it. Ain't that what business is all about?"

Questions

1. Is the North Carolina store owner deceiving customers about the product that he sells? Why or why not?

2. Is the grocer providing a useful product or service for customers? Is he supplying a product which some consumers want? Explain.

3. Is the grocer, to some degree, using the marketing concept? Explain.

4. Are there legal statutes prohibiting the sale of the product? If so, what? If not, would you propose one? Explain.

5. What action would you as an OCA board member take in this situation? Explain.

Incident 3: Advertising— Using Source Credibility

An outraged consumer, Mr. Jones, has raised a complaint concerning the ethics of a television commercial he saw recently. Mr. Jones' story:

"Let me start by saying that I'm a religious person. That's one reason why I feel so strongly about this commercial. You must have seen it. It's the one in which this person dressed like a priest is giving a strong pitch for an automobile. He says, 'You can take it from me as gospel that this car is a good buy.' Even though the commercial states that the person is a priest, I don't believe it's true. A priest just wouldn't do such a thing. I think it's just an actor giving a prepared sales talk.

"Even if this guy is some kind of priest who actually owns one of those cars, I still don't think the ad should be allowed. I was taught that doing what a priest said to do would help you get to Heaven. This commercial sort of gives you the feeling that buying the car is a religious obligation.

"At any rate, this commercial is in poor taste. It downgrades religion in general to have a priest act like a huckster hawking for products. I find it very offensive. It should be stopped."

Questions

Research in persuasion has shown that an audience is influenced more by a source they perceive as high in credibility (trustworthiness, expertise, prestige) as opposed to one they perceive as low in credibility. Given this "principle" of human behavior, answer the following questions.

1. Assuming the "priest" is portrayed by an actor, do you feel the commercial is illegal? Unethical? Why or why not?

2. Assuming the person in the commercial is a priest by profession and does, in fact, own the car, do you feel the commercial is illegal? Unethical? Why or why not?

3. Do you feel the commercial would be effective if the *target* audience perceives the priest as a credible source? Why or why not?

4. Are there any audience factors which could negate the priest's source credibility? If so, what are they?

Incident 4: Advertising—
Using Subliminal Messages

This case was brought to the attention of OCA by Mr. Ash, an employee at a television station. In the process of repairing a split in the film of a commercial, Mr. Ash found what he believes to be subliminal cuts. Ash describes the commercial as follows:

"The color TV commercial opens with a housewife and child leaving home and entering a new car. The woman is identified as Lee Breedlove, whose husband is a famous race car driver. As the woman looks at the instrument panel of the car, there is a quick cut, and for one-sixth of a second, a black and white image of Mrs. Breedlove in the cockpit of a race car is flashed on the screen. Then the commercial returns to color and shows a typical family driving scene. Then follows another cut in black and white showing Mrs. Breedlove adjusting a racing helmet just before the end of the commercial.

"These cuts are too quick for a person watching the commercial to see. I had seen the commercial many times without being aware they were there. If I had not examined the film closely, I would not have known of their existence. Even after I knew what to look for, I was still unable to detect the cuts when the commercial was shown on television. These cuts represent a deliberate attempt to provide the car with a racy image. Since the commercial communicates at a subliminal level, I believe the consumer is being manipulated without being aware of the fact that he is being exposed to the stimuli. This kind of mind control should not be allowed."

Questions

Subliminal perception concerns the reception and interpretation of stimuli at a level below the conscious threshold. Subliminal advertising transmits stimuli at a speed faster than the conscious mind can process it, but not too fast for the subconscious level of the mind.

1. Do you feel that subliminal advertising motivates consumers without awareness to purchase products? Why or why not?

2. Do you feel subliminal advertising is unethical? Why or why not?

The Second National Bank of Capital City: The Impact of Store Choice Behavior on the Adoption of Service Innovations

This case was prepared by **Dale M. Lewison** *and* **Roger Cannaday,** *College of Business Administration, University of South Carolina.*

The Second National Bank of Capital City in Columbia, South Carolina, was chartered in 1920 and is now the second largest commercial bank (in total deposits) in the state. The bank's current facilities consist of a central bank and twenty-seven branch outlets. The central bank serves as the center of banking operations and is located in downtown Columbia (Standard Metropolitan Statistical Area population 341,000), the state's largest city. Second National's statewide facilities consist of a centrally located outlet in each of the state's eighteen principal cities (populations ranging from 32,000 to 280,000).

In its early years, the bank's management philosophies were quite conservative under its now retired founder, J. P. Homestead. While the present board chairman, Arthur B. King, and the current president, Malcom S. Hargrave, have followed a somewhat more aggressive management philosophy, Mr. Homestead's conservative influence is still prevalent in many of the major policy decisions. Several of the bank's top managers feel that it was Mr. Homestead's conservative influence that helped Second National avoid the recent problem of overextending on high-risk loans, which led to the collapse of several banks during the 1973–1975 period, including one in Columbia.

Second National's current operating philosophy was described accurately by one competitor as "progress through discretion." In past years, Second National's management has adopted banking innovations only when there was sufficient evidence that the innovation was in the best interest of the bank and its customers. These policies have created a consumer image of reliability, an image most managers feel is one of the bank's strongest assets. Recently, however, there has been considerable pressure by some of the bank's younger managers to initiate more progressive policies. John F. Peterson, vice-president of marketing and research, feels that the bank's management should be more receptive to banking innovations. Mr. Peterson believes that increasing competition, in terms of new competitors and new competitive marketing strategies, will require early adoption of new technologies and approaches if Second National is to maintain or increase its present growth.

The Banking Industry

The trend in recent years has been toward greater competition among commercial banks as well as intensified competition with other financial institutions, such as savings and loan associations, mutual savings banks, and credit unions. From 1950 to 1974, the commercial banks' share of total deposits had dropped from 81.5 percent to 66.5 percent, while savings and loan associations and credit unions had gained and mutual savings banks remained about the same.

A comparison of branching practices among these financial institutions is presented in Table 1. The number of commercial banks initially declined, then increased slowly while the number of locations more than doubled from 1.3 to 3.0 locations per institution. This number is held down considerably by the thirteen unit banking states which allow only one location per institution, and by the nineteen states which allow only limited branching, usually countywide. In the more populous states where statewide branching is allowed, it is not uncommon for one institution to have 50 to 100 branches. The profit margins of commercial banks have been narrowed significantly in recent years, due in part to the rapid expansion of the number of banking offices.

TABLE 1   *Number of selected financial institutions and locations, 1950–1974*

SOURCES: Federal Reserve Board, U.S. League of Savings Associations, National Association of Mutual Savings Banks, Credit Union National Association.

Year	Commercial Banks		Savings and Loan Associations	
	Institutions	*Locations*	*Institutions*	*Locations*
1950	14,121	18,966	5,992	N/A
1960	13,471	23,954	6,320	7,931
1970	13,686	35,330	5,669	9,987
1974	14,458	42,890	5,102	13,922

Year	Mutual Savings Banks		Credit Unions	
	Institutions	*Locations*	*Institutions*	*Locations*
1950	529	742	10,591	N/A
1960	514	1,000	20,456	N/A
1970	493	1,580	23,456	N/A
1974	479	2,121	22,889	23,500 (est.)

The Product-Service Mix

Commercial banks offer a wide array of financial services to individuals, firms, institutions, government, and other types of organizations. These services include storage of funds for safekeeping in interest-bearing accounts (savings accounts), storage of funds in noninterest-bearing accounts (checking accounts) for day-to-day transactions, loans for a variety of purposes, trust services, safe deposit boxes for valuable personal items, traveler's checks and money orders, payroll check and check cashing services, financial planning, investment counseling, and similar services. While commercial banks offer a wide range of services to both commercial and retail consumers, not all services are offered by all banks. The product-service offering of each bank facility is shown in Table 2.

TABLE 2 *Product-service offering by facility type*

Service	Full Service Bank	Limited Service Bank	Automated Teller Machine	Point of Sale Terminal
Open accounts	X	X		
Make loans	X			
Cash withdrawals	X	X	X	
Deposits	X	X	X	
Transfers	X	X	X	
Loan payments	X	X	X	
Credit card payments	X	X	X	
Other bill payments	X	X	X	
Determine current balance	X	X	X	
Trust services	X			
Safe deposit boxes	X			
Financial counseling	X			
Cash third party checks	X	X		
Purchase traveler's checks	X	X		
Purchase cashier's checks	X	X		
Purchase money orders	X	X		
Check authorization	X	X		X
Credit card authorization	X	X		X
Debit card authorization (to allow immediate transfer of funds from buyer's to seller's account)	X	X		X

The Operating Environment

The overall environment in which the banking industry operates is illustrated in Figure 1. The general state of the economy affects the level of checking

FIGURE 1   *The banking environment*

SOURCE: Rex O. Bennett, *Bank Location Analysis,* (Washington, D.C.: American Bankers Association, 1975) p. 5.

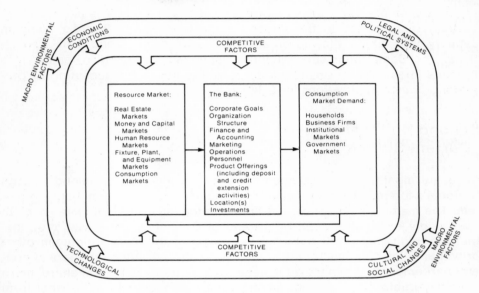

and savings deposits, the demand for personal and commercial loans, and the costs of resources. Cultural and social factors such as attitudes toward the use of credit, attitudes toward women as customers, pressure for greater social responsibility, and the continuing redistribution of the population into the suburbs affect banking operations.

As a quasi-utility, the banking industry has been subject to a high degree of government control and regulation. Regulatory agencies include the Federal Reserve Board, the Federal Deposit Insurance Corporation, the Comptroller of the Currency, and state banking authorities. As an example, national banks must obtain approval from the Comptroller of the Currency for the location of new branch banks.

Major technological changes affect the competitive environment of the banking industry. Electronic Funds Transfer System (EFTS) is an example. EFTS is an electro-mechanical method of transferring value, partially replacing the method of paper transfer of value (i.e. cash and checks).

One of these EFTS components has been classified as Customer-Bank Communication Terminals (CBCT) by the Comptroller. These terminals may be located on the site of an existing banking office or off-site such as a shopping center. They can be manned (operated by a bank employee) or unmanned (operated by the customer), on-line (connected directly to the bank's central computer) or off-line (self-contained). One type of CBCT is the Automated Teller Machine (ATM), which typically allows customers to make deposits, withdraw cash, pay on loans, and make account transfers. Another type of CBCT is the point of sale (POS) terminal which can be utilized at checkout counters in supermarkets, department stores, and other

business establishments. Retailers use POS for check or credit card authorization and for debit card authorization which allows immediate transfer of
funds from the purchaser's account to the store's account.

In December 1974, the Comptroller ruled that a CBCT is not a branch,
partially in response to the Federal Home Loan Bank Board's ruling in
January 1974 which allowed off-site CBCTs for savings and loan associations. The Comptroller subsequently suspended his ruling in response to
lawsuits in several unit-banking states and is no longer accepting or processing branch applications for CBCTs.

Second National's Current Situation

In recent months there has been considerable discussion among Second
National's top management concerning the need for additional banking outlets. The management concensus is that potentially profitable sites exist in
the rapidly expanding suburban areas of Columbia. Moreover, they feel
there is additional profit potential in several of the state's eighteen other
principal cities and smaller cities (10,000 to 30,000). Although there is general agreement that expansion is necessary to increase market share, there
is considerable disagreement among senior management as to what form
the expansion should take.

The need for a decision on the expansion issue has taken on greater
importance in recent weeks. Two of Second National's competitors, First
Central Bank (the state's largest) and First Farmers' Bank (the fourth largest), have been expanding their service offerings through the use of ATMs
in conjunction with their existing branch facilities. Just recently, Mr. Peterson
learned that First Farmers' intends to limit further construction of traditional
brick-and-mortar branches and embark on an ambitious expansion program
of off-site ATMs in shopping centers, employment centers, and other major
activity centers. Its expansion program is based on the belief that banking
services are primarily convenience goods; therefore, banking facilities
should have the greatest possible geographical distribution. Since ATMs
are available to customers twenty-four hours per day, seven days a week,
the marketing strategy appears to be one of creating greater spatial and
time convenience.

Second National's senior management is concerned about a recent
report which shows that market share of deposits peaked in 1970 and has
declined slowly since then. Management's assumption is that market share
of deposits is closely correlated with share of the total number of branches.
However, Second National's share of branches continued to increase in 1974
and 1975 while share of deposits decreased. Many of the larger banks in the
state experienced a similar trend. The exceptions to this trend were First
Central and First Farmers' which experienced substantial growth.

One of the stated goals of Second National is to maximize market
shares subject to a rate of return of at least 15 percent. In 1975, the market

share fell to 19.5 percent, under 20 percent for the first time since 1967, although the rate of return remained slightly above 15 percent.

In light of the situation, Mr. Hargrave has asked Mr. Peterson to develop and evaluate alternative expansion plans that would increase Second National's market share and rate of return. In addition, Mr. Hargrave instructed Mr. Peterson to consider the following issues:

1. Construction of a brick-and-mortar branch costs a minimum of about $250,000, or about five times as much as the cost of an ATM.

2. The chairman of the board has expressed repeatedly the opinion that ATMs cannot be cost-justified in terms of the profits they generate, an opinion shared by some experts.

3. Several of Second National's large commercial accounts have expressed a wide range of views as to the desirability of Electronic Funds Transfer System (EFTS).

4. At the recent conference of the National Association of Bank Managers, several experts expressed strong feelings concerning the problems of fraud, security, and malfunctioning of automated banking equipment.

5. Recent consumer surveys showed considerable mixed reactions to the use of automatic banking equipment.

6. Savings and loan institutions in several states are using ATMs, thereby allowing their customers to use savings accounts much like a checking account. In addition, two states are being allowed by federal agencies and Congress to experiment with negotiable ordering of withdrawal accounts which essentially are interest-paying checking accounts.

7. There is concern among several of our senior bank officials that any radical departure from current modes of operation might have considerable negative effects on the bank's image.

8. Pricing concepts in the banking industry are undergoing significant changes; whereas, most banks seek to make each application of each service profitable, some banks will adopt pricing strategies based on the profitability of the total customer and/or a total class of customers.

9. Point of sales terminals are used at check-out counters in retail stores and generally are installed with one terminal per check-out counter, or anywhere from one to twenty terminals per store.

In his initial meeting with the bank's Marketing Research Department, Mr. Peterson outlined the major issues of the problem as presented in the discussion above. He expressed the following opinion:

"Innovative expansion is the key to regaining and increasing the bank's market share. In order for any expansion program to meet the bank's market share goals, we must develop expansion alternatives which incorporate product-service mixes that not only satisfy the needs of our existing customers, but also provide the opportunities for attracting new customers. It is my opinion that the only way to attract large numbers of new customers is to create the image of a modern progressive bank. This type of image requires that our marketing programs be fresh and imaginative. Today's banking customer chooses and continues to patronize a bank for many different reasons; however, all of these reasons are strongly related to today's modern life styles. Hence, our expansion program must accommodate today's life styles. What I need from this department are innovative alternatives of expansion that are not only conducive to the consumer's modern way of life, but which will be acceptable to the 'dated' gentlemen upstairs. I believe that our current research files (see the Appendix) are sufficient for the initial development of these alternatives. We can always collect additional data later that would be more suited to whatever alternative we come up with. If you have any ideas as to what type of additional information might be required or if there are any specific aspects to the problem you feel should be drawn to my attention, submit them to me in writing by the end of the week. Otherwise, within the next six weeks, I expect from the department recommendations as to the most feasible expansion alternatives. Now, are there any questions?"

Mr. Sidewood: "How many alternatives do you want?"

Mr. Peterson: "I'll leave that up to you."

Mr. Sidewood: "Are there any specific issues you wish us to consider?"

Mr. Peterson: "I think we have at least mentioned in some fashion most of the issues pertinent to the problem. Again, I would think that consumer needs and responses might serve as the focal point in the development of the alternatives. However, that is not to say you should overlook all of the other issues that have been noted. Also, I am sure that there are additional issues that you might consider."

Mr. Sidewood: "One last question. How extensive an area should we consider?"

Mr. Peterson: "The entire state."

Mr. Armstrong: "As a resident of this state for fifty-five years and a banker for twenty-seven, I feel that I know the people of this state *and* the customers who bank with us. Although we want to think progressively, let us not forget that this state's population is quite conservative. These people are bound in tradition. They follow the habits of their grandparents, their great-grandparents! Why, twenty years ago most people thought the safest place for their money was a hole in the ground. It has taken this long for them to trust dealing with us. How long will it take to get them to trust dealing with a machine?"

Mr. Peterson: "You have a point. But people have changed. We have an influx of people from all parts of the country into this state. They don't have the same life styles."

Mr. Robeson: "As research analyst, I have data which supports both of your contentions. People in this state have been slow to adopt banking in general, and innovative banking practices in particular. However, the composition of the population has changed in the major cities of South Carolina. Companies from Detroit, Chicago, New York, Pennsylvania, and Connecticut, just to name a few, have opened major branches of their businesses here and have relocated many of their personnel as well. Although they represent a small percentage of the state's population, they have learned the advantages of using the new technologies in banking and draw high salaries. Their impact on the habits of other people in the state is difficult to assess."

Mr. Peterson: "Well, it is true that these people have been exposed to new banking techniques and do adapt to change more rapidly, but they are a minority. I think we should consider educating the rest of the population to the advantages of new banking technology. Just look at the strides First Central and First Farmers' have made."

Ms. Lucas: "Mr. Peterson, it is true that those banks have increased their market shares, but I agree with Mr. Armstrong. The people of this state are staunch conservatives, and particularly the customers who bank with us. If we try to become 'progressive,' as you call it, we will lose the solid image we have built with our loyal customers and they'll go elsewhere. People are reliable and trustworthy; machines are nothing but metal and electrical circuits."

Mr. Peterson: "But people of this state are changing, and people from out of state with more progressive views are coming in. We cannot continue to manufacture the horse-drawn carriage! Does anyone have any final comments before we adjourn?"

Mr. Robeson: "If I may make one last comment, let me say once again that I can see both sides to this question. As I view it, we are concerned with several issues. Each must be analyzed. We must consider changing life styles of bank consumers in this state. On the whole, are they changing rapidly enough to accept modern banking techniques in the near future? Secondly, what image do we convey and to whom? Third, can we educate people to accept and use machines? Their prior learning habits may not be easy to change. I don't presently have answers to these questions."

Mr. Peterson: "You've raised some good questions, Mr. Robeson. I feel there also are other questions we should raise and try to answer before reaching a decision. Let's adjourn and reconvene in two days."

Questions

1. What behavioral dimensions must be considered in this case? What information should Second National's Marketing and Research Department collect to consider in developing strategic alternatives?

2. Which behavioral concepts come to bear on Second National's strategy decision? Explain.

3. What alternatives do you propose and which alternative do you choose? What criteria did you use in arriving at your choice?

4. What are the possible effects of your recommended alternatives on the bank's (a) internal operations, (b) promotional programs, (c) product-service mix, and (d) pricing strategy?

Appendix

Marketing Research Files, Marketing Research Department

TABLE 1   Bank patronage reasons: retail and commercial consumers
SOURCE: Statewide Consumer Survey, Marketing Research Department, Second National Bank.

Patronage Reason \ Importance	First	Second	Third	Fourth	Fifth	Sixth	Totals
Location	42%	5%	19%	25%	3%	6%	100%
Hours	34	4	22	20	10	10	100
Services	10	43	15	13	11	8	100
Personnel	7	20	9	17	22	25	100
Reputation	5	7	10	6	21	51	100
Facilities	2	21	25	19	33	0	100
Totals	100%	100%	100%	100%	100%	100%	

TABLE 2   Consumer banking trip behavior: Retail and commercial consumer

Shopping Characteristic \ Type of Consumer	Retail Consumer	Commercial Consumer
Type of trip: I conduct my banking business in connection with:		
Trips between home and work	32%	10%
Special trips from home	30	8
Special trips from work	17	57
Shopping trips	18	—
Business trips	2	23
Other	1	2
Total	100%	100%
Trip frequency: I visit the bank:		
Less than once a month	1%	—
Once a month	8	—
More than once a month (less than weekly)	21	—
Once a week	51	1%
More than once a week (less than daily)	19	11
Once a day (weekday)	—	69
More than once a day	—	19
Total	100%	100%

TABLE 3   *Demographic characteristics of automated equipment users and nonusers*
SOURCE: Rex O. Bennett, *Bank Location Analysis,* (Washington, D.C.: American Bankers Association, 1975).

Demographic Characteristics	Nonuser	Infrequent User	Frequent	Total User
Sex				
Male	53.9%	64.0%	64.9%	59.1%
Female	46.1	36.0	35.1	40.9
Age				
21–34	36.8	49.3	54.5	43.4
35–49	47.4	44.0	39.0	43.4
50 and over	15.8	6.7	6.5	13.1
Social class				
Upper-middle	27.6	14.7	33.8	23.7
Lower-middle	38.2	53.3	39.0	45.6
Upper-lower	34.2	32.0	27.3	30.7
Marital status				
Married	86.8	85.3	87.0	86.9
Single	7.9	10.7	9.1	8.4
Widowed, divorced	5.3	4.0	3.9	4.7
Education				
Postgraduate	13.2	13.3	14.3	12.8
College graduate	23.7	32.0	29.9	27.7
Some college	28.9	32.0	28.6	30.3
Subtotal	65.8	77.3	·72.8	70.8
High school graduate	25.0	17.3	19.5	22.6
Some high school	6.6	5.3	6.5	5.5
Eighth grade or less	2.6	—	1.3	1.1
Income				
Under $5,000	2.6	4.0	2.6	2.9
$5,000–$7,999	3.9	6.7	2.6	5.1
$8,000–$10,999	21.1	22.7	10.4	17.2
$11,000–$13,999	19.7	24.0	15.6	20.1
$14,000–$17,999	13.2	10.7	18.2	16.1
$18,000 and over	34.2	22.7	44.2	32.8
Refused	5.3	9.3	6.5	5.8

TABLE 4   *Consumer bank selection criteria*

SOURCE: Statewide Consumer Survey, Marketing Research Department, Second National Bank.

Customer Type and Importance Rank / Selection Criteria	Retail Consumers			Commercial Consumers		
	First	Second	Third	First	Second	Third
Recommendation of friends or relatives	3%	4%	8%	—	—	2%
Recommendation of a professional acquaintance	2	6	1	11%	9%	8
Good reputation	4	3	—	9	8	14
Located near where I shop	10	8	3	—	—	—
Located near where I work	11	10	14	16	10	10
Located near where I live	18	16	10	—	1	1
Offers full service	11	13	11	29	22	13
Helpful personnel	8	7	4	6	15	10
Open during the evening hours	5	7	4	11	6	8
Open on Saturdays	7	4	6	4	12	6
Attractive facilities	—	6	3	—	—	—
Convenient automatic services	5	6	12	4	5	11
Interest charges on loans	1	—	1	6	7	9
Interest paid on savings	3	3	3	—	—	1
Availability of credit	—	1	—	4	5	5
Overdraft privileges on checking accounts	3	4	6	—	—	—
Premiums or gifts for new accounts	7	2	9	—	—	—
Convenient parking	1	—	2	—	—	1
Convenient entrance/exit	1	—	3	—	—	1

TABLE 5 *Likelihood of using automated teller equipment*
SOURCE: Rex O. Bennett, *Bank Location Analysis,* (Washington, D.C.: American Bankers Association, 1975).

Characteristic	Very Likely	Somewhat Likely	Somewhat Unlikely	Very Unlikely
Age				
18–34	34.1%	21.7%	11.2%	29.2%
35–49	33.2	18.6	11.3	33.2
50–64	19.8	12.5	14.7	49.6
65 and over	10.9	7.8	14.7	51.9
Income				
Under $7,500	15.2	11.0	11.0	51.7
$7,500–$10,000	25.8	20.8	11.9	37.7
$10,000–$15,000	34.8	17.4	12.1	32.6
$15,000–$20,000	34.1	20.3	14.8	26.8
Over $20,000	28.9	12.3	15.8	41.2
Sex				
Male	26.8	16.7	15.0	37.0
Female	28.0	16.2	10.5	40.0

TABLE 6   *Automated teller equipment: advantages vs. disadvantages*
SOURCE: Rex O. Bennett, *Bank Location Analysis,* (Washington, D.C.: American Bankers Association, 1975).

Characteristics	Advantages Outweigh	About Equal	Disadvantages Outweigh	Advantages Outweigh plus Equal
Occupation				
White collar	31.6%	38.6%	29.8%	70.2%
Blue collar	25.4	12.8	61.7	38.3
Professional	12.9	45.2	42.0	58.0
Housewife	23.6	31.1	45.3	54.7
Retired	23.5	5.9	70.6	29.4
Other	41.2	35.3	23.5	76.5
Age				
18–23	40.0	40.0	20.0	80.0
24–34	27.5	25.8	46.7	56.3
35–44	16.7	33.3	50.0	50.0
45–55	20.3	29.7	50.0	50.0
56–64	16.7	16.7	66.7	33.3
65 and over	33.4	13.3	53.4	46.6
Income				
Under $5,000	12.5	25.0	62.5	37.5
$5,000–$10,000	32.6	30.2	37.3	62.7
$10,000–$15,000	38.2	21.8	40.0	60.0
$15,000–$20,000	25.0	36.5	38.5	61.5
Over $20,000	29.2	33.3	37.5	62.5
Refused	17.1	31.4	51.4	48.6

Marketing the
Marketing Club

This case was prepared by **Denis F. Healy,** *College of Business and Economics, University of Delaware.*

Over the past few years, the University of Delaware's Marketing Club has struggled to become a viable activity area for a wide variety of students, in particular for those concentrating in the field of marketing.

To generate initial interest, the club has held mixers, beer blasts, brought in speakers of note, and the like. In addition, a variety of times and locations have been used. Initial interest has been modest in all cases with only a smattering of students participating in the early sessions.

Starting with a small core of interested individuals, the club usually manages to get off the ground with a business meeting in late September, and with concerted effort, a couple of programs are held in October and November. Those students who attend the meetings and programs seem interested, but there is high variability in attendance (10 to 100).

Frustrated by the participation and the amount of work involved in getting a club and programs together, the faculty advisor, who is growing short on patience and is pressed to do other things, begins to look for some reasons why participation is low. In addition, he begins to seek ways to stimulate interest and to market the club more effectively. In dealing with these issues, it finally occurs to him that the subject matter he preaches, namely consumer behavior and marketing management, might contain some ways of analyzing the situation and of presenting the club in a more appetizing way.

There is one thing you should know about the faculty advisor—he is lazy. Thus you are asked to:

1. Structure the issues in terms of consumer behavior and marketing management constructs.

2. Using the decision process model of consumer behavior, list or outline the steps one is likely to follow in deciding on club membership and participation.

3. Using your knowledge of marketing management, indicate the approaches you would make to formulate marketing strategies and segmentation plans. Consider each of the 4 P's (Promotion, Place, Product, Price).

4. Indicate areas where more research is needed and how you would obtain the information.